BEFORE I FORGET

BEFORE I FORGET

a boyhood of little drama

Tom Turkington

ISBN: 153959288X
ISBN 13: 9781539592884

Before I Begin

My parents never told me much. They talked to me often enough, or at least Mom did, but they never told me much about what I should do, or how I should be, or what the world was going to throw at me. That was fine, because I probably wouldn't have paid attention. They particularly didn't tell me much about their pasts, and that too was fine, because I wasn't very interested: not while I was growing up and concerned only with what happened to me, and not as a young adult when I was concerned only with what I was doing.

Something happens to many of us when we begin to crowd the outer edge of middle age. A sense of personal history begins to take shape, along with a feeling that our lineage is an important part of that history. Lineage is a lot more than the branches on the family tree. The events and actions and choices that made up the lives of those who came before me are a part of my life in a way that I just couldn't grasp when I was a younger fellow. By the time I wanted to know about these things, there was nobody around to tell me.

A few years ago, anticipating that my own progeny would doubtless delay their interest in my history until I wouldn't be here to fill them in on it, I thought it prudent to put some of my recollections, reactions and observations on the record. A modest enough initiative, maybe, but it got a little out of hand as one memory led to another, and another. What follows is a chronicle of the first 18 years of my life, drawn solely from what the recesses of my memory bank brought forth. There has been no research and no fact-checking except where noted. If I don't remember it, it's not in here. If there is anything that isn't entirely accurate, it derives from an accident of recall, not embellishment. None of the names have been changed to protect the innocent, or the guilty.

Before I Forget

I remember being baptized. It never came up in conversation when I was growing up, so it wasn't a memory I shared with anybody for a long time, but when I reached an age – my teens, maybe? – when my perspective had broadened sufficiently for me to realize that this was my first memory of life and therefore carried some significance, I mentioned it to my mom while sitting around before dinner. She was dubious, as was Dad. So I related some of the details. It took place at St. Barnabas in Falmouth. The Hopkinses were sitting in the front pew. Mom and Dad were up at the baptismal font with me. That's about all that came to mind, but it convinced the skeptics. I was a little surprised that nobody thought it remarkable that I'd retain a memory of the event, but some time later I found out just when I was baptized, and I was pretty old for it.

My first home was on Fairview Avenue in Falmouth center. Like most other hospital-born babies from the Upper Cape at that time, I first drew breath in the town of Wareham, at Tobey Hospital. I've been told that I began to make my presence felt on the Bourne Bridge, and waiting time for me in the delivery room was brief. In 1949 you could speed right over the Bourne Bridge on a midsummer day, and Dad took full advantage of that circumstance. A couple of Falmouth transplants have tried to tell me that I'm not a native Cape Codder, having been delivered on the mainland. Dad once assured me that newspaper and record-keeping protocol have it that your place of birth is wherever your home is at the time of your delivery. I'll buy that. If I want a copy of my birth certificate, I write to Falmouth town hall. So that settles it. I'm a native Cape Codder.

Dad grew up in Port Washington on Long Island with his older sister Lysbeth and my grandparents, Ola and Frederick sr. When my father was in his early teens, the family was unexpectedly blessed with the birth of a boy, whom they named Peter. Peter was a bright, lively boy who was loved by everybody but was especially close to Dad, whom he called Big Boy. There was something not right with Peter's eyes, and at the age of 7 or 8 he went in for an operation. They administered ether to put him under for the procedure, and he never woke up. The family was devastated, and never fully got over their sorrow.

When I was close to 2, I showed every sign of being an alert, engaged, cheerful little kid, but I wasn't talking yet, or doing anything that resembled talking. Examination revealed that I was just about stone deaf, couldn't hear much of anything, but that an operation of some kind on my ears would set me right. So they took me in to have it. Ether was still the anesthesia of choice; the doctor soaked a cloth with what he hoped was the right amount and held it to my face. I struggled for a moment, then went unconscious. I've never gotten so much as a whiff of the stuff since, but if I ever do, I'll know just what it is and I'll get sent right back to that very memorable incident. I came out of it fine, started jabbering away not long after and haven't stopped since. How do you suppose Dad felt when they wheeled me into the OR? How about when I woke up?

During the Korean War, Dad was called up from the reserves and we all packed up for Sumter, South Carolina, where we lived on The Base. As part of the Air Force's effort to make life enjoyable for families living on The Base, they screened films for the kids in an auditorium there. A bus went around on Saturday morning, picking kids up. The kids watched the films, then got back in the bus and returned to their homes. I was 2 1/2 years old, and on this expedition was put in the care of Eric, 4 1/2. The wisdom of that arrangement was called into question on at least two occasions. At one of the film days, if not all of them, they ran a Three Stooges comedy, and from the very first poke in the eye I started screaming in horror. I turned around in my seat, put my hands over my ears and cried like a baby, which I nearly was. I received no succor from Eric, who was mature enough to take pleasure in the Three Stooges. On one of these occasions – I can say with confidence this only happened once – the kids all got back in the bus to be brought back to their homes. The driver had many stops to make, and when he stopped at our street, Eric got off. I did not. The driver went on, finished up his route, and was left with me. We then spent quite a bit of time going back over the route, hoping that one of the streets would spark some memory of home in me, but none did until we went by a street corner where stood my mother, waving her arms.

Another day in Sumter, I was in the kitchen with Mom when Eric and a friend came in, asking excitedly for a jar to contain a really big worm they'd just found out in the back yard, near the woods. Mom looked around and found them a jar, but thought she'd go out back to have a look at this big worm before they brought it into the house. She got close enough to it to see that what they'd found was a rattlesnake. A short while later, a neighbor with a hoe was in the yard, hacking up that rattlesnake. A photograph was taken of the event which was in existence long enough to inspire retellings of the incident for some years after. There were neighborhood children and mothers standing to the side in this photograph, watching the man butchering the snake.

Other than my family, the only person I remember from the South Carolina period was a large black woman by the name of Betsy, who was a friend of Mom's. We were visiting Betsy at her home one rainy evening when I saw a small cow in a pen behind the house. I was with a boy a bit older than I who seemed to live there, who told me it was a horse. I didn't know much about livestock, but I knew this was a cow and told him so. He laughed then and told me he was kidding. Mom may have known Betsy through some campaign work she did for an opponent of Strom Thurmond, either when we were there or earlier on, before she had kids. In either case, old Strom prevailed, and did he ever: Mom went back north, gave birth to two boys, raised them to adulthood, had a long teaching career, retired from it, eventually got old and died, and Strom Thurmond resided in the U.S. Senate for every day of that, and more.

I have no idea what Dad's assigned chores were at The Base - he was about as far as you could get from the action in Korea - but I did learn at some point that he spent the latter stages of WW II in Medmenham, England, examining the photographs of German territory taken by Allied reconnaissance planes, either before or after our bombing runs. He joined other clever analysts in assessing the destruction and, maybe, seeing what we should target next. He put in a few more years as a reservist after Sumter, was away for some weekends and a couple of weeks once or twice, and seemingly kept getting promoted. I never saw him in uniform or heard of him speak of himself as a veteran.

Truce came to Korea and we moved back to Falmouth. We settled in at 14 Mill Road and stayed there for the next three years. Mill Road angled off from Woods Hole Road just a ways up from the house, so we weren't far from a fairly busy (by early 50's standards) road, but not right on it. The house was pretty old, judging by the style: a basic, narrow 2-story facing the road and a 1 1/2 story ell running out behind. There was a broad, screened full-length front porch with fluted columns that was probably an add-on, but enhanced and fit well with the front of the house, and was a favorite hangout of mine. We were about equidistant from Main Street and Surf Drive beach, either of which you could walk to if you didn't mind walking a ways, which most people didn't.

Inside the front door of 14 Mill Road, there was a living room with a fireplace to the right and an open space – foyer, maybe – that you crossed to get to the foot of the stairs. The stairs were the graceful kind that nice homes have, that run straight down about 2/3 of the way, then wind around and broaden out as they spill out on the bottom floor. They were spacious enough to be played on. There were bedrooms at the top of the stairs – one of them was mine – and a hallway that ran back to the ell, where my parents' bedroom was. That room seemed very big to me. The bathroom was off the hallway and looked out over the side yard. There wasn't a lot of yard, as there was another 2-story with ell just to our north, closer to the corner, and a dormered Cape with ell to our south, set further back from the road. Both places were pretty old and attractive. I never met the people to the north, but Amelia Turner and her mother lived in the Cape. Amelia was again a presence in my world when I did a little work on her house many years later. All I recall of her mother was that she had white hair and died some time when we lived there, because I saw somber-looking men going to and from their home one day and Mom explained that the old lady had died.

Just the other side of Turners' was a long drive that led to the old town cemetery. In the early days of Falmouth, this was just about the center of the village, and I'd assume there was a meetinghouse close by, as the cemeteries were usually set not far behind them. An alert historian might correct me on that. The cemetery was pretty big, with headstones dating back to the early 1700's, and the back end of it bordered Siders Pond. It had a sizable open area with no headstones right at the end of the drive, which was a fine place to play. I first swung a bat at a ball there. Houses on Pin Oak Way backed up to one side, and Mill Park on the other, but there were never any adults around.

There was no driveway to our house from Mill Road. To get there by car, you pulled onto Pin Oak Way, then right onto a road with no name that shortly turned to gravel and split into two drives, left to the Panises' little house and shop and right to Russell Hartwell Brown's barn and our back yard. Brownie's barn looked like a carriage house for a big estate, but there weren't any estates around. Maybe it was built to house some light industry, 19th century style. It had three very large pairs of hinged doors with arched frames, and a couple of dormers above, and a cupola, and a broad rear roof that we could get onto by climbing up a tree that was overtaking the place. It was just dangerous enough running around on that roof to make it exciting to be there. Russell Hartwell Brown was a talkative, intelligent, kindly, rather batty fellow who used the barn to hoard all his stuff. I was never inside it and never heard of bigger kids who were. It had a large door that led under the barn that was accessed by a long-overgrown drive, bordered by stone retaining walls.

Stavre and Gladys Panis were silversmiths who lived in a little cottage a short walk from our back yard. In the rambling workshop across their driveway from the house they each had a workbench littered with patterns for their pins and earrings and bracelets, which they produced in an Old World style that nobody else was able to do at the time, so they were well known among jewelry cognoscenti. We saw a lot of fancy cars going up their drive during the summer. Behind the jewelry benches was a shop for the more heavy-duty goods that the old man produced: candlesticks, ash trays and the like. There was a kiln there for glazing the ash trays and a number of power tools for fashioning the candlesticks. The place was heated by a woodstove. When I was in there years later, looking to order a silver bracelet for my flame at the time, I found I had to duck my head to get through the door. I could stand up straight inside with little room to spare. I'm not six feet tall.

Behind the shop they kept chickens and grew grapes and vegetables. Gladys was an intense flower and shrub gardener. Their cottage was ringed by shrubs and flowering trees, especially boxwood, and stuffed with plants; every level surface and much of the floor space was covered by something growing in a pot. I'd follow Gladys around sometimes as she made her rounds with the watering can. It was a task that took a long time and made her very happy.

The Panises had no children of their own and were absolutely delighted to see Eric and me every time we went over to see them. A couple of times when we wanted to get a gift for Mom, they'd let us execute Step One of the making of a pin, which was tracing one of their delicate patterns onto a piece of paper. They'd take it from there, but then we could say we'd helped make that piece. I don't know how long the Mr. lived. He seemed terribly old to me when I was very small: wispy white hair, missing teeth, weatherbeaten skin and hunched back. By the time I was grown and back in town, he was gone. Gladys, who by then was in the habit of joining us for Thanksgiving dinner, was still going strong and sharp as a tack into her 90's, turning out her jewelry and watering her plants. I cannot get a whiff of ripe grapevines or boxwood without being sent back to her home.

Eric and I vacated our bedrooms during the summer so that my parents could take in roomers. This was a common practice for homeowners in Falmouth who could free up a couple of rooms for tourists who were traveling on the cheap. You'd hang a little sign out by the sidewalk – "ROOMS" – and people would come and stay at your house for a fee. We boys were tasked with delivering glass pitchers of ice water to the roomers. Other than the right to use the house's only bathroom, I believe that was the only amenity offered. When we took in roomers, Eric and I slept on cots in an enclosed porch off of the kitchen that was usually used for storage of stuff. It was always hot at night when we slept there, always pleasant by morning. One day I woke up to the call of a bird outside the window. Its song was simple: a high-pitched cheep followed by a lower cheep, then a break, then the two cheeps again. It was the sweetest sound I'd heard in my young life, and the sun was bright, the air clear, and I knew that this was going to be a fine day. It was many years before I found that this was the call of the chickadee. They still sound like that.

Mill Road and Woods Hole Road met just up from our house at an oblique angle, which afforded a triangular location for a little park whose centerpiece was a monument to the sailors. The monument was a very large rock with an anchor on top and a plaque fastened to the side. Climbing on the rock and hanging from the anchor was one of our pastimes. One of my first recognizable signs of physical growth was the day that I could get the side of my foot up on the ledge at the bottom of the plaque and claw up the side of the rock with my fingers to grab the anchor, then pull myself up to the top of the rock and stand there like Hillary on Everest.

There were scads of kids in the neighborhood, as there surely were in any neighborhood in any thriving town in America at the time. The Haustons, the Langenheims, the Bailows, the Mullens, the Voses, the Richardsons, the Ketchums, the Struths were the ones whose homes were most proximate to ours. As hardly any families ever went anywhere, most of our activities took place in somebody's yard, or started there and spread out. We wound up at the beach sometimes, a little less than a mile away. Halfway there was a big estate that was unoccupied most of the year, if not all of it. The grounds ran down to Salt Pond, where there began trails that meandered through the puckerbrush and came out at the railroad tracks. Those tracks crossed Woods Hole Road across the street from our house, just the other side of the sailors' monument. We spent an inordinate amount of time playing on or around the tracks, considering it wasn't the most pleasant environment, given the rust and tar and creosote and crushed stone of the railbed. There was something a little daring about being there. We'd put our ears to the tracks and see who'd be the first to tell a train was coming. Then we'd see it from a half mile away, one bright light on the engine that could nearly blind you even in the daytime, and we'd wait on those tracks long enough to be afraid before we'd hop to the side of the railbed and feel that huge machine rumble past. Usually, the engineer would smile and give us a wave. Once in a while, there'd be one who'd shout "GET AWAY FROM THE TRACKS!!!"

There was a day care center of sorts that a lot of mothers brought their kids to. It took up a room in the Rec Center at the east end of Main Street, and it was organized and run by something called the Child Study Club. It may have been a drop-off center, or it could be that the kids' mothers all stayed and hung out there while their kids played. It was probably the latter; very few mothers of young children had jobs they had to get to. The CSC served as an escape from isolation for young mothers and their kids. Its most memorable feature was a couple of large (to a little kid) platforms on rollers that were shaped and painted to resemble turtles, which made a lot of noise and no little mayhem as they scooted across the floor with preschool kids riding on and falling off them.

The most exciting event of the day during the summer was the arrival of the ice cream truck. It always seemed to show up in the early evening; I imagine the driver got better trade during the day by cruising the beaches and the ferry docks. The truck had a rack of bells over the windshield to announce its coming, which we'd keep an ear open for it after dinner. A torpid summer evening burst into a frenzy of sprinting children at the first audible jingle, with kids racing first to their parents for ice cream money, then across whatever yards and stone walls stood between them and the truck's destination. The social aspect of the congregation was part of the attraction, but the true excitement was in having something sweet to eat, and paying for it with cold cash. It wasn't something we got to do very often, but the regs were relaxed a bit in the summertime. Those of us with nickels got Popsicles, and were silently envious of the richer kids who came with dimes, and got ice cream bars.

Another, less dependable communal event was when the DDT truck came down Mill Road, spraying the trees alongside with poison to kill mosquitoes, gypsy moths and what have you. It was just taken for granted that if your community didn't want irksome bugs pestering you all the time, you'd just go out and spray them. "Silent Spring" at this point was just a bee in Rachel Carson's bonnet. One DPW worker would drive while another held a hose that was fed by a compressor and a big tank of DDT, and he'd aim that hose up into the branches of the trees along the road. It shot pretty far, too. All the kids would run out to the edge of the yard and breathe in that sweet mist as it filtered down, a little pungent and a little damp. It didn't smell bad, it didn't smell good, it just seemed kind of cool to be sucking in this stuff that came shooting out of a hose in the back of a truck, and could kill bugs but couldn't hurt us.

A little way up Locust Street from our house lived Eddie and Jean Wright. Eddie was pressman at the Enterprise. He and Jean were a trace older than my parents, as close as anybody would come to being their friends, and as congenial and welcoming to two little boys as anybody could ask. They had a television, which forced them to welcome Eric and me into their home on a regular basis. We went there to watch Howdy Doody, the hottest thing going in children's programming at the time, and I assume from the fact that our visits went on for a long time that we must have brought with us a degree of charm. We did, of course, pester our parents about getting a TV so that we could watch it and many other shows at home. Mom once offered in the discussion that we wouldn't always want to watch Howdy Doody, that the time would come when we'd outgrow it. "Oh no! We'll NEVER outgrow Howdy Doody!" The show was a significant enough part of our lives that on one of our trips to New York to visit Mom's parents, we went to the network studio downtown and appeared on the show among the screaming kids in the Peanut Gallery. It was fun, and exciting, but my most lasting impression was of how little studio space it actually took to present all the action in the show.

My father smoked a pipe, my mother cigarettes, both with regularity. We spent many an hour gathered in the living room at 14 Mill Road, Eric and me on the floor with the funnies or comic books or a game, Mom and Dad in their chairs reading a book or the paper, one (usually Mom) speaking now and then of something in the reading. There was a lot of silence and a tremendous amount of smoke. It wafted in thick layers, drifting through and around the room on air currents generated by four people breathing, so thick you could barely see the other side of the room. As he smoked his pipe, Dad rhythmically released the smoke from his lips with a barely audible "bup", and I say barely audible, but in the silence you couldn't miss it. I wasn't old enough yet to get really annoyed at my parents' ways, lucky Dad. Mom was not quite a chain smoker, but when sitting around like this, she came close.

Life among the Turkingtons was generally pretty quiet and devoid of drama. Aside from an occasional breakout from Mom, who often did express her thoughts with wide-open eyes, grand gestures and amusingly affected manners, self-restraint prevailed. This was not wholly consistent with my own nature – out on the street, I could show anger, frustration, excitement or joy with the best or worst of them – but I got with the program at home early on and stayed with it. I don't believe anybody ever shouted at anybody within our walls. Whether because it was in their nature or as a matter of principle – probably both, since the one follows the other as the night the day – corporal punishment upon the boys practically never happened.

One exception was an evening, near bedtime, when I went into the home's only bathroom, latched the door and sat down on the toilet. And there I continued to sit, quite unnecessarily, until I was told from the hallway that it was time to get off, open the door and get ready for bed. This I would not do. The commands grew more insistent, but still I sat. Who knows why kids do these things? Soon, I was threatened with punishment if I didn't get up and unlatch the door. On the toilet I stayed. Eventually, I heard Dad outside with a hammer and screwdriver, knocking the pins out of the hinges. At last I had the motivation I needed to open the door. Unfortunately, just as I did, he pulled the last hinge pin, and the door fell on him and hurt him. He, in turn, hurt me with the only true spanking I ever got: sharp blows on the bare ass while suspended over the knees. I'm sure it didn't require that tanning to keep me from locking myself in the bathroom ever again – this was a one-shot deal – but who knows? Maybe it diverted me from a lifetime of locking out the world indefinitely while sitting on the can. Better get up and go, Tom, or you'll get spanked.

The first day of kindergarten was not without trauma for most of us. Though every kid there was socialized to some degree in his or her own neighborhood and circle of friends, most of us had never been to anything more structured than the Child Study Club's play group at the Rec. There was no attempt made to familiarize us with the classroom or the teacher prior to the day when we were expected to be there with her on a daily basis, sans Mom. Besides that, the room was full of strange kids. I didn't take it real well; cried my eyes out, in fact. I just couldn't abide by the idea that I was being left on my own in an environment that had nothing in it, aside from the clothes on my back, that had ever been a part of my life. So I cried. It was suggested that I might feel better if I came in with something from home, so we went back and got my Pooh bear. Whether we returned with it or came back the next day with it I don't know, but once I was at kindergarten with my Pooh bear to talk about and show to the other kids, I was off and running.

I was fortunate that my teacher was Miss Mcintosh. She was somewhat new to the game, but she managed to keep everyone active, and there were all kinds of different things to do in her classroom. Kindergarten classes haven't changed a whole lot. There were big block letters and numerals on the walls, one bulletin board with a variety of shapes on it, another with a bunch of colors. There was a library corner with books from which Miss McIntosh would read to us at the appointed hour. I spent my share of time in that corner. Having learned the rudiments of reading from an older brother and a collection of comic books, I was able to do more than look at the pictures. At some point during the winter, I went to Miss McIntosh and announced, "I can read every book in this room!" Rather than express the doubt she surely felt – learning to read was not in the first semester's curriculum – she led me over to the book corner and picked out one for me to read to her, which I did. And another. And another, until she was sure, by golly, the kid really can read them all.

She never asked me if I could write, but I was getting the hang of that too. One day when there was nobody around the house I decided to go on over to Jimmy Richardson's house, which was just a few backyards away and usually had something going on. I knew I should tell somebody, but there was no one around. So I left a note. In a corner where we kept our comics and games I found a Parcheesi board, and then I found a pencil, and I wrote on the back of the Parcheesi board in letters about 1/4 inch high, "i m at jimmies". Then I left the board where I'd found it and headed out. This seemed to me the best way of handling the situation. I got back around dinner time to a couple of stern parents. They started to talk to me about the importance of letting them know where I was, but I was ready: "But I left you a note!!" What? Huh? A note? So I retrieved the Parcheesi board and showed them, and next thing I knew they were laughing, I wasn't sure why. Maybe this was the first sign of intelligent life out of me.

My attendance at kindergarten also provided me with an early lesson in the power of our olfactories to cause us to connect with events in the past. It was in the cafeteria of the Village School that I first smelled what I believe now to be a cleanser or disinfectant of some kind. It was a powerfully acrid smell, to the point of irritation, and though it wasn't always around, it was present often enough for me to know it was there for a purpose. I reacted to it, as did other kids with whom I discussed the matter, somewhat the way I would react to Pine-Sol or Mr. Clean or bleach, but more repellently. It was really unpleasant to be around. What has always been a mystery to me is that I have smelled that smell in institutional rooms and hallways many other times through the years, but never in somebody's house and never in a high-class joint. After all these years, you'd think that everybody from the janitors to the principals would have found a less offensive way to get that cleaning done.

Falmouth got hit by a hurricane from time to time, and still does. There was a pretty big one by the name of Carol in, I believe, 1954. During the course of the storm, we weren't endangered, as the biggest trees around us were at some remove from the house. But the water came a little too close for comfort. We were fairly far from the beach, but once the Sound rose high enough to breach Surf Drive Beach and the meager sand dunes next to the road, there wasn't much to stop it, as the road was pretty level. At the peak of the storm, seawater was flooding the road to where we could see it from the front yard. That's as close as it got.

The next day, we walked down to the beach to survey the damage, as local folks were wont to do. I was walking barefoot along the shore with Dad when we spied what looked like a white, football-shaped balloon floating in the shallow water. Dad told me it was a Portugese Man-O-War, a poisonous jellyfish that didn't belong within a thousand miles of here but came up with the hurricane. He found a long stick, fished it out of the water and dragged it up on the beach. I asked him if it would die there, and he said yes. That meant to me it was as good as dead, so without a word I ran up to get a closer look at it, stepped on its tentacles with my bare toes, and experienced a burning pain of an intensity that has rarely been repeated in my life.

Not much about first grade has stuck with me, probably because I wasn't struck with separation anxiety on my first day and I was no longer the only kid who could read all the books in the room. Free of trauma, I was nevertheless struck with some disgust that first day while standing on the broad granite steps with a crowd of kids waiting for the door to open. There was pigeon shit all over the steps and landing, especially directly beneath the columns, atop which the pigeons roosted. I walked to school with Eric and whatever other neighborhood kids we met up with. It wasn't a real long walk, and when we took a route that went through some peoples' back yards, along a couple of trails by Siders Pond and through the back parking lots of Main Street businesses, it could be promising of adventure. The return trip was more promising yet, as there was no arrival deadline.

It was called the Village School still; all the kids in the center of Falmouth from kindergarten through 4th grade went there. This was a brick edifice with three stories above the basement, sided in brick in a neoGeorgian style that was often repeated in public schools built in the 20's. Each story had a central corridor lined with classrooms and with a stairway at either end. The classrooms were all exactly the same size, big enough to pack in about 30 desks, a big one for the teacher and a bit of room to walk around. Classrooms on the north looked out over Shivericks Pond, beyond which rose The Big School – Lawrence High, built in 1953 and still, to my mind, the best school building the town ever had. Classes on the south side had a view of the playground, which consisted of a large open field that staunchly resisted the growth of grass and a mixed bag of swings, seesaws, and jungle gyms at the west end. At the east end was the Hall School, about which more later. Beyond the playfield was the town library and Main Street.

This was a Main Street that politicians who have nothing worthwhile to say like to evoke when they talk about the greatness of America. Standing on the sidewalk in front of the library, you could see the three schools where were educated the children of Falmouth village between 5 and 14, and all the kids in the whole town of high school age. You'd see the library, and usually a goodly number of cars parked in front of it, this being only the dawn of the television age. Beside the library was Town Hall, and the police station behind. Next to town hall, the A & P, as close to a supermarket as Falmouth or most towns of its size had. In just a few years, there would appear a First National at the foot of Shore Street, which was a little bit more like one. There was Harvey's Hardware across the street, with not just hardware, no: toys, pets, linens, knickknacks, and a wonderful bike shop in the basement too. There was Davis's Furniture on the Shore Street corner with a display of big bureaus, big dining room sets, overstuffed chairs and overstuffed sofas behind huge plate glass windows right up against the sidewalk. A little further west stood the Methodist Church on its very small lot, a jewelry shop, Issokson's clothing store, Eastman's hardware (more inclined to the sporting/hunting enthusiast than Harvey's) a Western Auto and of course a J.J. Newberry's with a lunch counter where a kid with a nickel could get The Pause That Refreshes, with cherry syrup added. There were no cafes. There was no fine dining, though there was The New Yorker, later to become The Quarterdeck.

Following along the sidewalk past these utilitarian, locally created, long-established businesses the likes of which would be found in any town with a pulse, the stroller would encounter a spreading-out of establishments, a canopy of majestic elms and a sense of quiet grandeur surrounding the arrowhead-shaped village green. At its point was a public water fountain built of stone, roofed and inviting but seldom functioning. On one side of Main Street where it forks to accommodate the green was a bank and the post office; on the other, another bank and the Episcopal parsonage. Here was true landscaping and gardening brought into the commercial sphere as nowhere else around. Surrounding the rest of the Green sat the core elements of New England prosperity and righteousness: several fine homes, a few modest and ancient but wearing the years like a crown, the others of assorted vintage, gracefully large, likely built by seafaring traders to herald their success, now kept by bankers and doctors.

Facing off from opposite sides of the Green are the Congregational and Episcopal churches. The former dates from the 1700's and has all the visual features of the classic New England meeting-house-on-the-common. Bright white in modern times, it appears to be a dun brown in the early photographs. The Episcopal church will forever be a latecomer, though one with a presence. Leaning largely to the Gothic inside and out, it was erected by the Beebes, Falmouth's earliest wealthy summer visitors, so that they could worship in the faith while taking the Falmouth air. They endowed their church with a broad front lawn, quietly exquisite stone work, and altitude: the property slopes downwards to Shivericks Pond to the south, westerly to a fine captain's house, easterly to the parsonage and northerly to Main Street and the Green. The sidewalk abutting Main Street is as level as the sea for its entire length, except as it approaches St. Barnabas church. I was baptized in this lofty church.

I learned to ride a bicycle and swim at some point in the Mill Road period. In both cases, I was a willing learner but not an exceptionally quick one. Dad had me out on the lawn for the bike lessons. First he held onto the handlebars and the seat, then held me by the seat from behind as I pedaled, then one day let go of the seat without telling me. I went about 50 feet under my own power, looked behind me, saw him way back there, and fell over. I wasn't happy about the fall, but now I knew I could do it and only needed practice, so I was all set with the bike. I took to swimming without lessons, just a comfort with the water born of many expeditions to the beach. Wading turned to splashing and in time to holding myself up by the arms in knee-deep water while kicking like mad. From there, propelling myself by way of dog paddle was the next natural step.

The Haustons were neighbors. Their son Billy was older than me, and their daughter Beth younger, Martha younger yet. We were at their house for dinner one night when I felt I was being excluded or worse by the play of Billy and my brother Eric, and went whining to Mom about it. I did so more than once, I suspect, because it wasn't very much like her to snap back at me, but she did. She told me to quit complaining or I could go back to the house and have cold cereal for dinner. So that's what I did. I left quietly, walked back to the house, poured a bowl of cereal and milk and sat down at the table to eat it. A bit later, there was Mom at the door. She was part smiling, part crying and very kind. I went back to the Haustons' with her.

Mrs. Swift was my first grade teacher and my only clear recollection of my time in the classroom. She was short, had white hair, moved gently and never raised her voice. The name of Swift went back a long way in Falmouth history, maybe back to the first white settlers. Mrs. Swift had a pleasant smile, which I saw for the last time as she helped me zip up my jacket after a going-away party for me on my last day in her class. The Turkingtons were moving away.

* * *

My mother once told me, in slightly hushed tone even though nobody else was around, that my father didn't much like to talk to us about things that had happened in his life before he married her, and that she would always go along with this for his sake. What I didn't realize at the time, my family experience with them being the only one I was familiar with, was just how reticent he was about things that happened after he married her as well. For one thing, nobody ever spoke in my presence to the subject of why we uprooted ourselves from a seemingly acceptable life in Falmouth and moved to Seneca Falls, New York. Over time, I divined that Dad was feeling a bit underutilized at the Falmouth Enterprise and had a hankering to run his own newspaper. He may have had reason to believe that the Seneca Falls Reveille was on the block or about to be, and figured that he could sign on there, learn the ropes, line up financing and become its publisher, not to mention editor and chief reporter.

There were some connections to upstate NY that may have entered into the move. Nano – Dad's mother – grew up in or near Gouveneur, which is way up north, and my parents lived there after Dad got out of World War II service. Eric was born in Gouveneur. My folks attended Syracuse – both as fledgling journalists – met and fell in love there.

Some men in a moving van came to 14 Mill Road one day and took just about everything in the house away with them. We spent one night in a bare house, slept on blankets, got in the car the next morning and followed the route of the moving van. We pulled into the Latham Street driveway in Seneca Falls that night, walked in the door and found all the beds, chairs, rugs, lamps, dressers, the entire contents of the moving van piled up in the living room and parlor. The rest of the house was bare. I now know that this is not what moving companies lead their clients to expect, and better understand why Mom and Dad seemed annoyed upon walking in the front door. I was just glad to get out of the car and didn't much care that we slept another night on blankets.

The house turned out to have its share of charms. You'd walk in the front door into the living room, with the stairs to your left and a parlor of sorts further to the left. I'd now suspect that the parlor had once been a broad front porch that got closed in by a previous owner when broad front porches started going out of style. The living room led into the dining room – open concept! – from which there was a door to a little side porch that I don't believe we ever opened. The kitchen was behind the dining room, with a door leading to the back yard. The bathroom was beside the dining room, and featured the oddity of a sliding panel that led to the kitchen counter. If desired, a person in the bathtub could have dinner passed to him, straight from the kitchen. Could this have been a pantry, made over into the bathroom when indoor plumbing came into vogue? I would think so now; I didn't think much of anything about it then.

Behind the house was a good-sized barn left over from the days when even people in the towns – and this was definitely in-town property – kept horses and other livestock. This barn had a couple of stalls, a hayloft, and a sizable open area, none of which was used by us for anything but fun and games. There was a high, steep-pitched gable roof dead center, and a shed roof at shallower pitch running off to the left. Right next to the eave of the shed roof was a large tree with many limbs, which of course were there to provide access to the roof for daring young folk. One of the rites of passage into big-boy status in the neighborhood was to get up a good head of steam running up the shed roof, and scramble up the steep main roof to the ridge, from where you could see all around. You could also fall and get severely injured, but nobody ever did.

The barn was also the repository of many years' worth of scrap lumber, no two pieces of which resembled one another. Eric – being two years older than I and even then the organizer – got us started on applying the lumber to a series of structures in the back yard, and we built some substantial ones. Some of the neighborhood kids got involved too, but Eric and I were the ones who'd stay on the job. These shacks would not make it to the pages of Fine Homebuilding, or even the Seneca Falls Reveille, but considering we had no expertise and built them without any adult guidance, they came out okay. Our masterpiece was a triple-decker: four walls far enough apart to allow a child to lie down inside; a platform on top of that room; a similar room above, with a platform on it; and some rudimentary walls on top of that. We built a long house at one point, a one-story but with rooms. We were working on it one day – I was at the front entry, looking down through the rooms, and a couple of kids were on top of it – when the whole structure started leaning sharply to the side, and came crashing down. It didn't break our hearts or anybody's bones, but I think the discouragement factor entered in and we let off homebuilding in the back yard.

We were forever getting splinters, cuts and nails in the feet from those efforts and others. By nails in the feet, I mean big, fat rusty nails coming up through the shoe and poking deep into the sole of the foot. Everyone got their tetanus shot, and we made do with nails in the feet. I don't ever remember seeing a doctor about anything. One of our games was to see how many kids could ride on a bicycle. I was sitting sidesaddle on somebody's front fender one day, with somebody on the handlebars and someone else on the back fender and the biggest of us pedaling hard down the hill to Latham Road, when for some reason the bike tipped over and I slammed my head on the pavement. I wasn't knocked out or anything, but when I got up I put my hand to the back of my head and it came back dripping with blood. So I started screaming and ran to the house. I don't know why Mom wasn't home, but Eric must have got on the phone, because a little bit later Dad came home from work. He looked me over, and then he was on the phone for a couple of minutes. Then we went into the kitchen to wash off the back of my head, dried it with a towel, and then Dad went back to work, and that was the end of that.

Actually, Mom probably wasn't home because she was at the office too. I believe that she was involved in the effort to acquire the Reveille. She spent a lot of evening time doing something with boxes of file cards and lists of things, and typing stuff up. Now that both boys were in school and were otherwise safe at home playing on their bicycles or the roof of the barn, she was free to join Dad in the world of journalism for which they'd both been trained. We even had a cleaning lady come in once a week to vacuum the floors and what not. That was the only time in my parents' married life that they hired a housecleaner, and I don't know how long it went on, but it wouldn't have happened if Mom wasn't working at least a lot of the time.

Seneca Falls was the home of Elizabeth Cady Stanton and of the first women's rights convention. In postwar America, this distinction was of the magnitude of Carrie Nation and Prohibition: interesting bit of history, but what does this mean to me? Mom did once walk Eric and me over to a house that was either Cady Stanton's home or the meeting place of the convention – it was just a couple of streets away – and told us something about that history. Imagine the impact it had upon a couple of little boys in 1956. Seneca Falls was also bisected by a branch of the New York State Barge Canal, which some 140 years earlier had been dug in order to open up a water route from the Great Lakes to New York City, and was quite the busy waterway for many years following. By my time, it was pretty quiet, if not moribund. To me, the canal was a place I was really, really expected to stay away from. Given that our house was about 100 feet away from the bank, and the bank was steep and wildly overgrown, it's not hard to understand that keeping us away from it was my parents' primary safety concern. They told us there were water moccasins in it. I never tried to find out.

The canal was otherwise just a barrier between us and Main Street, which was the heart of town. To get there didn't take long: a short walk up a road directly across from our house, then a right and a slightly longer walk paralleling the canal, then across the bridge and there you were. Of principal, or exclusive, interest to me were the movie theatre, which was the primary source of community entertainment for kids, and the church, which we attended rarely, preferring to spend our Sunday mornings reading the news and the funnies in a parlor full of smoke. The Reveille office was thereabouts as well, and I had to have been there at times, but it left no lasting imprint. There was a Saturday afternoon one winter, when Eric and I were so determined to see that week's showing at the theatre that we slogged through a very harsh snowstorm to get there. We got to the ticket booth, excited to have made it and to be seeing some friends there, and realized we had no money. Somehow, the grumpy old fellow in a suit and tie who was always there got wind of our plight and gave each of us the 15 cents admission fee. He told us he expected us to pay him back, and we promised we would.

We had neighbors diagonally across the street who had a garage and a late-model car. On Saturday morning, that car would get backed out into the driveway and for the rest of the morning the whole family would set to work cleaning it. They'd clean it with buckets of warm, soapy water and rags and sponges and a hose running the whole time for rinsing. They'd bring out the vacuum cleaner and crawl around inside with it, and they'd open up the trunk and pull out the tire and clean that all out. When they were done, the car went back in the garage and the family went back in the house.

We had a next-door neighbor who had a kid who sometimes played with us, but who distinguished himself one time when he had a problem with his water supply or cesspool or something else deep in the ground. He had to dig a big hole in the middle of his driveway to get to it. All by himself, with no other equipment than a pointed shovel, he dug and dug for hours. The hole became an object of interest to the neighborhood kids and a few adults too. It was a steaming hot day to be digging a hole, but he kept going down until his head was well below ground level and there were tall heaps of dirt ringing the hole. We kids were standing on these mounds watching, when somebody sent a mini-avalanche down into the hole. It went down the man's bare back and into his pants, and he glared up and shouted, NOW YOU KIDS GET AWAY FROM THERE! I said to a friend as we walked off: What a grouch!

There was a family that lived at the other end of Latham Road, meaning about four houses down from us. They had a boy close to my age, so we were in each other's homes fairly often. His mother's name was Madeline. They had a puppy named Seasons who often joined us in our play. The family was away one afternoon when some of the neighborhood kids were hanging around trying to think of something to do. Somebody suggested we should go to Madeline's house and feed Seasons, since nobody was around to do it. Finding the doors locked when we got there, one of the kids climbed in through a cellar sash and came through the house and let us in. We played with Seasons a little, then I went pawing through their stuff in the back room, looking for dog food. When I heard everyone scurrying around and the side door slamming, I went into the living room to find out what was going on. Just as I got to the front door, it opened and there was Madeline. She looked like a giant, an angry one. She grabbed me by the arm and shouted WHAT ARE YOU DOING IN MY HOUSE? What could I say? "Feeding Seasons".

Later, I gave Madeline further cause to think I was a rotten kid. Her son's birthday was coming up, and she and her husband bought a toy rifle for him, then hid it in the garage. A friend of mine was snooping around in their garage one day and found it, and took it. He showed it to me in the barn, and though I knew there was something not quite right about the way he'd acquired it, I took a "what's done is done" attitude towards it. Our yard backed up to the home of a nice family with a boy a little younger than my thieving friend and me. We went over to see if he wanted to play guns, but what we wound up doing was terrorizing him with it in his playhouse. We were playacting, but he didn't know the gun was a toy and he didn't know we were playing, so when we threatened him he got really scared. We finally got the sense that we shouldn't be doing this, so we let him go and went back to the barn. Of course, the kid told his mother, and the next day my parents were asking me about the incident, and the heat came down on my friend, so he threw the gun in the canal, and a little later I was in Madeline's living room, playing with a nice barnyard and miniature animals that I was giving her son as restitution for the loss of his toy gun and the part I'd played in it. Everyone was being nice to me, and I had the feeling that things were being set right, and I felt it was okay that I should give the boy one of my favorite toys.

During our summer in Seneca Falls, my family took a week's vacation at a cabin in a campground a little bit uphill from Cayuga Lake. It may have been a state park, because there was a large paved parking lot at the bottom of the hill and renters of the cabins walked up dirt paths to their cabins. Across from the parking lot was a sizable installation on the lake: a drive-up dock big enough to accommodate several boats and a paved drive/bulkhead along the shore that led to what I believe was a bathhouse. We got ice cream there a couple of times. The swimming was nice enough, though the water had a lot of sausage-sized clumps of dirt or organic matter floating around in it. They weren't turds, but it was hard not to be suspicious. Our cabin was one room, as they all appeared to be. It may have had a propane campstove, but the only eating that I recall was at a campfire outside the cabin, where potatoes wrapped in foil in the coals came out utterly charred, but very tasty inside.

Our toilet needs were served by a communal latrine that had a single bare lightbulb, a distressing aroma and clouds of mosquitoes with the wingspan of hummingbirds.

A couple of significant material acquisitions attended our time in Seneca Falls. We acquired a 1954 Ford sedan, copperish in color, that stayed with the family for several years and served us well. We also bought a television, also copperish in color, a little bit smaller and lighter than the Ford and destined to outlast it. The time period between having just a few friends with a TV and being one of the few families without one was very brief. The cultural benefits and educational opportunities offered through ownership of a TV were being widely trumpeted, and the Turkingtons got on board.

The Turkingtons also moved on again after just about one year in Seneca Falls. Again, there was no discussion of the move that made any sort of impression on me. A little while before we moved, the boys were told we were going to move. Our next home was to be Elkton, Maryland, where the Cecil Democrat may have looked like a more agreeable candidate for a friendly takeover than the Reveille had turned out to be. Or was it something else entirely? Nobody ever told me, and anyone who knew isn't talking any more.

* * *

Between Seneca Falls and Elkton, everything I know about myself and can recall about the two towns would suggest that Seneca Falls was the cooler place, and more my kind of town. But Elkton really stuck with me; I retain more powerful, enduring images and impressions from Elkton than either my time there or the depth of my experiences would seem to call for. It may just be that there is something about the ages of 7 and 8 that activates a lasting sense of selfhood, and that one's surroundings and accompanying events right at that time have an impact beyond warrant.

Other than being the county seat of Cecil County, the northeasternmost county in Maryland, Elkton's principal distinguishing characteristic was that it was for many years known as the place to go for a couple that wanted to get married in a hurry. Municipal districts everywhere then had, and maybe still do, a waiting period of some kind between the act of taking out the marriage license and actually tying the knot. This was not the case in Elkton, so a lot of impatient, often eloping couples came from distant places to become man and wife there. Some pretty famous people passed through town on this mission. I don't imagine this did a lot to boost the economy of the town - it's not as if any of the newlyweds stuck around for their honeymoon - but it got its name out there among the impulsive set.

Our home was at 139 West High Street, in the center of town. The High Streets ran parallel to Main Street and were a couple of blocks away. Our place was a duplex, as were at least some of the others on our block. The houses were so close together that nobody had a side yard, the road behind so near that nobody had much of a back yard either. We had a small front porch about 8 feet from the sidewalk, from which you entered the living room, which was pretty small, then past the stairs into the dining room, about the same size, then straight through a door into the kitchen. From the kitchen there was a back door that led out to a shed-roofed storage room, then to the back yard, which was the width of our half of the duplex and maybe 40 feet deep. The stairway was steep and kind of narrow. My bedroom was on the right at the top, looking out over the street; a hallway ran to the left past the bathroom, Eric's room and my parents' room, in that order. There was a large metal grille in the floor of the dining room, under which was a smelly furnace that blew hot air up into the room and was the house's only source of heat.

Knowing what I've since learned about how even relatively unmaterialistic people feel about their home, I can't help thinking that 139 West High Street was not quite what my parents would have had in mind for their living situation at this stage in their lives or that of their kids. It could be that their effort to assume the reins of the Reveille involved some sacrifice on their part that didn't pan out, though here they were doing it again, if in fact they were trying to do what I suspect they were trying to do. More likely, they'd come up against the cold facts of the cost of living and the difficulties of meeting those costs with one wage-earner in a field that is not lucrative, and two young boys who want things that cost money.

Kids, fortunately, don't – or didn't at the time – give much thought to the level of grandeur of the place they lived. The TV networks were just beginning to introduce shows that displayed happy white kids having fine times in splendid homes, so we kind of took what we got. There were certain highly desirable elements to our situation there that may not have been seen as big plusses to adults, but scored high with me.

Behind all the homes on our block was an unimproved little road that served to provide access to everybody's parking spaces and back yards, such as they were. On the other side of the road was a very large brick building that may have been a warehouse or a shuttered industry of some kind. There was never any traffic to, from, or in or out of it. I never knew anybody who was ever in there, which surprises me now, knowing what I do of my peers' limited degree of respect for private property. The place had a big gravel parking lot that was directly behind our house and was big enough to turn tractor-trailers around in, if any had ever shown up. The lot wasn't very level and its surface was pretty rough, but it served well for playing ball or racing around on our bikes. The east end of the lot was bounded by a corn crib that was often half-filled with corn cobs. When it was, we could often be found – or what was better, not found – waging corn cob wars inside it.

Right behind the warehouse and corn crib were a few parallel sets of railroad tracks. Shortly after we moved there, the tracks got dead-ended to make room for Elkton's first supermarket. We were there for its grand opening, where I got a free ice cream cone. The remaining tracks were not entirely inactive, though nearly so; a freight train would pull in now and then to serve an establishment that we called the feed mill. This was a going, though not seemingly very busy, concern that must have served farmers and horse people. There were big stacks of burlap bags filled with animal feed all over the place, and lots of tools for digging or shoveling for sale. Most of the time, there were a few overhead doors open to the street on the other side, and we felt we could wander in and out pretty much at will. There was a nice, earthy smell inside, and a Coke machine we patronized, and usually a few old fellows sitting around waiting for customers or the freight train. They weren't hostile to roaming neighborhood kids, but they didn't let us play hide and seek in there, though they had the perfect setup for it.

Around the corner of the brick warehouse, tucked between it and the remaining railroad tracks, was an outdoor storage depot where the phone company kept a lot of their equipment, or so I now surmise. To us at the time, it was just a bunch of unattended, unwanted gear. Immense spools of all sorts and sizes of wires and cables stood here and there in disorderly fashion. There was a stack of creosoted phone poles with grass growing all around them. Best of all, there was a big pile of green glass insulators that they used to run the wires around as they were strung from pole to pole. You'll see them in collectibles shops now, but then they were used on the crossbars on every phone pole, and here there was a big pile of thousands of them. We stood about twenty feet away and heaved them at the pile, one at a time, to watch them smash to bits. And why not? Nobody ever told us not to.

I think it was early winter when I became the new kid in the 2nd grade class at the Howard Street School, which was on the other side of the center of town from where we lived, maybe a fifteen minute walk. The school was a cubic brick building that harkened back to earlier days of public education: two classrooms, no office, no assembly hall, no amenities whatsoever beyond a coatroom and adjacent bathroom. I believe the other classroom was also 2nd grade. They were upstairs, we were down. We had separate recess times and therefore had nothing to do with each other. If I had to guess how many kids were in our classroom, I'd say fifty; it was a very big room, and except for a little reading area at one end it was packed with desks, row upon row of them. Our teacher was Miss McLane, tall, dark-haired, younger than most schoolteachers were at that time. She was not terribly strict ("strict", "not too strict", and variations on the theme of strictness were the most commonly used assessments of our teachers), but the class stayed under control. Miss McLane was warm and pleasant enough to make us want to please her, but disconnected enough to make us fear what she might do if she got really upset. There were times when the entire class was doing the same activity silently at their desks. I would look up sometimes and see her at her desk, looking into a compact mirror and brushing her hair or touching up her lipstick.

Recess was by far the most memorable time of the day, not least because for a little while there developed intense boy-girl interactions in the schoolyard. Innocent games of tag evolved into kissing games, in which each gender in turn would chase down the other, corner them and give them a big smootch as an emblem of success in the chase. The boys chased the girls, the girls chased the boys, and it was just incredibly exciting while it lasted. I try to imagine this activity being allowed to go on now, and can't picture it. There was an alpha female in the group by the name of Roseanne, known to all as Rosie. She was very pretty, had neatly cut and brushed red hair, always dressed well and was laden with self-confidence. She lived in one of the finer homes in Elkton, a little ways down from Main Street. My friend Reggie and I did on a few occasions get home from school, dress ourselves up, comb our hair and go to visit Rosie. She had a couple of friends named Brenda and Susan who joined us once or twice for play in her big yard. Then, a couple of times, we were told at the door by Rosie's mother – a smiling, gracious, red-haired 35-year old version of Rosie – that Rosie couldn't come out today, and so we gave up on that.

Another playground episode – less rewarding than kissing girls – came about one day when somehow I accumulated three one-dollar bills and decided to bring them to school with me. Three dollars was a lot of cash for a 7-year-old kid to be flashing around, but I wanted to show off and I wanted to enact an image I'd acquired from some cartoon or comic book, of a wealthy man with currency visibly sticking out from his pockets or from under his hat (!). I enacted this at recess time, and got some laughs. I also drew the attention of a kid who asked me if I wanted to buy a watch with those three dollars. He showed me the watch, and it looked pretty cool. I'd always thought it'd be fun to have a watch, so I gave him the three and he gave me the watch. As he walked back into the school, he shouted to me: "The mainspring's busted!" "No it's not!" I shouted back, but it turned out the watch couldn't keep time, busted mainspring or no. Somehow, I revealed this sad exchange to my parents after I'd determined that the watch was no good. Dad took it upon himself to call the kid's home, talked to his mother and explained why he felt that I ought to get my money back. She insisted that I made the deal of my own free will, and her son was going to keep the money. Nice try Dad, but I'm not sure you know what you're dealing with here.

To get to the bathroom from our classroom, you walked out into the entryway, then took a right into the coatroom where we hung up our outerwear, then into the bathroom. One time Miss McLane excused me to go there, and as I entered the coatroom I saw all the coats piled up on the floor in front of a window with a wide sill that looked out on Howard Street. One of the boys from the other class was jumping from the windowsill onto the pile of coats. When he saw me come in, he left without a word. I went in to take a leak, then on the way back decided to have a jump on the coat pile. I climbed up onto the sill, heard a noise and saw in the doorway the school district superintendent, who made it his business to stop by from time to time to see how things were going at the Howard Street School. Every classroom had a paddle ready to hand for such occasions as this, and the superintendent went on in and got it, came back and whacked me good and hard on the ass many times. He disbelieved my assurances that I had nothing to do with this, then made me hang all the coats back up, which I did, sobbing all the while.

Elkton's public library was just past the little business district on Main Street, and a charming place it was. A stone wall that was chin-high to a 7-year-old curved in from the sidewalk and led to the front steps. The wall was topped with pointed stones like the back of a stegosaurus, and the building on its little lot was surrounded by trees and bushes. It wasn't a big place, but it had two stories and was broken up into lots of little rooms, so there were nooks and crannies and spots to explore all around. In the largest room, the one with the big window that looked out on Main Street, was a finely carved, full-sized lion that was irresistible for a kid to sit on. I don't think we were supposed to do that, but the librarian was kindly enough to look the other way most of the time. Years later, I read a short story about a guy in New York City who somehow achieved invisibility. Now he could do something he'd always wanted to do but didn't want to be seen doing, which was to climb up on the back of one of the stone lions in front of the New York Public library. So he did, but while he was up there riding, he suddenly became visible again. People saw him and shouted at him with good cheer, encouragement even, so he didn't get down because he realized that everybody had the same fantasy. Mine was fulfilled many times at the Elkton Public library.

Being just a couple of blocks from Main Street, my time at West High Street was as close as I had ever come to urban living, or would for a long time. I spent a fair amount of after-school time downtown with a friend or two, roaming around aimlessly. Except for the library, there wasn't a place in town where unsupervised kids were welcome. The 5&10 – I think it was a JJ Newberry's – had an automated puppet in a glass case that hopped around to the tune of "Turkey In The Straw" for a nickel, but nickels were valuable and the puppet's act got old fast. Usually when we were downtown, we walked around outside hoping to see something interesting. I was wandering through an alley with a friend one day when we started poking through some trash cans and came across several sheets of 3-cent postage stamps. What a find! There had to have been many hundreds of them, and stamps then were the next best thing to cold cash. Some of the ads for junky kids' stuff in the backs of the comic books directed the buyer, Cash or Stamps Only Please! Later on, when as a young adult I was first paying bills and buying things through the mail, a lot of the invoices said, Cash or Check Only! No Stamps Please! Which would imply that 15 years later the practice was only beginning to go out of style. And here we were with armloads of them!

We divvied up our find and went homeward. I knew there'd be no way to turn my stamps into cash except through my parents, so I showed them to them. To my surprise, they didn't react with joy, but something more like consternation. They questioned me closely as to where and how we found them. They called the other kid's parents and talked to them. Dad told me he was going to talk to the businesses that backed up to that alley – The Cecil Democrat was one of them – to try to find who was missing them. A few days later, I was cleared. Nobody claimed their loss, and Mom and Dad deposited the value of the stamps in my savings account. So I got the rewards of my good fortune, but it surely did suck the pleasure out of it to face such doubt and well-intended investigation on my parents' part. We could have been prancing around the house in ecstasy, but instead everybody was Doing The Right Thing.

Elkton Elementary School would have been visible from our little back yard if the feed mill hadn't been in the way. It was an aging place, somewhat smaller than Falmouth's Village School but with an identical layout: stairway at either end, hallway in the middle, classrooms either side, all alike. What Elkton had done to try to keep up with the surge in the population of little kids was to add on a multipurpose assembly hall with a stage at one end and a lunch kitchen at the other. The space served as cafeteria, gymnasium and auditorium and was not well suited for anything. It was connected to the old classroom building by a flat-roofed hallway with big fixed-glass windows on either side. It was the first touch of modernity I'd experienced in my schooling life.

The principal of Elkton Elementary was a gracious lady named Rose Ricuparo, who was well regarded by the new second grade teacher, Dorothy Turkington. How Mom could move into town with no teaching training or experience and six months later be handed the reins of a classful of kids, I do not know, but I'm sure Elkton was facing a dilemma shared by many school districts in the 50's: hordes of kids to educate and not enough teachers to educate them. My 3rd grade teacher was Mrs. Lort, who was not new to the game but good at it. She was kindly and encouraging and personal. Not very strict, except when she had to be. Eric was a big 5th-grader now, up on the top floor. Mom made mention once that the written comment from his teacher at the end of his first marking term was, "Eric is a nice quiet boy". He's the smartest kid in your class, for Christ's sake, lady. Is that all you can think of to say about him? That comment is mine, not Mom's. She just smiled and shook her head at the time.

In Mrs. Lort's class, as no doubt in all others in Elkton and probably the length and breadth of America, our day started with a salute to the flag and the Lord's Prayer. Most everyone knew the Lord's Prayer from Sunday School, and anyone who didn't picked it up pretty quickly, because we recited it every day. When we did, we folded our hands and bowed our heads with our eyes shut tight. One time during the prayer, I heard a slight noise from the next row of desks. I opened my eyes a crack, looked to my left, and there was Jimmy Barnes, standing up and doing the hula in the aisle. He had a big grin on his face, and I wondered how God would choose to punish him for his blasphemous behavior.

Here and in all classrooms that have ever existed, an earnest effort was made to inculcate our fertile minds with the things we'd need to know to make it in society. A lot of what we were taught was surely exactly what kids everywhere were learning. Then there were those materials that were somewhat open to interpretation through regional or local points of view. My first awareness of the Civil War was gained in third grade, where Mrs. Lort assured us that all the fighting really had nothing to do with the issue of slavery, but was all about states' rights. The southern states wanted to hold onto the rights they'd always enjoyed, and the northern states wanted to take them away. It seemed simple enough to me, and well worth fighting for. Elkton sits just a few miles from the Mason-Dixon line, and Maryland was forcefully persuaded not to secede in 1861, but this was a southern town and culture. During music time, a lot of our songs were from Steven Foster: finely composed, sentimental pieces about the antebellum South. A lot of others drew amusing caricatures of black people. I prefer to believe we'll never again see the likes of a roomful of white 8-year-olds singing:

> Two little chillun just a lyin' in bed, one of 'em sick and de other 'most dead.
> Call for de doctah and de doctah sed, Feed dem chillun on shortnin' bread.
> Momma's little baby loves shortnin', shortnin', momma's little baby loves shortnin' bread. (repeat)

It was in the classroom one day that I was given some early insight into the nature of intelligence. We were doing some science learning, and Mrs. Lort asked every kid to give her the name of an insect. Up and down the aisles we went, naming insects or creatures that were so like insects that Mrs. Lort refrained from correcting the confused by telling them, "Oh no, a spider is an arachnid". She just let it go. But then it was the turn of the girl in front of me, and she said "Uhhh…bug?" And I was really stunned, that she should be so unable to see that "bug" was categorically different than "moth" or "ant" or "bee" or whatever else she'd been hearing. Nice girl, not bad to sit behind, but boy, was that a clueless answer.

At one point, Mom's sympathetic heart led her to open up our home to a boy in her class and his younger sister, who were among the poorest of the poor in the school. They came over once in a while so Mom could fix up some food for them, or cut the boy's hair or brush the girl's, or let them wash up, or find some clothes that I'd outgrown that they liked. Eric and Mom and I got back from school one day to find the back door open. When we went into the house, we found our dog Jingles cowering in a corner of the kitchen. There was a baseball bat on the floor and some drawers and cabinet doors were open. Mom and Dad did some inventory that night and figured out that a bunch of silver dollars that we boys had been given by our grandparents were gone, along with a few other things of little value that I've forgotten. The police came by, took some notes and said they'd investigate.

Mom did some investigating of her own and became convinced that our two waifs did the deed, whacking Jingles with the bat when she tried to chase them away. How it all played out I don't know and never did, but one evening soon afterwards there was a meeting in the living room with a cop and the kids' mother. By Mom's account, the officer assured her that they would keep trying to find the perp, but that those two kids didn't do it, of that he was sure. After he left, the kids' mother said to Mom, "Please don't press charges. We'll get the silver dollars back." With some cooperation from the police force and the merchants who distinctly remembered just when and from whom that silver dollar came across the counter, they were all returned. There was nothing in the way she treated troubled kids later on that would suggest that Mom lost any of her faith in young people over this episode, but her heart had to have been bruised.

At some point during our time in Elkton, my family took a couple of days to visit Baltimore. We'd done this sort of thing with New York a couple of times and would again, but that was always in conjunction with a lengthier stayover at my mom's parents' home in Great Neck, on Long Island. This Baltimore trip was out of the blue, as we knew nobody there and had no connection with the city. It was undertaken with the aim of showing the boys a more cosmopolitan side of life and seeing the sights. We viewed the USS Constellation, an early American battleship that did service in the War of 1812, I believe. It was, naturally, on the Baltimore waterfront, amid rotting wharves and sinking piers and all the detritus of a broken-down, unneeded, untended anachronism long removed from the glory days of a thriving harbor scene. The ship itself was in the very early stages of restoration, but all the more affecting for its decrepitude. Very few historical sites in the 50's were fixed up, glitzed up and friendly to the fastidious; they showed their age and their wrinkles, very often in a setting that had lost all evidence of importance.

We toured Fort McHenry, the fort that withstood a night of bombardment from the British and in so doing inspired Francis Scott Key to pen what would become our national anthem. There were ramparts and cannons and a few displays of artillery. A visit to the Fort was a self-guided affair, or maybe we were there in the offseason. Dad took pictures of us in various locations, which he later developed and printed in the darkroom of the Democrat. I brought one in to school to accompany my recounting of the trip to the class. In this photo, I was straddling a cannon with my hands on its sides in front of me, grinning at the camera. When I passed it around the class, there was a lot of snickering and even some outbursts of laughter that I couldn't understand until I'd given it a little reflection. It was actually a pretty funny picture. I'm surprised my parents didn't intercept it on its way to Elkton Elementary.

We went to a rather hoity-toity restaurant named Miller's one of our evenings in Baltimore. We didn't eat out a whole lot, but so far in my life, whenever we had, I'd ordered from the children's menu. The same was probably true of Eric. I don't know at whose volition it was that tonight we'd be ordering from the main menu, but that's what we did. With encouragement from Dad, who assured us that Miller's was known far and wide for its chicken pot pie, we each ordered that. Well, this Miller's chicken pot pie was an immense quantity of food. The dish it came in could have been a salad bowl for a large family. And it was very, very tasty. We ate and ate, and with some determination managed to polish it off. We had a bit of dessert, then Mom and Dad lit up and lingered at great length over their coffees, as was their wont, while Eric and I left the table to roam around, as was ours. We took a quick tour of the restaurant, then went out into the street to explore. We must have been gone quite a while, because when we got back to Miller's our parents were waiting stiffly at the door with their jackets on. There was no scolding, but we could tell.

My best friend in Elkton was a classmate named Bobby Jones. I was a pretty sociable kid at 8, got along with most everybody and hung out with a lot of different kids, but Bobby Jones was the guy I'd sit with at lunch, and head out to the playground with, whose home I'd bike over to on Saturday and whose family I got to know pretty well. The Joneses lived at 245 East High Street, which was the slightly more hardscrabble end of the street. On our block, there was a car behind every house and all the men got up to go to work every morning. The houses had paint on them, and the front porches were in good repair. Not everyone on East High Street enjoyed such prosperity. The little front yards were more dirt than grass. You'd see cardboard where there was a broken window pane and smell kerosene when you walked in the door in the winter. There was no sharp distinction between the two neighborhoods – mind you, my home was about a quarter mile from Bobby's – but things were a little more downtrodden at that end of the street, and I noticed it.

Bobby had a brother named Curt, who was in my mother's 2nd grade class, but was big for his age and a good kid, so he often wound up playing with us. He had an older sister whose name escapes me who was in Eric's class. I saw a lot of his mother, an expansive and welcoming woman of some spirit. His father, I was told at the time, had a job as treasurer of their church, and I may never have interacted with him. I did once see the parents both seated at the table, busily sorting a pile of coins. The Joneses had at least one luxury that the Turkingtons did not: a bigger back yard with a garage. The garage wasn't big enough to do much of anything in, though we did sometimes enjoy the challenge of seeing who could piss highest up on the wall.

More than anything else, we played baseball. If there were just the two of us, we'd play catch. Add another, and someone could hit. Add a couple more, and we could play bataround, which is the most rudimentary form of a real baseball game. Add a few more, and bataround starts looking like the real thing. A few more, and you can start thinking about two teams. Whatever congregation of kids might show up in the same place at the same time was a random event, determined entirely by the laws of chance. There was Little League, or perhaps a more local organization, that had tryouts one day in the spring. I went to the tryouts, but being among the youngest was completely ignored by the coaching staff. I found myself filling up the outfield with at least a dozen other little kids, waiting for someone to hit the ball out there. The only activity was initiated by a husky kid a little to my left, who kept shouting HUM BATTER! HUM BATTER BATTER! HUM BATTER! After a while, tryouts were over and I went home, not to return.

I bought my first of many hundreds of packs of baseball cards in Elkton. Some other kids I knew had started accumulating them, and they were about baseball, so I was pretty excited to have some of my own. I opened that first pack up in my room, and there on the top was Johnny Logan of the Milwaukee Braves. The part of me that is capable of instant loyalty rushed to the fore at that point, so Johnny Logan became my favorite player for the rest of his moderately distinguished career, the Milwaukee Braves my favorite team for many years. Bobby Jones's favorite player, and that of most other Elkton boys, was Harry Anderson, who'd grown up nearby and was at that time enjoying a pretty fair season or two with, I think, Cincinnati, before drifting out of the majors. All the other kids were Harry the Horse when they came to bat in a ballgame. Not me, though; I was Johnny Logan. His nickname was "Yatcha", and at an old-timers game in Fenway Park decades later (Johnny had played for the Braves before they left Boston), he hit a home run over the left field wall. I ill-advisedly sold the bulk of my baseball card collection in about 1982, but I held back some representative cards from every year along with samples of some of the biggest names: the Stan Musials, Hank Aarons, Ernie Bankses, Warren Spahns, Ted Williamses, and Johnny Logans.

Baseball cards weren't my only interest. Eric, for reasons long forgotten, started up a collection of Indian head pennies, inspiring me to join in the world of numismatics with a collection of Lincoln pennies. Bad move, Tom. The Lincolns were very easy to come by, of course, but few of them had much collectors' value and, since they've never stopped making them, never achieved the cachet that discontinued coins would. People at that time still would often find Indian heads in their pocket change, and those who knew of Eric's interest would save them for delivery to him. The object of collecting a particular coin was to garner one sample from each year and each mint (Philadelphia, Denver or San Fransisco) that issued them.

In time, we both came pretty close to completing our collections. Dad helped in this effort by bringing home the mounds of change that the newspaper carriers brought in to the newspaper office. Eric and I spent a lot of Saturday mornings rummaging through all these coins, looking for vacancies in our collections or anything else that had collector's value. This little touch of graft rewarded us one day with the discovery of a 1916D Liberty head dime. Even in its worn condition it was worth serious money, so on our next trip to New York we brought it to Gimbel's, an immense department store in Manhattan. Can you imagine a department store with a numismatics section? Gimbel's had one, and it wasn't shoved over in some corner either; it had aisles and display cases and counters and dignified workers. They gave us a cool ten dollars for the coin, which covered the cost of treating the family to lunch at a swanky joint in midtown. I was more of the opinion that Eric and I should split that ten-spot and buy what we wanted, but Eric was all for doing the gracious thing and I went along without complaint.

Back before I started kindergarten, I picked up rudimentary reading skills via comic books, which I continued to enjoy for years afterwards. At first, Eric read them to me as I followed the artwork, then I went solo as soon as I was able. I've often thought that early childhood education should recognize the potential benefits of starting little readers in on comic books. They match up the written narrative with a series of panels that depict a story unfolding before the reader's eyes. Most children's books also do this. The difference is that a kid looking at a comic book really wants to know what's going on, a motivation that very few children's books are able to excite, hard though they try. All the Disney characters had comics in their own name, as did all the Loony Tunes figures. Then there were a whole lot of others who existed no place other than in the world of comics: Baby Huey, Richie Rich, Little Lotto, Gyro Gearloose and many others too numerous to mention or remember. At the time, the only superheroes known to me were Superman (and Supergirl and Superboy) and Batman (and Robin). Marvel Comics was beginning to widen its cast of characters, but my full awareness of them came later.

More sophisticated than those comics from the rack at the drug store were the Pogo books, which started commanding my attention at about this time. These were compilations of Walt Kelly's all-time greatest comic strip about the critters in the Okefenokee Swamp. They were hip, wise, hilarious and meaningful on many levels. I knew as I read them that there were political and cultural references that were beyond my understanding, but I loved them and bought or received as gifts all that were available. Even the most insipid strips nowadays seem to warrant being compiled in a book, usually of coffee table book dimensions, but then it was just Pogo and Peanuts in little paperbacks. Pogo was my choice and remained so for years. It seems that there is currently a series of hardcover books under way that intends to reprint all the Pogo strips from the beginning. I'm on it.

My stage of reading the comics/funnies never truly ended, but by now I usually had a real book going as well, and not solely because a certain amount of storybook reading was expected of me at school. The only book I retain from my youth is a first edition of Charlotte's Web, still intact but somewhat damaged from an attack of mildew on the cover, suffered no doubt due to improper storage at some point in its past. It sits prominently on my bookshelves now, along with a few solemn-looking young people's books that must have been hand-me-downs from my parents. Except for Doctor Doolittle's Garden, I never read them - Rudyard Kipling didn't have much to say to American baby boomers - and probably never will. I'm afraid to touch them, actually; they're practically 100 years old. Alongside them sits The Common Sense Book of Baby and Child Care, by Dr. Spock. This was certainly not the first book of child-rearing advice, but it was probably the most influential. It was encyclopedic, revolutionary and wildly popular. If you think of the children of the 50's as the Cuckoo Generation, blame it on Dr. Spock and the Rolling Stones.

Elkton was not an extremely small town - it was the county seat of Cecil County, supported two newspapers and a department store, and had a short but busy Main Street with shops, restaurants, clothing stores, a sporting goods store, a hardware store and some bars. There was a hospital – a decent-sized one for those days – between our place and Main Street, and an auto dealership on the corner in the other direction that took up very little space and sold Opels, or tried to. There was a lot of country just outside of town, though, including a horse farm a few miles off where Mom and Dad decided that their sons would learn to ride. So for a lengthy spell of Saturdays, Eric and I went out there and rode horseback, western style. I thought it was a lot of fun, though I'm not sure how much instruction there was. Actually, I'm pretty sure there was none. We spent most of our time there riding single file on the trails behind more experienced riders. As soon as we got back, we'd get off our horses and go home. They always put me on Chief, who was a rust-colored and amiable old cayuse who they felt would be good with a little guy like me. And they were right; Chief and I got along fine.

So the horseback riding was cool, until the ranch held their annual rodeo where their riders got to show off their skills. I had no skills! I was at that rodeo, decked out as a knight in shining armor, meaning aluminum foil, watching with dread as the older kids took their horses around a long line of poles, like skiers in a slalom race and almost as fast. When it came my turn, they put me on a strange horse and slapped him on the rump. The horse had no idea where he was supposed to go and I had no idea how to tell him. We roamed this way and that around the ring for an agonizing minute or two before a ranch hand took him by the bridle and led us to the fence where my parents were. I thought I heard people laughing, and I was utterly humiliated and in tears. As soon as my feet were on the ground, I said to the ranch hand, Get Chief. He started saying that Chief wasn't riding tonight and Mom was there telling me what a nice job I did, and I stood there and said, GET CHIEF! So there was a little parley, and a few minutes later there was Chief all saddled up, and they put me on him and we headed towards the poles. We went between a few at a walk, missed a couple, weaved between a pair or two at a trot, got to the other end, turned about and came back in similar fashion. I rode him to the fence, brought him to a halt, dismounted, heard some applause and wasn't crying any more. But Mom was.

Elkton wasn't far from Chesapeake City, which was at the foot of the Chesapeake and Delaware Canal, which provided a calm water route between those two great bays and cut off the Delmarva Peninsula from the mainland. There was a funky little marina there that was overseen by Captain Bob, who always wore a sailor's cap and had a face that looked like it had never been out of the weather. He was a kindly old fellow, and Dad bought a boat from him. Dad acquired a love of boats one summer in his late teens, when he crewed a charter sailor that cruised up and down the New England coast. If this was wish fulfillment, I give him credit for accepting such a modest beginning. The Pickle, as we named her, was an aluminum skiff, maybe 14 feet long, with a 5 horsepower outboard motor and a set of oars and oarlocks for use when the motor broke down. This was what might be called a starter boat, but it provided the essential service of recreational boats everywhere: it got us to places we'd never have gotten to by land. The principal such place, in our case, was the middle of the Chesapeake and Delaware Canal within a mile or two of Captain Bob's marina. The way was not without its charms. A favorite of mine was an embankment of dense orange clay that sloped sharply upwards from the narrow clay beach. With a wet swimsuit and a touch of courage, a boy could climb up to the top of the bank and slide down at high speed. Over and over and over, he could.

Dad further catered to his devotion to watercraft by subscribing to Yachting magazine. I don't think I ever heard the word "yacht" spoken in our home, and if I did, I detected no connection between the word and the magazine about boats, which in my mind I pronounced exactly as it was spelled: "yach-ting". Having begun to get out on the water, I was developing an appreciation of boats that led me to take an issue of Yachting magazine and a pair of scissors up to my room, to cut out pictures of the ones I liked. It didn't occur to me that anybody would mind, but I guess Dad did, for reasons I fully understand now. A few days after I took the mag, Mom asked me very pointedly whether I'd seen the latest issue of Yotting magazine, and since I didn't know what she was talking about, I said I hadn't. A little later, Dad came into my room as I was sitting at my desk with a bunch of cut-out pictures of boats and his shredded magazine in plain view, and asked me with great solemnity if I'd seen his Yotting magazine anywhere. I said no. He told me to be sure to get it to him if I saw it, and I said I would. He must have left my room thinking, That son of mine better learn to tell the truth, because he sure is a piss-poor liar. And I'm thinking, I've never heard of this magazine they're talking about, why do they keep bugging me about it?

There were black families in Elkton; there were probably quite a few, but I can't guess at how many there were because I seldom saw evidence of them. I heard reference on occasion to "the colored school", to use the polite term, but I had no idea where it was or what it was like. The civil rights movement was beginning to make news in faraway places, but it engendered no discussion among the kids about the whys and wherefores of it, among ourselves or with the guidance of our teachers. Whether segregation was a legal fact of life in Maryland in 1957 I don't know, but it might as well have been for all the interaction there was between the races. Bobby's home may have backed up close to the black section of town, because it wasn't unusual for our baseball games to include a few black kids from nearby. The closest we generally came to a discussion of ethics or morals was when we were passing around a bottle of soda and questioning whether what was gained by wiping the neck of the bottle with your hand (removing the germs) was worth the implied insult to the last guy who'd taken a swig (who put the germs there). I don't believe we ever settled that one.

Adults, presumably, had loftier questions on their minds, and I have my suspicions that my parents never felt wholly comfortable with the mismatch between the operative racial values of their adopted community and those that they held. Neither of them would ever tell either of their sons what he ought to think or believe, but they – or Mom, anyway – did make an observation once in a while, or ask a question, with the objective of investigating what we were hearing or beginning to believe. And I don't think they would have been entirely encouraged by the feedback, such as it was. We plunked ourselves down into a culture with a powerful racial bias, and surprise! The young boys showed signs of absorbing it. There may well have been other issues, but I know my folks were connected with a number of good families and thought well of the school and the library, but decided to move on from Elkton at the end of my year in third grade.

Eric and I were informed of this next move some time before it was undertaken, and I retain at least one shred of insight concerning the reasons for it that derives, as do so many, not from anything I remember thinking at the time, but from the consequences of an action I took that indicated what I was thinking. Towards the end of third grade, I was at Bobby's house, in his front room, with his mother and siblings. The subject of my departure came up, and Mrs. Jones asked me why we were leaving Elkton. I told her, well, one thing my parents don't like is that they've heard me using swear words I've learned from kids. She asked me, Really? What kind of kids are using swear words around you? And I went and said, Well, Bobby and Curt do. Can you believe I said that? Neither could I as soon as the words came out. Vulgarities and little boys have an attraction to each other, and a lot of cross-fertilization goes on in the process of learning them, and the Jones boys were no more guilty of their dissemination than many of us. But I couldn't have explained that at the time, and Mrs. Jones would have been in no mood to listen. I can still see the horror in Bobby's face as she came at him with the paddle. She really let him have it, then Curt in turn, and up to their room they went, with promises of more to come ringing in their ears. I looked over at their sister as I headed out. She was half smiling, half grimacing and fully shocked.

When I saw Bobby in school the next morning, he had a somber look about him. He asked me why I'd done what I did, and I told him I didn't know why. I mean, what could I say? His mother asked me a question, and I answered it without thinking of what would happen. I'd never been and never was much for telling on kids, given that there were usually things kids could have told on me about, and most of them didn't. I just screwed up on this one.

I was sorry, but didn't know how to tell him so. Tongue-tied a day too late.

* * *

Here I make two reference breaks. One was inadvertent and in the course of my normal life, so it's not a true violation of my rule against gathering ex post facto information. The other clearly is.

As part of my ongoing interest in what is going on in the world of baseball, I have often throughout my adulthood bought a little red paperback book entitled "Who's Who in Baseball". This is an annual compilation of the lifetime professional stats of major league players. Whichever is my most current volume I will read through at uncommitted times, such as while eating breakfast or sitting on the can. One of those issues, probably in the early 80's, presented a tiny photograph and the pro stats of a less-than-full-time major league outfielder/first baseman by the name of Robert Oliver Jones. His birthplace was Elkton, Maryland. He was born in 1949. He was once my best friend. He was up and down from the minors many times, some with the Angels, mostly with the Rangers. He never made it big, but he made it.

My other reference break on the subject was an unabashed Googling of my old buddy. He was drafted in the 36th round in 1967 by the Washington Senators. The 36th round. He debuted in MLB in 1975 and played his last game in 1986. In 2010, the good baseball people of Oklahoma City held a day for him to celebrate his 10 years as manager of the Rangers' AAA affiliate in the Pacific Coast League. The club flew in his sister, whose name is Rita, from Elkton, and Curt from New Jersey. People said all kinds of laudatory things about the work he'd done and the kind of person he was. I believe he had at that point been a professional player, coach or manager since he graduated from high school.

A life in baseball. Nice going, Bobby.

* * *

With the upcoming move, and with it a return to the associate editorship of the Falmouth Enterprise, Dad started taking some trips to Falmouth to get things set up there. The rest of us had a school year to finish. He took some pretty good chunks of time there, it would seem, because he and Mom were communicating at least in part by mail. Long-distance phone calls were not easy to make, often full of interference and extraordinarily expensive. We all learned in our childhood that you must never, ever ask to make a long-distance call from another person's phone. It was about like asking them to buy you a meal at a ritzy restaurant. Many of us never unlearned that, even though communications technology has brought us to where it's more costly nowadays for a host to give you a glass of water than for you to call California on their phone. So, we got letters from Dad in Falmouth. Among other things, he reported on his househunting. In one celebrated letter, he spoke of two places he'd looked at. One was on Allen Avenue: near the harbor, recently built, in a neighborhood of tidy homes, a mix of ranches and Capes, on similarly-sized lots, all the same distance from the road but no two alike. And every one of them a good deal nicer than 139 west High Street in Elkton. The other was on Scranton Avenue, built in the 20's and showing its age already, lacking in amenities and not in a neighborhood per se, but right across from the boat yard. As he described the properties, he segued from Allen Avenue to Scranton Avenue: "Now to turn from the sublime to the ridiculous..." I don't need to tell you where we wound up.

I'll take a step back here to reflect on that business of telephone usage. There was one phone company, nationwide, known corporately as The Bell System and familiarly as Ma Bell. They had a monopoly, and they were quite in your face about it. You could not own a telephone; you had to rent it from Ma Bell. You could not run a phone line to another phone in your house; you had to ask Ma Bell to send out a technician to run that wire, and then rent that second phone from them. These requirements had the force of law behind them. In Falmouth, and maybe everywhere, you couldn't call the business office if there was a problem; you had to show up in person. The monopoly was sustained by the Bell System's insistence that taking any of the process out of their hands would lead to chaos and terrible disruptions in service. Eventually, as the consumer movement acquired muscle and potential competitors grew in number and influence, the antitrust laws were applied to Ma Bell and the telecommunications world came into the modern age, with options for the consumer and dramatically lower prices and better service for all. Conservatives could view this progress as a triumph of free enterprise, liberals as a success story for intervention by a government agency. They both have a case.

Having settled in at the Enterprise and secured a home across the street from the harbor, nothing would do but for the Turkingtons to come into ownership of a little more boat than the Pickle. Vineyard Sound, the Falmouth shoreline, the Elizabeth Islands and Buzzards Bay offered seafaring opportunities that the Chesapeake and Delaware Canal just couldn't match, but a family of four couldn't very well explore them in a little skiff with a 5-horsepower motor and expect to live to tell about it. It's a little late to ask Dad why he chose to look for our next boat in the area we were about to leave, rather than in the town and the waters where he expected to spend the rest of his life. I wouldn't have thought to wonder about it then. All I knew was, we were going to find ourselves a bigger boat.

To that end, we all trotted off to a bigger boat yard than Captain Bob's to attend a boat auction one spring day. The boats for sale were in dry dock and fully congested the yard. Eric and I scrambled all about that yard, shouting "Here's a boat! Daddy, here's a boat!", indicating all the boats that were far newer and spiffier than anything the Turkingtons were looking for. What we wound up with was a 26-foot wooden cabin cruiser built by Colonial in 1932, with a 95 horsepower inboard motor that could propel the vessel at about 10 knots at full throttle and high volume. It had a semi-enclosed cockpit somewhat like a lobster boat, and a lift-top bench at the stern. The cabin had a narrow mattress for a bunk on one side and a little table that could be folded up and converted to a slightly wider bunk on the other. The head (toilet, ye landlubbers) offered half the dimensions and twice the aroma of a porta-john. By working a pump handle, the user ejected the contents out of the basin and into the ocean. Forward, two very short and narrow bunks met in a V at the prow. In theory, four people could bunk down under cover in the cabin. In fact, they sometimes did. The cost of the vessel was $1750. Its name (something in me wants to say "her name", but the feminization of seagoing vessels never took hold with or made much sense to me) was to be "Swash", which is a real word that can mean something akin to the splashing of water, as well as and probably more importantly, an elegant feature of a particular typeface. To deepen the mystery of the word, think of swashbuckling sailors or pirates. I watched the artisan apply the slightly ornate block letters of the new name in gold leaf to the transom while it was still in drydock.

The Swash was anchored at Capt. Bob's little harbor only briefly, as there were big plans for our new boat and they were soon to be put into effect. There may have been a shakedown cruise on the Chesapeake and Delaware or maybe, with our newfound capability, into the Bay itself. But the school year was over, we had a home in Falmouth and Dad had a job there, and there was no time for lollygagging around. We were due in Falmouth, and we were going to get there by boat. How the Ford and all our belongings got there I cannot imagine – somehow, they did – but we were taking the water route.

There were many times in the first eight-plus years of my life when my family was thrown together in a confined space for some length of time. Most mornings for breakfast and most evenings for dinner, there we all were, sitting quietly around the table breaking bread together. We'd been on some long car rides, of which the trip from Falmouth to my grandparents' house in New York, then later from Elkton to the same destination were the most common, and we all were pretty good at sitting quietly in the car as the miles went by. And there were the countless Sunday mornings and weekday evenings, smoking and reading in the living room, the silence broken by occasional verbal spontaneity from Mom, less frequently by Eric or me, and rarely by Dad. But we could be around each other, frequently and at length, with a modicum of comfort and little acrimony.

Togetherness on a small boat can be something else entirely, because there is absolutely noplace else to go, nor any possibility of one materializing, and nothing to do but look around. When looking around while cruising north along the Atlantic seaboard, there is the shore to port, open ocean to starboard, the sky above, and that's about it. The view of the shore changes with forward progress, but at a glacial pace. The sea and sky change with the weather, which is also a very gradual thing, except for when it's not, and that's usually a time to worry. Reading would have been difficult, because it's nearly always windy out there, and was inadvisable anyhow for people just getting their sea legs under them, as focusing on the printed page while being pitched this way and that is the quickest route to seasickness, which is unbearable. On top of all that, conversation was next to impossible. The engine, which sat under a box in the middle of the deck, was terribly loud. We could communicate when necessary, but only by raising our voices to a shout close to the ear of the listener. It was not the environment in which to share our innermost thoughts, which we wouldn't have done anyway.

Even in those simple times, a couple of boys approaching 9 and 11 years of age really had a need either to be entertained or to have the means to entertain themselves. At sea on the Swash, Eric and I had neither. I can't understand why we weren't mad with boredom or bitter with resentment that we'd been dragged off on this pointless expedition, but we managed pretty well. Dad may have been somewhat sensitive to the likelihood that his traveling companions didn't fully share in the excitement he surely felt of being on the high seas in a boat of his own. Most days, we put in to port well before dark and didn't set out again until we were well into the next morning. There was a practical reason for that, though: preparing a meal on the Swash and cleaning up afterwards, though theoretically manageable, was a time-consuming and unsatisfying chore. The galley consisted of an icebox, a sink, a propane heating element, one shelf and one cabinet. Every one of these accoutrements was very, very small and right tight against the others. Mom was a good sport about putting together a decent lunch, but breakfasts and dinners were usually had ashore.

Not a whole lot of events on the trip have stayed with me, probably because there were so few. We had a nice evening in Cape May, though there was a mishap in the morning that was never forgotten. Dad was looking for something in the aft storage bench with the heavy, hinged lid pushed up. That lid had a metal strip along the edge, and when it dropped down unexpectedly, the edge caught dad on the bridge of the nose and cut deeply into it. He put a bandage on it, and after a while it stopped bleeding and never became a problem, but he carried a big lump just below his eyes for the rest of his life.

Further up the Jersey coast, we caught some rough seas off Sandy Hook that severely tested our mettle. We were so far offshore that we were completely out of sight of land. I'm not sure why we were that far out to sea. Maybe there were shoals to be avoided, or maybe there was a current pulling us out with greater force than the Swash's engine could counter. Unable to see anything around us but the briny, and getting a good rocking and rolling from the waves, we all got seasick except for Dad. Anyone who has never been seasick cannot appreciate how awful it feels. Given the option, I'd rather pass a kidney stone or land a 3-pound hammer square on my thumb than be seasick. I think anybody would. Fortunately, I haven't had to deal with it often, but I sure did in the Swash off Sandy Hook. At one point, I was throwing up over the side of the boat with Mom weakly gripping the back of my pants to keep me aboard. I was thinking that it just wasn't possible to feel sicker than I felt, until I looked in the cabin and saw Eric. His face was actually green, and he looked terrible, just terrible. Any seasick person would rather be dead, but Eric looked like he actually was. No land in sight; pitched and tossed around in a little boat by an angry sea; three-fourths of my family dying of seasickness, and the other just plowing ahead as if it didn't matter; oh, the horror!

Just as all good things must come to an end, so does a bout with mal de mer. We approached land again, the seas calmed and there was the Statue of Liberty to port and the towers of Manhattan dead ahead. With everybody feeling a little more chipper, we listened to Mom shouting out the sights to us as we paraded up the East River, which of course is not a river but a strait that leads the sailor to Long Island Sound and its protected waterway to Rhode Island. Our last overnight was passed either at Block Island or Cuttyhunk, and we reached the Falmouth shoreline in the middle of a stellar June day. There, Dad uncharacteristically made mention to me of his summer long ago working on a charter yacht, and the feeling he got when he first saw these shores, that it was the most beautiful place he'd ever seen and that he wanted to live there someday. So here he was, home, and so were we.

Home, this time, was 287 Scranton Avenue. The street paralleled Falmouth Harbor and was 3/4 of a mile long, almost perfectly straight and level. It ended at Main Street at its northern end and ran to the mouth of the harbor. Harborfront property was not considered to be an especially choice holding among the locals, and especially the acreage along Scranton Avenue. Open land close to the center of town was being broken up into house lots at a rate that was only accelerating with the arrival of the baby boom generation, but Scranton Avenue had been shunned, and continued to be for many years. At the Main Street end of the road were a seasonal restaurant/night club and a gas station. Heading south, there were a laundromat and a fleabag motel close to Main Street, but once you reached the foot of the harbor there was just polluted wetlands for much of its length. Across the street from the harbor there was just open, unwanted space for nearly half a mile. Suddenly there appeared five shingled houses in various states of repair, so tightly clustered together that three of them barely had room for a driveway. The first of these was #287.

One could charitably describe our house as a Craftsman style home. We in the trade would apply the judgmentally neutral term, foursquare. A cynic might call it a box. It had four sides of equal length, which may have been as much as 24 feet. It had two stories and a pyramidal roof. Except for the front porch, which ran the length of the house and had a shed roof, there were no breaks in the planes. Nor was there any ornamentation. The place was built in 1926 and exhibited no signs of any maintenance work or updating when we moved in, in 1958. The original wiring was in the walls, the original furnace in the basement, the original cast iron stand-up radiators in the rooms, the flooring underfoot, the primitive sheetrock with lattice tacked over the seams, all the windows, all the doors: all these things came in when the house was built and there they stayed as long as there were Turkingtons within, and they remain there to this day. 287 Scranton Avenue ought to be in the National Register of Historic Places, as a display of middle-class home construction, design, materials and workmanship in the 1920's. No restoration work or historical research necessary. In 1958, my parents took possession of the property for the sum of $10,500.

There was another hip-roofed foursquare among the tightknit string of houses that began at #287. This one was actually sided in clapboards, a rare find on Cape Cod. Clapboards require paint, and this place didn't appear to have had any paint applied since it was new, probably in the 20's. Many of the clapboards were missing, others badly split, or askew. There was a side porch that was clearly returning to the earth. The roof had holes in it that were noticeable from the street. There were a number of missing window panes and many broken ones. The place looked like the sort of sadly abandoned homestead that Walker Evans might have made famous in a photograph during the Depression, yet it was inhabited by Russell Hartwell Brown, who owned the big barn that stood behind our previous home on Mill Road. Brownie was probably well into his 60's, with a Fu Manchu mustache and a mane of gray hair flowing down to his shoulders long before there were hippies, and the cheeriest disposition I've ever encountered. He'd been a working architect in his productive time, and he retained from those days a professionally lettered sign that read "Russell Hartwell Brown, Architect", which he displayed in his front window, perhaps in the hope of drawing in trade. What he drew instead was the amused attention of pedestrian passersby, who we often saw taking a picture of that sign with the crumbling house as backdrop.

Another colorful feature of the neighborhood was the fish market and clam shack at the mouth of the harbor, about 300 yards from our place. I sometimes hung out there at the end of a summer afternoon to watch the sportfishermen come in with their catches of swordfish. These were hugely impressive fish that seemed then to be plentiful in the waters not far off our shore. Bud Tietje owned that fish market and was only too happy to haul the fish onto the dock, weigh them, buy them and sell them as steaks in his market. He also carried many other varieties of fish, shellfish and lobster, probably from local suppliers though I wouldn't know.

Part of his business was to serve up takeout seafood dinners, mostly deep-fried and served with French fries and coleslaw. Some things are too good ever to change. There was real enjoyment to be had in walking back from Tietje's with a tub of fried clams and extra tartar sauce for dinner. They were pretty costly then, as they are now, so we didn't get them often, but they were always a hit when we did. My craving for fried clams and tartar sauce is a subliminal trait that surfaces rarely, but it has never left me.

This was not the first time the Turkingtons took up residence on Scranton Avenue. The uninhabited wasteland between us and Main Street had been, for one brief shining moment in the late 40's, the most densely populated neighborhood in the whole town. Whatever federal agency came into being for the purpose of providing cheap housing for returning veterans built a colony of concrete-block row dwellings there. When Mom and Dad and baby Eric first moved to town from upstate NewYork, that's where they lived. We did not coddle our young veterans; life here was rather spare, and the grateful residents moved out as soon as they could find something better, which in our case was the house on Fairview Avenue, just down the street, my first home. The block dwellings were demolished when the need for them passed, but one dominant structure remained until the early 60's. It consisted of one very large room with a couple of little ones at one end. I'm guessing now, but it may have served as a play and gathering place for the residents. So here were rows of apartment-style dwelling units, with a community recreation building, open space all around, and an unobstructed view of the harbor. Dig it: a rock-bottom, low-budget, disposable development for penniless veterans served as the model for the vacation communities for the bourgeoisie that now infest practically every harborfront site in New England and beyond.

A distinguishing feature of life in Falmouth center that we shared with everyone for a mile or two around was the intensive, indiscriminate use of the whistle at the fire station on Main Street. It had a sound midway between a foghorn and a racing fire truck, and the volume of both combined. It blasted twice at noon (Time for lunch, people!) and twice more at 4:30 (Quittin' time, everyone!) But it really got a workout when there was a fire somewhere; every location in the entire town had a designated three-digit code number, so that when a fire broke out near that location, the whistle would signal where it was to all the volunteer firefighters who no longer existed, as Falmouth had ponied up for a full-time force some years before. If the code of the fire's location was, say, 653, we'd hear six blasts, short break, five blasts, short break, three blasts, long break, then the whole sequence all over again. Those who thought they might want to go see a fire, such as a newspaper reporter, kept a signal sheet nearby with its hundreds of signals and their corresponding locations listed on it. Those who only wanted to get a good night's sleep must have just gritted their teeth and put up with it, because the practice went on for years after there was no longer any reason for it.

The front of our house faced Falmouth Marine Railways, an ample and busy boat yard. It was owned and profitably run by Fred Wormelle, whose family lived in a sharp-looking prairie-style house diagonally across the street, visually protected from the ramshackle houses in our row, and from the bothersome workings of the boat yard, by tall fences and taller bushes and trees. The boat yard itself consisted of a couple of very long, very high and deep boat sheds that provided space for machine shops, engine repair bays, sail lofts, woodshops and what have you, and ample cavernous cover for winter storage of the boats that rented the many FMR piers during the summer. The railways in the corporate name referred to the method of getting the boats in and out of the water: a dolly of appropriate size ran on steel wheels down railroad tracks until it was deep enough in the harbor for the boat to motor onto it. Tide went out, boat nestled in dolly, and back it came, into the shed. This whole rig became obsolete a few years after we got there, when the yard acquired a Travelift, which could drive out onto the piers on either side of a slip, drop two immense canvas straps into the water, pick up a boat and take it wherever they damn well pleased. A good metaphor there for the abandonment of the railroads, which was already well under way.

The Swash was not docked at one of Mr. Wormelle's piers, but was moored out in the harbor along with scores of other vessels of modest mien. FMR kept a floating dock next to the main pier to accommodate the dinghies that transported the hoi polloi to their moored boats. We could see the Swash from the house, due to the happy fact that there was a parking lot directly between us and the water, tucked in between the end of the storage sheds and the Wormelles' fences. Now that we had an oceangoing boat and had all developed our sea legs, most of the fair-weather Sundays saw us abandoning the smokefest in the living room for adventure on the high seas. I can't say I ever took to the journey itself with much enthusiasm. The wind in the hair, the sun on the face, the roll of the ship and seasickness but a memory, I did like all that. But no matter what you did on the Swash, it was like doing it next to someone operating a chain saw. The engine just could not be tolerated. But there were a number of appealing destinations that I came to know and looked forward to seeing again.

I sometimes wonder, now that my life is starting to become something I can look back on, whether settling in on Scranton Avenue contributed to a couple of traits that started showing up in my adolescence and have accompanied me ever since. These traits go hand in hand, which could be a stroke of luck. I have not, since I was a young boy, had much of a tendency to put myself out in order to socialize and generate activities with other people. Not that it never happens, or that I don't draw pleasure from the company of others, but I seldom take steps to initiate it. At the same time, I don't have trouble finding things to do by myself. Solitary time rarely induces loneliness in me and very often proves rewarding. I don't know whether the demographics attendant to Scranton Avenue led me this way, or whether that's when it began to come out, but it would not have been a good place to harbor a craving for companionship. Propinquity tossed me together with Jimmy and Gail Wormelle from across the street. Jimmy was a bit younger than I and Gail younger yet, but they were generally enjoyable kids and we hung together pretty amenably, though not regularly. There was always the reality that most of what we did together, we did in or around the boat yard, which belonged to their father, so we couldn't ever completely avoid the question of whether what we were doing was okay to do. I wasn't used to this.

Other than them, the neighborhood was bereft of kids around my age. Between us and the shore, there was a big cluster of handsome old summer homes, but there were only kids living there a couple of months a year, and they didn't mix much with the locals. Between us and Main Street – well, this was Scranton Avenue, where nobody wanted to live. Between us and the heart of town were some built-up family neighborhoods within an easy walk, but as fate would have it, not much good-friend material. And to the east was Falmouth Harbor. Not much socializing to be had there. The primary locus of 50's suburban American lifestyle was in Falmouth Heights. The true "Heights" was a late-1800's summer colony that blanketed a bluff overlooking Nantucket Sound. There were several dozen vacation homes of all shapes and sizes, packed pretty closely but charmingly together. They were unoccupied most of the year. The part of the Heights that was being built up and drawing families was the flats between the old Heights and Teaticket. It was a mile's walk away from my home, very negotiable, and a lot of families of boys my age moved in there the first few years that I was back in town, but there seemed to develop there a society of its own. I could and did at times interact with it and them, but I always had the feeling that there were things going on I didn't know about and didn't know how to access. This was a feeling that deepened in me as time went on in many avenues of my life, and caused me considerable discomfort until I began to get rid of it, or used to it. What I can see now is that there was no good reason for it. Most of my peers liked me and some thought well of me, but I demanded proof.

Such adolescent angst wasn't complicating my life yet. I entered fourth grade in the fall, back in the Village School. Mrs. Leonard was my teacher, a short, plump, kindly lady approaching retirement. Other than that, not much from my year in fourth grade remains with me except for my constant puzzlement at the persona of Margaret A. Mullen. She was the principal of the school, which later was renamed in her honor, and had been in the business for a long, long time. It amazed me that anyone could be so old and still be up and about. I was also amazed by her hair, which was blinding orange and coiffed high upon her head, and by her dress, which was a rich purple from collar to hem. If she had other dresses, they were all exactly alike, because she never looked any different on one day than on any other day. She stood inside the main entrance to her school every morning and greeted every kid who walked in. As the doors were wide and the kids full of energy, the stream of kids could flow pretty fast, but she'd figured out how to say "good morning" in rapid-fire fashion without flubbing it. At the end of the day, she'd be there again: goodnightgoodnightgoodnightgoodnight...."

From time to time, the school conducted an air raid drill. Being very close to Otis Air Force Base, Falmouth kids were accustomed to seeing and hearing fighter jets screaming overhead, so the notion of being attacked from the skies was not wholly theoretical. The Cold War was quietly raging, and even the most ignorant of children were well aware of the existence of nuclear bombs, of planes and missiles that could deliver them from the other side of the world, and the consequences of putting them to use. We got it from a number of authoritative sources that those dirty Russkies wanted nothing more than to blow us to smithereens. Which made the old-fashioned air raid drill seem quaint and pointless, but we had them anyway. The horrifically loud buzzer sounded, Mrs. Leonard shouted for us to get under our desks, and we sat there on the floor with our heads between our knees and our arms over our heads. Even at that tender age, we saw some black humor in this: Draw up your feet, put your head between your knees and kiss your ass goodbye.

It was not only foolish people who felt that a nuclear exchange would be just one of those bumps in the road that could be dealt with if you were properly prepared. Many sensible, prosperous families dug up their yards to put in fallout shelters: underground concrete bunkers with air vents to the outside that were filtered by some means to keep out radioactivity, in which the family would live until Civil Defense announced over the transistor radio that it was safe to come out. Better lay in a good supply of batteries for that radio, because the power outage is expected to be a long one. Many people of lesser means, such as my parents, did what they could to prepare for the worst. One partitioned corner of our little basement was stocked with jugs of water and cans of Spam and sardines for the occasion. I was down there sometimes looking at all that and thinking, What the hell? The idea was that in a nuclear war, the country that is the quickest to get its survivors back above ground and rebuilding a modern society would be the winners, so it was all Americans' patriotic duty to enhance their chances of living through it. This was probably a remote corner of life that adults could cope with in a rational way, but to kids who had only recently outgrown Howdy Doody, it was very real.

Some good did ensue from the worldwide paranoia attached to the potential outcome of a nuclear exchange. A number of comfortable families found themselves in possession of outstanding wine cellars or rec rooms as it became clear that the whole idea of survival was silly. On a more subliminal but wider-spread scale were the stirrings of recognition that some of the wondrous technologies and industrial advances that were coming into use just might not be all to the good. With a few older cousins who were growing fast, I didn't often shop for new clothes, but shoes don't hand down very well, so we'd usually buy those new, at John's Shoe

Store on Main Street. When I was little, I could try on a new pair and proceed to John's x-ray machine, where we could all look down and see just how well my feet fit into them. I could see the bones and everything! This was cool. I was pretty disappointed when the day came that John told me they weren't doing that any more; he said they weren't sure it was good for me. In our science books, we were starting to see mention of smog in Los Angeles and dead rivers in the Northeast. There wasn't any talk of remedies; these things were just an unfortunate aspect of modern life. The word "pollution" was just beginning to get used. Earth Day and "ecology" were years away yet, but the need for attitude adjustment was beginning to dawn on people who thought about these things.

Not much new entered my life around this time, but I did find myself starting to play the flute. I'm sure my parents gave all due consideration to the question of whether I should take up a musical instrument, and if so, which one it would be. But to me it was just something that happened one day. I was given a flute in a little black carrier, and one day a week I walked over from the Village School with Kathy Cooper and another girl from my class who later moved away, to the adjacent Hall School. There, in a little room underneath the balcony of the auditorium, we met up with Conrad Rosello, who introduced us to the playing of the flute. Mr. Rosello was a small, balding European man who spoke with a considerable accent, always wore a suit and tie, and like many adults trying to cobble out a living from a unique proficiency in the music business, could not hide his love of the subject or his frustration with the shortcomings of his youthful charges. He wasn't a total hardass, but he certainly let us know when our work didn't measure up. I don't think any teacher could get away now with saying "It's no good!" when his student messes up, but he said it a lot. I believe my progress pleased him at least as often as it upset him. I was pretty good with rhythm and not bad with fingering, but had to work on clarity of tone. At some point along this time or a year later, I became part of a junior high band/orchestra that performed on rare occasions in the Hall School auditorium and gave our parents one of their few opportunities to turn out and see what our teachers hath wrought with their students.

Once again, Mom applied for a teaching position shortly before school started and was hired immediately. At least this time she had a year's experience on her resume. Woods Hole still had an elementary school and Mom was enlisted to teach the 2nd and 3rd graders, who constituted one class. One of her innovations was to teach everybody how to play the Flutophone, which was a cheap plastic recorder-like instrument about a foot in length. It cost 50 cents and came with a primer on how to play it, and everybody got one. Mom put a lot of herself into her teaching role. She had a lot of imagination, and could recognize when the customary way of doing things wasn't the best way, at which times she'd do things her way. She was greatly appreciated by most of her students, because she had a lot of respect for them and their talents, and showed it. She wasn't especially geared towards a certain age group. After a few years with the little kids, she took a position at the high school teaching freshman English, where she stayed until retirement. After I moved back to Falmouth as a young adult, any time I ran into someone I hadn't seen in a while, they'd ask me, "HOW'S YOUR MOM??? She was the best teacher I ever had!"

There weren't many out-of-school activities for elementary school-aged kids in Falmouth in the 50's. There weren't many in school either, but once Miss Mullen said goodnight to you, you were either under the watchful eye of your parents or on your own until the end of the day. For most of us, that meant being on our own. Very few fathers were at home before the end of the work day; most mothers were, but not too many expected to know where their kids were all the time. Sometimes by school dismissal time I'd have plans made to go home with a friend, sometimes not. When I didn't, I walked home and puttered around, usually outside, often along the edge of the harbor or along the private beach at Belvedere Plain, a beachfront community of fine old summer homes where nobody lived during the school year. We had a dog named Jingles who came to Eric and me as a Christmas present when we were little, and often when I was going someplace interesting she'd come along with me. Jingles was a mutt, fairly entertaining and dependable about coming home after being on the loose, but not the loyal company you'd like to have in a dog. She wasn't disposed to identify a whole lot with people, including her own.

Late in the spring of '59. we took to getting out in the Swash every weekend. I was still a couple of years away from resenting being told what to do with my time or being in the presence of my parents, so this was okay with me. The south shore of Falmouth is all outwash plain: a series of peninsulas separated by large tidal ponds, but connected at their south ends by a barrier beach, on which was lain the shore road. The ponds are surrounded by clam beds, sandy beaches, salt marsh, and houses behind all that. A couple of the ponds with the wider inlets to the bay could be entered by the Swash. A row to shore in the dinghy, some swimming, beachcombing, a picnic lunch ashore and some time to explore, all could make for a pretty nice day. Washburn's Island was my favorite stop along the Falmouth shore. Washburn's had been used during WW II for amphibious landing training, I was told, and bombing practice. It was said that there remained some unexploded ordnance on the island, which lent a bit of excitement to our explorations among old foundations, fiddler crab colonies and oceans of poison ivy.

My parents rented out our house for four weeks in July that summer. The house was no prize, but its location right on the harbor and near the beach was quite attractive to prosperous summer visitors, even though it met with scorn from the locals. Mom and Dad spent the four weeks living on the Swash, while Eric and I were packed off to Camp Clark in Sandwich. It was to be the only overnight camp experience in my life, and I'd do it again now if they'd let me. The camp was well out in the woods, on the shore of Lawrence Pond. Mind you, on Cape Cod every body of water is a pond, even if it's a mile or more across, and Lawrence Pond was that and more. It was your basic no-frills summer camp, but it had everything a kid could want. We slept in bunks in rustic cabins that smelled strongly of wood then and probably still do if they're still there. We got to them via footpaths leading out from the center of the camp. The mess hall was in the middle of things, serving up small quantities of budget food, but it was the one time the entire camp was under one roof, and the senior counselors usually had a show of some kind at dinnertime, so it was a good place. There was one spot of level land big enough for a ballfield, and we played a lot of baseball. There was a crafts cabin where we made crafty things, most of them of gimp. The pond had a stretch of sandy beach and a long dock that accommodated a bunch of sailboats and rowboats. The cost to the parents for all these amenities was $35 per camper per week.

There was surely a schedule of sorts in effect at Camp Clark, but the only routine that sticks with me was Reveille early every morning, when we ran out to salute the flag, then headed into the mess hall for breakfast. There were probably also rules about where we could and couldn't go, but I know for sure that I often headed off for hours at a time with a friend or two, wandering around the overgrown dirt roads that wound through the scrub oak and scrub pine woods outside the campgrounds. One quirky thing they had us do was to take our clothes off on Sunday morning and run into the pond for a swim, every kid in camp. The idea, we assumed, was that this kind of thing toughens you up. Years later, when Scott Brown was first running for the Senate, he famously revealed that he'd been fondled by a counselor at Camp Good News, a Christian camp that was just up the road from Camp Clark. Who knows? Maybe there were pedophiles among the camp's brass who wanted to get a look at the young fellows in the buff on Sunday mornings. These days, that suspicion, or assumption, would be out there. Nobody there ever bothered me.

Show me a Scotsman who doesn't love a thistle,
Show me an Englishman who doesn't love a rose,
Show me a true heart, the son of Camp Clark,
Who doesn't love the spot (CLAP CLAP CLAP)
Where the Lawrence waters flow

Fifth grade was easy to get excited about, as my classroom was in the Hall School. The Hall was located at right angles and close to the Village School, just off Main Street in the center of town. I'd always liked the looks of the place. It was entirely of brick, but with a fair amount of detail to it. It had a domed cupola and a particularly welcoming entrance to the lobby. Its roof was flat, or close enough to it so it looked that way. It was long, lean and low-slung: two stories, the first of which was partly below ground level. The booklearning part of the school was a long, wide hall, classrooms either side, upstairs and down. Attached at one end was the auditorium with a real stage, a few hundred wooden seats, and a balcony. Matching it at the other was a gymnasium. I'd never been in a school with either of these features before. Even to the untrained eye of a child, it was pretty obvious that much of the place was in disrepair, but that didn't matter. When you walked in there to start fifth grade, you could rightly feel, maybe for the first time, that you were getting to be a big kid.

My teacher was Mrs. Goulding, or was it Miss? She was on the young side, not fresh-out-of-college young but lively and un-jaded. She genuinely liked the kids, didn't insist on doing the same thing at the same time every day, knew how to improvise, laughed a lot, and best of all, was not too strict. By this time, they were starting to track kids according to their perceived intelligence, so the makeup of the class was somewhat highbrow, and Connie Goulding was equal to the task. The details escape me, but there was a pretty good feel in the room most of the time. Not that we never had our differences. The class was playing dodgeball out in the playground one recess, when I made a quick turn and got crashed into from behind. I shouted "HEY!", then turned around and saw Sandy Nickerson on the ground. To Mrs. Goulding's eyes, I'd knocked Sandy down and then shouted at her. She shouted at me: "YOU SAY YOU'RE SORRY!", and I shouted back at her, "I DIDN"T KNOW IT WAS SANDY!". A bit of a non sequitur there, but it was enough to get me sent back up to the classroom for the rest of recess.

Back to the classroom I went, feeling dissed and wronged, as would any normal fifth-grader whose behavior has been criticized. Annie Ackeburk (sp?) and Robin Gordon were there, working on a project of some kind. Annie was a very special girl. She was short and blond, smart and well-behaved but not about to take any guff from anybody. She could play sports with the boys or talk Barbies with the girls. Even among the boys who disdained the girls as goody-goodies, which meant most of us, it was okay to like Annie. So I walked in on her and Robin, sniffling and obviously upset, and Annie asked me what had happened. I told her about the collision and Mrs. Goulding's reaction to it. Annie said, "She's such a bitch!" It was a show of solidarity that made me feel better, though we both knew it was a stretch. Good old Annie. She moved away after that year, sadly. It's my guess that she welcomed the coming counterculture with open arms.

This was the year we were to start receiving foreign language instruction. Our curriculum consisted of all the fifth-grade classes piling into the auditorium at the beginning of the school day to watch a talking head on a 21-inch television screen that was placed stage center. The teacher was a middle-aged French woman with deeply lined, highly protrusive lips, the result of a lifetime stressing the "eu" sound. The class had to be first thing in the morning because that's when it was broadcast. There was no way to see anything on television except to tune in to the station that was broadcasting it at that moment, and we couldn't view it in our separate classrooms because the school had only the one TV. In recognition of the fact that 120 kids were scattered around an auditorium watching a television up on the stage, the volume was turned way up. This added considerably to the annoyance factor, not at all to the instructional value. All I learned from it, and I learned it well, was the French word for "listen", as the only action on the screen was when she'd point to her ear and say, "Ecoutez".

Organized sports entered the picture for me in the form of Little League baseball, which started up late in the spring. Assignments to teams were made according to location of the player's home. Falmouth had not yet outgrown its status as a collection of discrete villages, and each village had a team, except for Falmouth center, where the demographics warranted three. Further, each team had a majors squad for the better ballplayers, and a minors squad for the poorer ones. I was assigned to the Tigers' minors team, which was to be expected since that's where most newcomers started out. Everett Lumbert, who'd been coaching young ballplayers since time began, was the overall head of the Tigers. The minors coach was a Mr. Szymanski, who had a couple of kids on the team and was a very nice man who made it fun to be there. He had a lot of faith in me, used me as a middle infielder and played me a lot. I was fairly good at that level; I could catch anything that was reasonably catchable, throw the ball in the vicinity of where I wanted it to go, and knew what was going on in the game. Many on the team did not have these abilities.

There is only so much you can do on your own to improve your ballplaying skills, but I worked on mine as best I could. My parents' reticence about telling me about family history was matched by their willingness to allow me to go on doing something that was extremely annoying, without interference from them. To get practice catching fly balls, I spent lots of time in the back yard, throwing a ball against the upper reaches of the back wall of the house. Being sided with wood shingles, the wall did not have a smooth surface, so the rebound often went in an unexpected direction. I got pretty good at tracking balls in the air that way. Another feature of wood shingles is that if you hit them often enough with a hard object such as a baseball, they will shatter, and after several blows will fall off the house. And I can only imagine the effect that all those impacts against the wall had on people pursuing quiet activities within. I did this a lot, and was never chastened.

Perhaps in an effort to forestall an expensive reshingling job, Dad took to going out in the side yard with me and throwing fly balls my way. He may have seen this as a father-son bonding thing before many people thought too much about bonding with their kids. I was always up for it; I was like many peoples' dogs, who will just keep chasing a ball that is thrown for them for as long as it keeps getting thrown, or until nightfall. This was not tossing a ball back and forth; this was throwing long fly balls out to where I had to run for them. Having performed the same drill in my own yard with my own kids, I now have a real sympathy for the ligaments in Dad's shoulder and elbow. And appreciation for the fact that he did it at all.

Hitting was not my strong point, though I drew a fair number of walks (as who doesn't in the minors?) and could usually put the ball in play when the slower pitchers put it near the strike zone. What I lacked was the confidence to take a hard rip at a good pitch with the expectation of hitting it. There can't be many actions in the world of sport that reward confidence as much as hitting a baseball thrown in earnest, or that so punish lack of confidence. Maybe when a big-time quarterback fires a pass to a receiver who has defenders close by, then an instant's hesitation, a trace of self-consciousness will reveal itself as clearly in the resulting failure. I don't know. All I know for sure is that I never, ever was excited about going up to bat against a pitcher with ability. I played pretty well for the Tigers minors team that summer. The following summer, I was playing better, and got called up to the majors. I sat on the bench for a game or two, then was sent up to bat with two outs in the final inning of a close game. The pitcher was Paul Ingram of the North Falmouth Rangers. Paul was my age, but a profoundly talented athlete known as the fastest Little League pitcher in town. He may have figured I was too scared to jump away from an inside pitch, because he threw me one high and outside. I swung at it anyway. The next pitch was a little further away, but I swung at it too. His third pitch was so far high and outside that his catcher couldn't reach it, and I heard it whistling as I swung at it. Game over. The shame.

I spent a lot of my summer days hanging out at Surf Drive Beach, which was a public beach a mile from home. The town had a multifaceted raft about 50 yards offshore that offered all kinds of opportunity for fun. It had a diving board just a few feet above the water, a platform about six feet up and another about ten feet up. And it had a long slide with a shiny metal surface that had a couple of burrs on it that you had to watch out for or you'd rip your bathing suit on the way down, if not your flesh. It floated on two massive pontoons which, as long as they stayed watertight, kept the raft a foot above the water. This allowed daredevil boys to dive off the raft, swim under a pontoon and come up for air under the raft. We played a lot of tag on that raft. There were all sorts of tricky, extremely hazardous ways to tag someone if you were It. One was to jump off the high platform and tag a kid standing on the raft as you went by, then swim under the pontoons and get away. This meant that you'd be jumping from ten feet up, missing the edge of the raft by inches, then going underwater and not being seen again for a while. The Beach Committee provided this raft for the amusement of their beachgoers, with never a thought for liability. Accidents? That's what lifeguards were for.

* * *

Ken Ketchum was a friend and classmate who I often biked over to visit for the day. He lived in my old neighborhood, a stone wall and driveway away from 14 Mill Road. The Ketchums' house was an antique Cape with additions, where there was always some activity. Ken had a number of siblings, most of them younger. His mother was usually at home, busy trying to keep up with the requirements of a large family. She liked talking to her kids and their friends, in a way that respected their selves and their intelligence, of which there was plenty in that crowd. There was an out-of-the-mainstream feel to that home that appealed to me. The kids all had unkempt hair and the little ones sometimes ran around naked. There were musical instruments around, and books, and some disarray, but not a lot of toys.

A fantastic climbing tree grew in front of the house. We could get way above the roof of the house before running out of branches. Ken had a slightly dour demeanor, but recognized humor when he saw it. Even at the advanced age of 11, he could get down and do make-believe with the best of them. Our friendship was based as much as anything else on the fact that we were each other's intellectual equal. He was, and always remained, somewhat more highbrow culturally. He was onto folk music and topical humor when they were just beginning to make themselves felt in post-Red Scare America. He once solemnly assured me, before we knew better: "Rock and roll will never take the place of Big Band."

Mark Denman was the oldest of – let me guess – seven kids. He was a slightly clumsy, large-boned kid with a broad face, piercing eyes and jet-black hair. His father, Nat, was an intense, volatile man who was proprietor and sole employee of a research entity known as Basic and Experimental Physics, which he operated out of a little house next to the family home near the center of Falmouth village. Nat Denman was known as the town crank, forever speaking up in a losing cause at Town Meeting or hauling people or institutions into court for reasons that made perfect sense to him, but not to anybody else or to judges and juries. Being the child of a known misanthrope, and suspiciously intellectual, and not very good at sports, Mark was the frequent target of jibes and ridicule from his peers. I was no less likely to heap scorn upon him than anybody else, but we actually had quite a lot in common and spent a lot of time together. Mark handled the slings and arrows that came his way far better than I could have. He was forever unbowed, taking the hits and prepared for more. He faced the world on his own terms and in his own way, and his spirit never flagged.

Mark's home was cramped, cluttered and unimproved, but with uncoordinated activity going on at all times, I felt I could come and go as I pleased. His mother often seemed to be in a state of borderline despair, what with all the little kids and the shortage of amenities in the home, but there was a place at the table for me any time I wanted it. The most intriguing feature of the Denmans' place was the attic, which had full headroom, lights, windows and a ladder for access. It stored boxes and piles and shelves full of books and magazines, including every issue of MAD magazine since that august publication came into being. Our adolescent souls ached for signs of irreverence toward, and parody of, a society whose strictures were beginning to chafe us, and MAD understood us very well. We both followed baseball, especially the statistical and card-collecting aspects of the game, though neither of us was achieving great success on the field. For reasons never clear to me, Mark was a Yankees fan. This defect in his character informed much of our dialogue, usually to my chagrin, as the Braves were heading towards mediocrity (and later, Atlanta), and the Yankees were perennial World Series champions. My contempt for the Yankees, a birthright of most New England natives, came to full flower then and stayed with me for many years.

Chip Papp was one of the most amusing kids I ever knew. He was one of those people who are funny not because they can point out the funny side of everyday things, but because their whole take on the world is funny. Chip would go ahead and do what it pleased him to do without regard for its appropriateness, or the consequences. It was very easy to fall in with him because what he wanted to do was usually fun. This was not always to my benefit. I took my first and only ride in the back of a police cruiser with Chip. He lived on a short road in inland Falmouth that deadended at the town's largest gravel pit. To get into it, we crossed his road, beat our way through ten feet of woods, then slid down a 50-foot embankment to the floor of the pit. There were huge mounds of sand, gravel and crushed stone all around, amid the buildings that housed the machinery that created those mounds.

One day when the pit wasn't operating, we climbed a ladder up to one of the operator's shacks, went in and crawled onto the conveyor belt that hauled the sand skyward, got out to the end of it on hands and knees and dropped into the sand pile below. We fell in up to our knees, then slid and crawled down the pile until we got to the ground again. What a blast! Dangerous as hell! After a while of that, we headed back, but came upon a policeman at the terminus of the road. He directed us into the rear seat of his cruiser, got our names and addresses and phone numbers, and drove us the

50 yards to Chip's house, where Mrs. Papp was in the front yard. Oddly enough, neither she nor the policeman seemed angry at us. They just didn't want us risking our lives foolishly. They rightly figured this was a good way of making a lasting impression.

I learned a few other of life's lessons from Chip, not always in quite the way they were intended. He once related to me his mother's account of a Kennedy sighting. Apparently, this was at the thrift shop in Woods Hole. This thrift shop was a little rummage-sale store in the basement of the Church Of The Messiah that served as a fundraiser for the church. By Chip's account, his mom, or a friend of hers, saw Jacqueline Kennedy there and reported her to be not nearly as charming as most people were led to believe by her publicity, nor as attractive. Uh huh. Jackie Kennedy. Alone. Bitching about the merchandise at the Woods Hole Thrift Shop. Looking like hell. Innocent and gullible was I, but I had my limits, and this tale did not fall within them. A life of skepticism was born here.

The Papps were Red Sox fans who often made a day of a trip to Fenway Park. I was invited a few times that summer. Mrs. Papp could put together a scandalously good picnic lunch, which we'd stop at some interesting spot to eat on the way to the game. Mr. Papp, who worked for the Post Office, was an earthy man who smiled easily and demonstrated to me some of the finer points of baseball fandom: things to look for on the field that the Sox failed to do which cost them the game; following the minors for upcoming talent; moves made by the manager – there was a lot more to this game than could be found on the back of a baseball card. We were at the ballpark one Jimmy Fund Day. Ted Williams – in his last year as a player – gave a speech down on the field, then headed up through the stands to get to the press box. Chip and I leaped out of our seats and raced up the aisle to try to intercept him at the top of the grandstands. I got there a little quicker, just as The Kid had started up the enclosed stairway. I leaned through the door and said, "Hey Ted!". He turned around and gave me a big smile, reached down to shake my hand and said, "howya doin' there, fella?" My hand got lost in his. What a presence he had.

In at least one small way, I was looking forward to going back to school in the fall of 1960. It was to be my second year at the Hall School, with which I was now very familiar, knew where everything was, knew everyone on the staff, knew the routines, but above all was going to be in the most senior class in the building. There is a distinct feeling of elevated status when one is part of the most mature class in any school, a feeling undiminished by the fact that the school serves only two grades. But it was not to be. Sometime during August, the building was given a routine inspection by the state to ensure that everything was up to snuff. Said inspection included an examination by structural engineers, who determined that this structure was not a safe place in which to house a few hundred kids for the next nine months. The Hall School needed major repairs of a nature that would render it off limits for the school year. School was about to begin, and ten or a dozen 5th and 6th grade classes had to find new homes right away.

There exists no protocol for dealing with such circumstances, and I'm sure nobody was wholly pleased with the solutions, but somehow classroom space was found in or near the center of town for all those kids. I believe that classes were set up in a couple of church parish halls, in the dilapidated recreation building, maybe in the Chamber of Commerce building, anyplace they could find room for 30 desks and a few shelves. The classes of Mrs. Pederson and Mr. Kenney wound up in the National Guard Armory. I was in Mrs. Pederson's class. What the Armory had to offer was a function room that was divisible by an accordion door. Closed, the door afforded just, just barely enough room on either side for the students' desks, a teacher's desk and a table or two. Visitors to the second room got there by bobbing and weaving through the first room, freeing up the latch on the accordion doors, pushing them open and inching through.

Educationally, the situation couldn't have been up to even minimal 1960 standards. Administratively, I'm sure it was a nightmare. To the students, it had a lot more plusses than minuses. Most of the Armory building consisted of a cavernous hall spacious enough for training Guard units and for storing heavy artillery, with plenty of room left over for games. Outside was an expansive open area of pavement and gravel surrounded by chain link fence, which contained all the war equipment Falmouth needed to fend off an invasion of the town by the Russians. We had tanks, howitzers, and many camouflaged personnel carriers right there in our playground. In the parlance of the day: Cool, or what?

Mrs. Pedersen bore some resemblance to Lewis Carroll's Queen of Hearts, if you can factor in a softness to her visage that revealed sympathy for, perhaps even understanding of, all of her students, even the ones such as myself who made her job difficult at times. She was given a thorny assignment and handled it well. At the Armory, we had our half of the function room for academics and the rest of the building and grounds for play. There was nothing else: no library, no auditorium, no art room, no principal's office to send an unruly boy to – no blackboards! But the year went pretty smoothly, all that considered. She was a Yankees fan.

When her favorite team was about to meet the Pirates in the World Series, she bet the class an hour of recess time that they'd win it. Being Yankee-haters for the most part, we foolishly took her up on it. Miraculously, the Pirates stretched the Series to a seventh game, which I was watching on TV at home when Bill Mazeroski popped one over the wall to win it for the Pirates. With no audience, I leaped all around the living room in exaltation: Yankees lose! Bragging rights over Denman! Extra hour of recess! We win! Hooray!

We didn't have a wager on the 1960 presidential election, but Mrs. Pedersen once again found most of her pupils rooting against her. Some of our fondness for JFK derived from a natural inclination to support the home team: he was a Massachusetts boy, his family's vacation compound was just down the road, we knew people who talked like him. Yet even a bunch of unsophisticated sixth-graders could sense the composure and intelligence in the man, and feel that we'd prefer to be growing up in a world with someone like him at the wheel. There wasn't a great deal of talk of politics at home, but there was some. It was pretty clear to me that Dad felt a little more highly of what JFK might become than what Nixon had already proven to be, though not strongly so. To Mom, who judged from the heart as well as the mind, there was no question. She liked the way that JFK and Jackie both carried themselves, their style, their respect for others, and who cares if it was noblesse oblige? So, in my first season of heightened political awareness, I found it easy to get on board with JFK and the Democrats. And that was before I saw the debates with Nixon. They clinched it. Sorry, Mrs. Pedersen. It's been a bad season for your favorites.

The other teacher in our one-room schoolhouse was Ray Kenney. Male teachers at the elementary level were even rarer then than now, so his presence alone would have been a notable change even if he didn't connect well with the kids. But he did. He got a couple of activities under way that had never been a part of school before. He introduced us to soccer, strictly as a recess thing, but we played it often. He made up a couple of goals and taught us the rudiments of the game and let us go at it. He also started up a chess club, and was able to line up a few matches with other schools, which we won easily, much to our collective surprise. Rick Hill was our best player, while Mark Denman and I fought it out for second. We'd all learned the game from our fathers and played in school from time to time, and I guess that's all it took to be the best 6th-grade chess players on the Upper Cape. Our introduction to away meets came with trips to the Otis Air Force Base school, and maybe Barnstable. We dressed in jackets and ties, and wiped our opponents right off the chessboard.

There was a Mrs. Plemmons who came to the Armory once or twice a month to give the combined classes a science lecture. It was generally naturalist-type material, plants and animals and their ways, never anything about astronomy or magnetism or the elements, but her visits were a break from the routine and so held some interest. She had one big impediment as a lecturer, and that was that she said "um" three or four times in every sentence. It was as noticeable and pointless as the modern-day "like", but even more frequent. She had to have been aware of this, but she couldn't stop herself from doing it any more than we could stop ourselves from noticing it. It made it hard to pay close attention to her train of thought, and if you do something to make it hard for kids that age to pay attention, then they're just not going to pay attention. I counted her ums once. A sheet of paper on the desk, pencil discreetly held out of view, a little tickmark every time she said it, for a grand total of 685 ums by lecture's end.

One pleasant spring day, Mrs. Plemmons brought the classes out to the fields outside the chain-link fence for some exploring. There was just too much freedom in this for everyone to stay in line, but we were all being fairly cooperative. Or so we thought, until Mrs. Plemmons started getting mad at us. So we all calmed down and shut up, but she kept on scolding us. What did this woman want? Mrs. Pedersen finally broke her silence and angrily defended our behavior to Mrs. Plemmons, who shouted at her, so she shouted back. WOW! Two teachers going at it! That's not something you see every day. That was the last we saw of Mrs. Plemmons, but the demonstration of filial loyalty gained Mrs. Pederson some points with her class.

This was the year when I started playing some basketball. There was a net inside the Armory – these Guardsmen had all the perks – so Mr. Kenney could get a game going at recess when the weather was bad. The kids from the Heights were the experienced ones. Dave Swain, Bobby Olenick, Jack Carreiro, Larry Ferreira, Steve Paltz and others all had nets near their homes and played the game a lot. I was less klutzy than most of the beginners and could play without embarrassment. There was a recreation-level hoops program on Saturday mornings at the high school gym that I went to during the winter. Except for Little League and Cub Scouts, this was the first organized extracurricular activity I was ever part of. It was ably run by Joe Allietta, a math teacher and baseball coach at the high school whose son Bobby was a year behind me.

Mr. Allietta was a Vince Lombardi type of man, and not just because he resembled him: he could laugh and he could joke around, but he could be hard as nails when he needed to be. He liked kids and understood them, but when they stepped over the line he wasn't delicate about letting them know it. One of the few times my dad scolded me was one Saturday morning when he heard me calling Mr. Allietta at 7:30 to ask if there'd be basketball that day. There was a full-scale blizzard hammering us at the time. Bobby Allietta wound up playing pro baseball years later, and spent some time in the majors.

I was a serviceable enough athlete to join in on ball games with other players my age, and I really did enjoy the challenges of sports, despite the occasional moments of humiliation that all but the most talented kids had to face. There were not a whole lot of peak moments when I could feel I'd done something really well. But there was one that came my way in an entirely unaccustomed area. As part of our physical education assessment, all the 6th graders had to run a mile. The boys, that is; it was commonly known that most girls couldn't run a mile, and those that could, shouldn't. Since we were scattered all over town, they arranged for us to gather on the field at the Village School one day, where they'd set out cones that described a loop which we were to run six times. They lined us up, shouted Go!, and sure enough, the star athletes took off, the really unfit kids dropped back, and there I was about in the middle. For a while.

Then I noticed something odd happening: the kids around me started slowing down, and the ones in front stopped pulling away. Another lap, and I was gaining on them, then catching them, then passing them, and I wasn't speeding up at all, just running steady.

I was getting short of breath and feeling pretty hot, but I so liked this feeling of passing other kids that I let it hurt and kept going. I approached our gym teacher, thinking she'd shout some praise, but what I heard was, "Tommy! You're too hot! Stop and walk!" I gasped out to her, "No, I'm okay!" Then Mrs. Pedersen: "Your face is all red, Tommy, you'd better stop." Such encouragement! But I made it all the way, red face and concerned teachers notwithstanding, finished behind a couple of kids of even less athletic repute than I, but left everyone else back there. I got a bit of acknowledgement of my success from a few quarters, but didn't need much. They saw me go by. Too bad this isn't a real sport, I pined. I bet I could be good at it.

I had a couple of other little successes far outside the world of sports. The Knights of Columbus offered a small monetary reward for the best sixth-grader's essay on "What Columbus Day Means To Me". I can't imagine what I could have said about Columbus Day, which meant nothing at all to me, but my essay was the chosen one, and Mom took me to a K of C meeting where I read it out aloud and got a polite round of applause and a little cash. I was also chosen from our class, along with Chip Papp and Lanny Anderson, to perform in a production of The Emperor's Nightingale. Lanny played the emperor, Chip and I a couple of courtiers of some kind. This was a one-shot deal, not the doing of any ongoing children's theatre group. Organizations like that didn't exist yet. We rehearsed a number of times in the Academy building off of Main Street and performed at Highfield Theater. Our director was Irva Levine, who was an impatient sort and taught chemistry at the high school. Why she did this play I can only guess, though she had young, pretty twin daughters, Ruth and Becky, who were in the play and she may have been trying to introduce them to the theater world. Doing the play was a nice break from a monotonous routine, but it did nothing to redirect me.

The Falmouth Enterprise was published on Tuesdays and Fridays. It covered, and still covers, only local news, but Falmouth has been a big enough town to support it for many generations. Its delivery system consisted of kids of 11-14 years who brought the paper to subscribers' doors after school. For most of those kids, myself among them, it was the initial foray into the world of work. I took the job on with few reservations, though I couldn't help thinking that there'd often be things I'd want to do other than deliver the Enterprise at the assigned times, and I wasn't sure I liked the idea of going into the homes of total strangers, especially to collect money. I was assured that my reluctance would pass, and for the most part it did. Making money was the big draw. I had 42 customers, hence 84 deliveries to make per week, and got three cents out of the dime each paper cost. The math: $2.52 a week if everybody paid me, plus there were always some tips. Not bad, not bad at all.

I performed the job diligently. Tuesdays and Fridays after school, I walked or biked straight to the Enterprise office just past the west end of Main Street, picked up my 42 papers and got right to it. The paper was not to go on the front lawn or into a tube; it was to go inside the storm door or into the house. No soggy Enterprises for our loyal customers. My route started about a mile from the Enterprise office, at King Street and Main. I covered King Street, Queen Street, Allen Avenue, Robinson Road and a few little side streets. It took an hour and a half if I kept moving. I was businesslike about the performance, but not the finances. On my way along Main Street to the route, I always stopped at a bakery for a Bismarck, which was a sandwich-sized pastry filled with whipped cream and strawberry jam, absolutely irresistible to a hungry growing boy. I usually stopped at the Sandbar, a variety store-cum-lunch counter run by Ralph and Helen Sullivan, to buy a pack or two of baseball cards. Mark Denman often came along with me, ostensibly to help me get the work done but in fact for the mutual companionship, so I felt obliged to give him fifty cents.

Another barrier to big profits was one section of my route where extracting payment from my customers was difficult. Halfway up King Street stood Robbins Laundry, a spread of a couple of acres of single-story sweatshops that had once been very busy, but was now entering its final years, as homemakers acquired automatic washers and dryers. Across King Street from the laundry were half a dozen derelict little houses, arm's length from one another and all painted red, where resided the unfortunate women who staffed the laundry, and the children of those who had them. They were never at home on Friday, which was pay-for-your-paper day, but I knew where to find them. Across the street to the laundry I went, dreading every second of the next five minutes. I hated intruding on them as they starched shirts, pressed pants and folded sheets; hated that I made them scowl when they saw me coming; hated being told so gruffly to come back some other day; hated knowing that I was going to keep knocking their debt down so that I wouldn't have to ask for so much. I just didn't know what to do. Stop delivering the papers, said my parents. Stop delivering the papers, said Frank Souza, the circulation manager. But I hated more than anything else the thought of those women coming home on Tuesday and Friday and not finding the Enterprise inside their door. They seemed to have had enough disappointments.

A little ways down King Street from there was a modest Victorian where Mrs. Irons lived in an attic apartment. To deliver the paper, I went around to the back of the house and up a steep, enclosed stairway to a landing by her door. Sometimes the door was open, and Mrs. Irons was sitting at a table in her kitchen, expecting me. I joined her at the table, she poured me a glass of soda, and we chatted at some length. She told me she was 92 years old, which I believed based on her appearance, but found extraordinary. As far as I knew, people just didn't live to be 92, but there she was, taking care of herself, reading the local paper and happy to shoot the breeze with an 11-year-old boy. If Mark was along that day, he'd know to keep on delivering the papers and I'd catch up to him in a little while. On days when Mrs. Irons's door was closed, I always found a little dish of unsalted peanuts by the door. I didn't much care for them, but I ate them because that's what they were there for.

There was a curious little advertisement that regularly appeared in a quiet corner of The Enterprise. It read as follows: "Are you having a problem with alcohol? Do you want to do something about it? Call KI8-xxxx". That was it. I wasn't sure what to make of it, and apparently worldlier minds than mine weren't either. The New Yorker frequently lifted published items or quotations that were considered so peculiar or amusing that they merited reprinting as space fillers at the end of an article in that venerable weekly. One day, I ran across that familiar item from the Enterprise while leafing through the magazine in search of humor. The notion of admitting to having a problem with alcohol, and of deciding to do something about it, was a laughing matter.

My parents' efforts to expose Eric and me to a little culture didn't end just because they both had full-time jobs and had settled into their lifetime home. With Mom's folks still living in Great Neck, we went to visit them, probably once a year, and always worked in a couple of trips to Manhattan during our stay. Usually we went by car, but that was an unpredictable and time-consuming proposition, this being before the age of interstate highways. Somewhere along the way, you knew you were going to come across a poorly-marked detour; no effort was made to keep half a road open when it was being worked on, the work took long enough as it was. This could be a real problem at night, because there were few road signs, they were unlit, and the off-limits sections of road were marked only by smudgepots, which were oilcans the size and shape of a bowling ball with a little flame on top to warn drivers of potholes, craters or worse. Any trip that required going very far on local roads was most wisely planned for daylight hours. Passenger trains were hastening out of style, but they still provided service to most anywhere, and I know we did at least a couple of New York trips by rail.

Most of the time, though, we hit the road, and there was very little anyone could do to ease the boredom. Eric and I weren't too bad about asking repeatedly when we were going to get there, but the subject did come up, and Mom always had the road map at the ready to show us where we were and how far we'd gone since the last time we whined. That was a smart move, as it provided incentive to hold off on asking how far there was to go, so that the progress portrayed on the road map would be better. Dad always drove, and Mom always smoked. I sometimes got a touch of carsickness from the smoke, but it never occurred to me to ask her not to, or to her to offer not to. I just had to tough it out. At one point on one of these expeditions, I noticed that Dad looked up into the rear view mirror about every five seconds. This led me to look back at his eyes through that mirror to see what else he was looking at. He was like a hawk looking for prey: he looked left, then forward, then right, then forward, then behind, then forward, ever vigilant for the whole six-hour trip.

On some of the trips, probably before puberty set in, we brought along a jar for Eric and me to piss in rather than stop the car. A lot of the Falmouth-New York route went through town centers and populated neighborhoods, so there weren't many places you could pull over, head for some bushes off the road, and expect not to be seen hanging it out. There were plenty of gas stations, but they didn't all have bathrooms and many of those were filthy. So, the boys pissed in a jar. Every family has its own peculiar ways of dealing with circumstances common to all, and that was how the Turkingtons dealt with the kids' need to urinate on a long drive. I suspect not too many people followed suit, but I'll never know.

My Hedner grandparents – Grandma and Papa to us boys – lived in a compact post-Victorian on the edge of Manhasset, where Papa was a volunteer fireman for many years. What he did for a living during his working years was never made clear to me. Grandma was a saleslady at Lord and Taylor, a department store for the comfortable, where she was able to and expected to indulge in her favorite pastime, which was talking it up with strangers. She was somewhat straight-laced in her attitudes, but probably no more so than most women of her generation. She was generally of good cheer and impossible to ignore. She was American-born, but her parents were German. Papa sailed over from Sweden when he was a little kid. He was the namesake of Eric, who still has the steamer trunk that accompanied Papa to our shores. He was taciturn and thin as a rail, but had a good sense of humor when he used it. He developed diabetes as he got older – most certainly not brought on by obesity – and I happened to see him shooting himself up a couple of times, and heard him talking to his doctor on the phone about the results of whatever tests he was self-administering. He was a devoted semi-pro ballplayer as a young fella. He and Grandma never seemed to talk to each other very much, at least not when we were around. I'm not sure if they liked each other.

Grandma had a number of startlingly thrifty habits that may have been expressions of her nature, but probably were boosted by the family's passage through the Depression. There were rubber bands looped over all the doorknobs in her house. She tucked used Kleenex into her cuffs for future use. On one of their visits to Falmouth, I wound up going to the supermarket with her, where she demonstrated how to be sure you're getting a good tomato: you stick your thumbnail into it to determine if it's over- or underripe. If it's either of those, you put it back and try another. There was something not quite right about this method, though I wasn't sure what it was at the time. It's my suspicion that her money-management ways had a lot to do with her family coming out of the Depression with ownership of their home and the means to send their daughters off to college. This would have been an accomplishment. She also had the means, on Christmas of 1957, to give her children, their husbands and all of their children a crisp new $100 bill. Multiply by ten or more to approximate today's dollars.

Papa's honored position as a longterm volunteer in the Manhasset fire department provided wonderful entertainment opportunities for his grandchildren. There was a large recreation room in the basement of the firehouse where I learned to play pool and ping-pong. These are useful skills for a growing boy to be able to put on his curriculum vitae, and I don't know where else I would have picked them up. Pool and ping-pong tables were unknown in anybody's homes that I knew of, and the big kids at the Falmouth Rec Center never let the little kids have the cue. So we begged a trip to the firehouse every chance we got, for the games and for the – get this – color TV! Color sets were incredibly expensive when they first came out, and this had to be an early one. They were also incredibly bad at reproducing color. I don't know why it was any more exciting to view a dumb TV show in green and purple than in black and white, but it was. Our most thrilling trip to the firehouse came one Christmas vacation, when the firemen had a party for all the families, during which they let the kids loose in the garage. There were three or four shiny red fire trucks in there, and we swarmed all over them. We blew the horns and leaned on the sirens and yanked on the bells and screamed, and I don't think I've experienced such an ear-splitting din since, though a couple of rock bands have come close.

Grandma and Papa were probably in better physical condition than most folks their age, but there was no question in my mind that they were old, and I mean old. When they went to sit down in an easy chair, they approached it with deliberation, turned around gingerly, spread their hands out to catch the arms of the chair, aimed their asses at the cushion and plopped down into it while exhaling a satisfied "Aaaahh". Getting up again required the full use of knees, hips, shoulders and a few seconds' time. Papa was active at times: he had a cherry tree that he'd go out to pick from in season, he kept the tiny lawn mowed, and I know on a visit to

Elkton, he got out in the vacant lot behind the house and threw the ball around with us at least once. But for the most part, he puttered around the house, as did Grandma when she wasn't at work They were approaching seventy.

Over time, primarily between the ages of 8 and 12, I saw a lot of the sights on our forays to Manhattan. The Museum of Natural History was full of dark oak display cases, dioramas, Gothic arches, and creaky hardwood floors. The dinosaur displays knocked me out, as all things dinosaur have grabbed all young boys for many years. Who cares if they were inaccurately interpreted and assembled by impulsive, overconfident paleontologists at the turn of the century? Their fossil skeletons were set up in the great hall to blow people's minds, and that they did. We also went to a Planetarium show, where I was appropriately transfixed except for the unavoidable intrusion of the projector in the middle of the theatre-in-the-round, like a giant deep-sea diver who refused to sit down.

We made a couple of trips to the Metropolitan Museum of Art, where the main attractions were the mummies in the Egypt collection, big landscape paintings, Northwest Indian totem poles and statues of naked ladies. We were there around Christmas once when I spent a long time looking over all the details of a Bethlehem installation in one of the big entry halls. This was a nativity scene with exquisite little figurines of all the principal characters in the Christmas story, with the town of Bethlehem around the stable and the hills and fields around Bethlehem, and the magi off in the distance. With the star way overhead and choral music all around, it had a real You Are There feel to it. Almost 40 years later, Becky was 2 1/2 years old and we were in that museum at that time of year. I had no active recollection of the nativity scene, but as soon as we walked into that room I was overwhelmed with the feeling, I've Been Here Before. Becky, too, spent a long time looking it over.

Soon after moving to Falmouth, the purchase of a hi-fi (high-fidelity, that is: the marketing name for an upscale record player) added a new element to Turkington culture. On nonboating Sundays now, we had three things going on: smoking, reading the paper and listening to music. My parents had a pretty fair collection of 78-RPM blues and jazz records which I'd love to get my hands on now, but they played modern albums of show tunes more than anything else. I knew by heart every word of every song in The Music Man, My Fair Lady, Camelot and The Threepenny Opera by the time I was 12. On one of our New York trips, we went to see The Music Man at the Majestic Theatre. Robert Preston, alas, was on leave and didn't play Professor Harold Hill, but otherwise the show was entirely up to my expectations. One of the kids in River City was played by a girl named Dusty Worrall, who had a great voice and a pile of energy and who I had a big crush on immediately. I walked out of her life at the end of the show, but the moment refuses to die. And that's what I retain from my youthful attendance at a major Broadway production.

We went to the top of the Empire State Building. I think we just walked in, went over to the elevator and headed up. Maybe it wasn't quite that uncomplicated, but I know we didn't stand around very much. There were not many other people at the outdoor terrace at the 88th floor, and when we went up to the enclosed room at the 102nd, we stayed as long as we wanted. A similar visit with my kids 40 years later was quite different. Then, we paid a lot of money, then sat around in a waiting room with hundreds of other folk waiting for the ride up. As soon as we got out on the terrace, we had to start moving along with the stream of tourists, and never did get to the top. Back now circa 1960, we went on a tour of Rockefeller Center which included a trip to the outdoor courtyard at the top floor. This wasn't the Empire State Building, but it was still very high up. What was amazing to me even at the time was that the only barrier to falling to the street below was a masonry wall not much higher than my waist, and I was nowhere near full-grown. A little bit of horseplay, a daredevil move by some nutty kid, an ill-timed slip on the ice or an unfortunate moment of inattention and it's Goodbye Charlie. Eric and I could, and did, lean out over the barrier to get a look straight down to the sidewalk, much to Mom's quiet distress. That was my first experience with a creepy urge I can get, to jump from a very high place. Something in me is deeply curious to know what it would feel like to hop off the edge. The urge to go on living was and has always been stronger, but it's rather disconcerting to sense that the argument is taking place within.

We made a trip to Nantucket in the Swash. I must have missed some school for this episode, because there are no lengthy vacations for a while after school opens, and I'm pretty sure this was in the fall. Nantucket was a very cool place to visit then, years before it evolved into the happening place for the wealthy to keep a home on the waterfront, and for the bourgeousie to keep a home someplace, anyplace on Nantucket. There were a few functioning piers on the harbor and a few decrepit ones. The main town still had its cobblestone streets and poorly-maintained whaling captains' homes, because neither the town nor the current owners had the money or the will to pave the streets or fix up the homes.

The populated area of the main village ended abruptly about a quarter mile from the harbor. From there, you could bike through the moors along a paved road, one heading east about 5 miles to Siasconset, the other south maybe 2 miles to Surfside, and not see a house anywhere except for an untended Victorian rising incongruously from the moor halfway to Surfside. These were two little settlements, largely but not entirely unoccupied in the offseason, that faced the open Atlantic. The moors covered most of the island and consisted of a vast spread of heath: hardy little shrubs maybe two feet high, uninterrupted by trees, hills or domiciles.

Mom and Dad stayed on the Swash on this trip, but they set Eric and me up in a rooming house on the harbor at off-season rates, and a fun place it was. The kindly old innkeeper couple showed us to a hidden door and rooms that were part of the Underground Railroad for escaping slaves in the 1800's (Nantucket was for generations populated almost entirely by Quakers, most of whom were staunchly abolitionist). We rented bicycles and pedaled out to Surfside, stopping along the way to take in the annual sheep-shearing festival, which drew a lot of visitors, most of them townsfolk. We did a tour of one of the finer captain's houses, the whaling museum and the historical society. At the latter, we were the sole visitors, so the gent in charge showed us all around. On one wall hung an 1858 map of Barnstable, Dukes and Nantucket counties – the Cape and Islands. The map was about 5 feet square and was covered with insets that highlighted all the villages, every home in those villages, and the names of the owners of those homes. We all oohed and aahed over this map, and our guide told us, "We have another. Would you like it?" Wull, yeah, we sure would, but…no, he just wanted to give it to us. Dad made a $10 donation to the Nantucket Historical Society, our guide seemed very pleased, and we hustled out with our fine map, which was in better condition than the one on display. It took up a lot of wall space at 287 Scranton Avenue for the next 44 years, and has been doing so at Eric's house since.

I joined the Cub Scouts a year later than the norm, but moved pretty quickly through Wolf, Bear and Lion and all their attendant baubles and badges, and had a good time doing it. My first den mother, Mrs. Kress, lived in a house on Palmer Avenue that Dad's parents rented a little later on. She was a lot of fun and her son was a good kid, so it was too bad that they moved. Our next den mother was Lee Savery's mom, and she was good too. We didn't do much of the outdoorsy, man-building stuff you might associate with scouting. But there were always a couple of engaging activities set up for us, and good snacks, and most importantly, a couple of pinball machines in the Savery basement. I'd never played real, full-sized, electrified pinball before, but I found it very entertaining. Den meetings at the Saverys' were not to be my only experience with this activity.

Being a big sixth-grader now, and having met all the challenges offered by Cub Scouts, it was time to move up to Boy Scouts. Falmouth village had the largest troop in town, but not the most vibrant one. Joining it was kind of a letdown. We had a troop meeting once a month in the Methodist Church hall. These meetings were devoted primarily to ceremonies, uniform inspections and marching practice. The only adult at these meetings was our troop leader, an impatient little guy, red of hair and face, who could often be heard shouting at us. Some years later, it occurred to me that he was probably half in the bag most of the time. I know that some of my troopmates stayed with it, advanced through the ranks and got a lot out of it, but the troop meeting is really the home page of local scouting, and to me it kind of sucked. I was in a patrol – a subunit of the troop – that met one afternoon a week without adult supervision. Maybe that was the idea, that we'd learn how to dream up and carry out activities on our own, but if it was, it didn't work. Not many showed up usually, and those of us that did just horsed around. I earned a few merit badges, got as far as Second Class but couldn't work up the enthusiasm to pursue this any further.

One benefit that did accrue to me from my scouting experience was a sizable addition to my baseball card collection. I'd begun to accumulate a lot of cards by this time, thanks to those many bicycle trips down Main Street to undertake my paper route, but all I had was what I'd bought. There was a kid in the troop, Billy Clark, with whom I was once discussing my avocation, who told me he had a pile of old cards. I told him I'd like to look at them. He asked me if I'd like to have them. I said sure. Next month, there was Billy with a shopping bag full of baseball cards from the late 40's to the mid-fifties. They were a little beat up, but what did I care? I stupidly let a lot of the valuable ones go when I sold off much of my collection later on, but I held onto the rookie cards of Hank Aaron, Ernie Banks, Roberto Clemente and Sandy Koufax. There were a couple of Ted Williamses in there too, and a Willie Mays. I still have them. Thanks, Billy.

* * *

Dad's parents lived in Falmouth for as long as I can remember being there. They may have retired there when we lived on Mill Road, stayed put when we left and were still there when we got back. At first, they lived in the downstairs apartment of a big white colonial, classic in both style and era. The place was on Locust Street, just down the road from the village green. Later on – not too long after we moved to Scranton Avenue – they relocated to a ranch house set back from Queen Street. The Colonial got torn down to make way for a convenience store. Their new place was pretty nice, with a fenced-in yard big enough for throwing a ball around and for my grandmother's flower beds. They had a lot of mementoes, but didn't clutter the house up with them. We joined them for dessert most Sundays after dinner, but didn't see a whole lot of them otherwise, even though our homes were a quarter mile apart. On those Sundays, we had dessert, then sat around talking for about an hour, and of course I was bored out of my skull the whole time, but I was mostly able to refrain from feeling resentment over being there. I knew they all meant well, and the air of gentility called for good manners all around.

Grandpa was Frederick George Turkington. He grew up in Lurgan, Northern Ireland, and came to the States as a young adult. In keeping with, or perhaps in establishing, the family trait of reticence about one's earlier life, I never heard much about what he'd done with his first 70 years, but he very much saw himself as an Irishman. He looked and sounded the part, though he was of the

Episcopalian persuasion. He was largely bald, rather gruff in manner and stern in outlook. It's been intimated by some in the family that he wasn't easy to grow up with. Whether he was mellowing a bit with age or he knew better than to be too critical of his son's kids I don't know, but we got along pretty well. I'd say anyone who loses a child due to someone else's failure is entitled, if not to be grumpy the rest of his life, at least to be tolerated for being grumpy.

One big piece of evidence that he was an impressive young man is that he got Ola Thornton to marry him. Nano we called her, and whatever fine human traits I may recognize in any of her progeny, I attribute in large part to her. She was raised in upstate New York, orphaned at seven, educated at a convent, studied piano at Oberlin Conservatory, and wound up working in New York City, where she met Grandpa, who was importing Irish linen. His business was good for a while and they got a comfortable start, but it petered out, so she started baking and catering to make ends meet. She was very good at it. I caught her culinary skills at the tail end, but they were outstanding. One of the nicest features of my birthdays growing up was getting a cake from Nano, made to order. She produced extraordinarily intricate hooked rugs, embroidery and crewel work. She never had a harsh word to say to her grandchildren or a bad word to say about anybody. She laughed easily, induced others to do the same, and could speak knowledgeably and thoughtfully about anything. She made no pretense of being better than anybody else, but in fact she was.

I watched television about as much as other reasonably bright, active kids my age did, meaning not a whole heck of a lot. Just entering adolescence, I was still up and about before the rest of the household on weekends, so I was familiar with the Saturday morning cartoons. They just ran them one after another, with no commentary or studio settings involved. There could be a couple of LoonyTunes followed by a few from the archives, like Betty Boop or Popeye or early Disney. There were ads, mostly for flashy, unattainable kids' toys, but I liked the older cartoons best. Hannah-Barbera was about to move in with their highly simplified, vastly inferior mode of artistry that required very few creators to produce, hence was far cheaper. The madcap, finely detailed animation that I was watching on Saturday mornings was a spectacular art form and a dying industry, though I didn't know it at the time.

The same could be said for some of my favorite prime-time shows, though here it wasn't the industry that was dying, far from it, just the normal retention of the popular shows and termination of the less popular ones. There were a lot of shows that depicted normal, wholesome, upwardly mobile families of northern European descent living in the suburbs. "The Donna Reed Show" was one of the best of them. The parents and two kids were a little less contrived, the humor a little sharper than the norm. "Ozzie and Harriet" was very formulaic in its storylines, but had the distinction of portraying a real, true-to-life family, one of whose kids was a deservedly popular teen heartthrob. Ricky Nelson was the good boy's Elvis; he had the curled upper lip that demonstrated an inner cynicism, but not too much of it; rebelliousness suggested by a coif of long black hair, but neatly done; and the sleepy eyes and saunter that let you know he was cool, but wasn't going to pick on you or beat you up. He had a lot of good songs and boy, could he sing them. The last two minutes of the show had Ricky singing his latest in one venue or another, usually a high school dance, and even when the show stunk, it was worth waiting for.

A large proportion of America's youth tuned in to watch the maiden episode of "Bonanza", whose opening shot of a map of western

Nevada catching fire has to be one of the all-time great lead-ins. The show could be pretty good, too. Some of the writers of other westerns were serious about their art. "Maverick" could sometimes present the plotline of a standard western in a dark, ominous tone that was outstanding drama. "Tall Man" did some nice work with the high-tension friendship of Pat Garrett and Billy Bonney. "Gunsmoke" had its game very well together, and it just went on and on. There were not many shows that I really made a point of watching every week. One was "The Many Loves of Dobie Gillis", which portrayed and discussed teenage life with unerring humor and thoughtfulness, and taught a generation the meaning of "propinquity". It wouldn't be too great a stretch to say that Zelda was the first feminist to show up in a popular TV serial, and Maynard G. Krebs the first hippie, though he was presented as a latter-day beatnik. My other must-see was "Secret Agent", wherein Patrick McGoohan played a highly unBondlike British spy. They could pack a mountain of tense, soft-spoken, mysterious action into that half hour, and Patrick was always just barely equal to the task of figuring it out. The musical intro to the show was quite original, later to be put to words and popularly recorded by Johnny Rivers. When I heard the show was on its last run, I actually wrote in protest to the network, and someone there actually wrote back. They told me they appreciated my loyalty to the show, but that I'd probably like their replacement for it even more: "Mission:Impossible". Nah. You bastards did it for the ratings, didn't you?

At the west end of Falmouth village, between the railroad tracks and Buzzards Bay, was a vast undeveloped tract of land known as Beebe's Woods. The Beebe family, rich merchants from the mainland who financed the Episcopal Church on the green, built a couple of mansions up there and cut in miles of serpentine carriage trails during their heyday in the late 1800's. The Beebes were long gone, the mansions – Highfield and Tanglewood - boarded up and untended, the trails overgrown, but all the land was still unmolested. In the middle of it all was the Punchbowl, a deep, circular pond a couple of hundred yards across. It was what is known to geologists as a kettle hole: a place where, as a glacier in the last ice age got as far south as it was going, an especially large section of ice came to rest, awaiting Phase I of global warming. When it all melted away, here was this big depression in the terrain. At the bottom of it lay the Punch Bowl. It wasn't easy to get to – you had to know the trails and walk quite a ways through the woods, which grownups never did – but for someone looking to get away from life's complications and adult oversight, it could not be beat.

Mark Denman and I hiked up into Beebe's Woods fairly often, not always with a trip to the Punchbowl in mind, but we usually wound up there at some point. Our main activities were skinny-dipping, smoking cigarettes when we could procure them, catching and releasing bullfrogs, throwing rocks, making funny sounds and listening for the echoes. One fine June afternoon, we were swimming in the middle of the pond when we heard shouts from the little rocky landing at the foot of the trail:

"DENMAN! TURKINGTON!"

We looked over and saw Donnie Couto and Jimmy Cary, two kids a couple of years older than us, standing on the rocks.

"WE'VE GOT YOUR CLOTHES!"

And so they did. By the time we got out of the water, they had a long head start and all of our duds, shoes included, and we had that empty feeling that befalls us all from time to time, usually when we least expect it: this time I'm really screwed. Walking unclothed through the woods wasn't the problem; we were unlikely to encounter anybody there. The problem was, what happens when the woods end? Getting to Mark's house was our only viable option, as he lived pretty close to the edge of the woods. Trouble was, once we were out in the open, we would have to cross the railroad tracks, run down a short unoccupied dirt road, then get to the other side of Palmer Avenue, which was Route 28, which was the busiest road in town. However we got through all that, we then would have to cut through a neighbor's yard to get to the little wooded area surrounding the Denmans'. And then what? Hi Mom, I'm home and I'm stark naked! So's Tom!

Well, we had plenty of time to think all this through, and what we came up with was, we'd skulk through the back yards of some of the homes this side of Palmer Avenue looking for laundry we could steal from somebody's clothesline to cover ourselves up with. If we couldn't find any, which we probably wouldn't, we'd crouch in the bushes beside Route 28, in broad daylight in a heavily populated section of town, hoping to remain unseen until there was a break in the traffic. Then we'd streak across the road, through the neighbor's yard, to Mark's house, get some clothes on and catch hell. It wasn't much of a plan, but it was the best we could do. Then just a while before the end of the trail, we saw something up in the branches. A pair of underpants! And look over there – a shirt! And a pair of sneakers in the middle of the trail! What good guys! Thanks,

Donnie. Thanks, Jimmy. Sorry about all those awful things we said about you hiking back from the Punchbowl. It's truly amazing how, when a distressing situation appears to be heading for the worst, and for some reason the worst doesn't come to pass, we not only are grateful for whatever prevented the worst from happening, but wholly unresentful of whoever created the distressing situation in the first place. Relief is surely one of life's most rewarding feelings.

Embarrassment in front of one's youthful peers is one of the worst, and Mark and I got a good dose of it the following morning. The class was sitting around on the grass next to the Hall School, waiting for the bus that was going to take us on our end-of-school-year class trip to the outer Cape. At a quiet moment, Rick Hill suddenly shouted out: Hey everybody, listen to this! Mark Denman and Tom Turkington were skinny-dipping up in the Punchbowl yesterday when Donny Couto and Jimmy Cary....yadda, yadda, yadda. This revelation to the crowd didn't spoil my day, but it sure was humiliating at the time. Rick Hill was an interesting kid. He was totally unself-conscious about expressing whatever might cross his mind. This could at times be an honorable trait, but often when he saw an opportunity to get under someone's skin, he'd take advantage of it. He was never vicious, and I suspect he saw his troublemaking as a sort of practical joke. Like many a practical joke, it can be funny to everyone but the target. About as often as you wanted to slap him for stirring up trouble for somebody, you'd want to praise him for being so much his own, unfiltered, forthright self. These things may have balanced out, but throw in the fact that he was a small but talented athlete, and that he had an older sister and brother who introduced him to the ways of the big kids, and I'd guess he scored well above the median in the acceptability ratings.

I spent most of that summer after sixth grade occupying myself with going to the beach, doing my paper route and making a little extra money mowing a few lawns in the neighborhood, such as it was. Fifty cents an hour was about the going rate for kids doing menial work, but I didn't have much to spend it on, so my bank account grew incrementally. As a condition of borrowing the family lawn mower for personal financial gain, I was expected to keep gas in the tank and change the oil from time to time. Dad showed me how to do that. You got the mower a little ways off the ground, unscrewed the drain plug and ran the dirty oil into a pan or wide-mouthed jar. Then you dug a hole several inches deep in the ground a little ways from the house. Then you poured the oil into that hole and filled it back up with dirt. This way, you didn't have to worry about tracking dirty motor oil into the house. My parents were well-read and thoughtful people who would have been well up on environmental consciousness if there'd been any, but there wasn't, except among a few crackpot scientists. We were also good about filling our empty beer or soda bottles with seawater before we tossed them overboard, so that they wouldn't float around and pose a hazard to propellers.

I started heading out in the evening from time to time with Chip Papp or Mark. Heading out meant walking up and down Main Street observing the ways of the many college students who were starting to infiltrate the Falmouth summer scene. Cruising was the big thing, at least in the earlier evening hours when kids like me might still be on the scene. Main Street was always jammed with cars, many of them convertibles, loaded with randy young folks checking out and being part of the action. From the village green to the Heights corner, the cars inched along, everybody conducting the first stages of finding a party, many of them drinking already, shouting back and forth, not usually causing any trouble but annoying the hell out of residents who had their own reasons for wanting to drive on or get across Main Street, and undoubtedly leading many to wonder: what the hell is this generation coming to? These were not baby boomers; they were born in the late 30's or early 40's, nor were they a big demographic bubble, but they were the first large wave of idle, pleasure-seeking young people to find Cape Cod in the summer a good place to look for fun. They were not the crest of the wave.

The scene at Surf Drive beach was considerably more wholesome, though age-appropriately self-indulgent. When I went there, which was often, I brought a beach towel and enough cash for a visit to the concession stand, and usually spent most of the day there. At that time, I was still comfortable mixing in with whatever collection of adolescents might show up on a given day. Such collections usually consisted of townies, with a liberal sprinkling of summer kids. There was beginning to be some blending of the genders in our age group, and though I wasn't sure about how to deal with the company of girls besides showing off, I didn't notice that the other boys had much of a better handle on it. It felt nice to be sharing space with the girls and there was some degree of interaction, but I didn't see any signs of pairing up. We still conducted long games of tag out on the raft, played a lot of rundown with a tennis ball, got dirty looks from some of the older folks nearby, and could still let the day go by without self-appraisal.

Dad's boss at The Enterprise was Jack Hough, the editor and publisher, whose wife Molly was a good friend of mom's. There was a forecast of a beautiful upcoming Saturday one week, and mom got the bright idea of inviting Molly and the Hough kids for an excursion in the Swash. Dad was going to be unavailable, as he worked Saturdays, but we'd all gone through all the routines of a boating trip and thought we'd be fine without his expertise. The day turned out as nice as predicted, the Houghs showed up, Mom and I got the boat loaded up and started and out of the harbor and into the Sound without any glitches. We anchored about a half mile off shore a little ways down from Nobska Point, had some lunch, did some swimming and readied for our return. We started up the engine without checking to see that the line to the dinghy behind us wasn't so located as to snag in the propeller. It was, and it did. That rope got threaded into the propeller shaft and the Swash stopped cold. I volunteered to go overboard and try to free the line from the shaft, but it was no go. It was really caught.

We drifted for a while, then decided we'd better drop anchor until someone came along to help us out. We were in deeper water now, and the anchor didn't reach bottom, so that was out. We had with us a big, long horn that made a loud tooting noise that was supposed to be recognized as a distress signal. We also had some measly flares in the S.O.S. kit. What we didn't have was a ship to shore radio. There were boats of all kinds motoring and sailing not far from us, and we shot those flares and blew that horn till our faces were purple, and everybody just waved in greeting. Meanwhile, we were drifting out into more open water and getting nervous. After some time, a larger cruiser came along, the skipper heard our story and offered to tow us back to the harbor. We gratefully accepted, but as we progressed we noticed that the dinghy was now getting pulled on a short line and taking on water. I got in the dinghy with a bucket, tied a longer line around one of the seats and freed the dinghy up from the short line that was snagged in the propeller. I started bailing with the bucket when, RIP the seat got torn out and the dinghy was no longer attached to the Swash. I dove for the seat now skipping over the waves, caught it with my fingertips and pulled myself hand-over-hand up to the transom of the Swash, where many hands pulled me back on board. Mom was laughing, crying and in shock all at the same time. For a moment at least, she'd faced the prospect of seeing her younger son treading water a mile out in Nantucket Sound as the Swash was getting towed to shore. She told me later she thought I was very brave.

The move into 7th grade brought big changes in my academic life. The biggest was that I was now in Lawrence Junior-Senior High School, a handsome and highly functional edifice that was built in 1953 to accommodate the 7th through 12 grades for the entire town and was by this time bursting at the seams. With a surprising but widely shared lack of anticipation, the town was only now working on plans for a new junior high school, but there's a long lead time in that sort of thing. In the meantime, we were on split sessions, wherein the high schoolers started early and got out early and the 7th and 8th started late and got out late, with as many as possible of the activities that didn't require classroom space scheduled during the overlap. The logistics of fitting nearly 1200 kids into a school building built for 800 probably kept some administrators awake at night, but to those in attendance, it was what it was and it seemed to work out okay.

Why Lawrence? Wasn't this a Falmouth public school? Good question. Let's see if I have it right. Back in the mid-1800's, it was decided that Falmouth needed a public secondary school. A Mr. Lawrence put up a big chunk of the money needed to build it, or maybe all of it, under the condition that it be named after him. Thrifty Cape Codders were only too happy to accept his generous offer, so the first high school in Falmouth was Lawrence Academy, which still exists as the Chamber of Commerce building set back from Main Street on Shiverick's Pond. When it came time to build a new high school, the name came with it. The school kept moving; the name stayed. I imagine that there was always in town a hard core of Lawrence High alumni who grew up cheering for and singing about and being loyal to Lawrence High, and damned if they weren't going to let their kids enjoy the same experience. It never made much sense to me. When I was on a team that had a lot of success, I found that many people thought that my teammates and I were from the city of Lawrence. Many others thought we were some kind of hotshot prep school, Lawrence of Falmouth. Those in the know were aware that we represented Falmouth's public high school, but they were a minority. Competing in high school athletics - or marching band, or quiz bowl, or debate team – always generates a certain sense of going out there and representing your school, a sense that is diminished when most of the people paying attention either don't know where your school is, or what it is. When the latest high school was built in 1973, it was named Falmouth High School. I guess folks figured that we'd more than met our obligation to Mr. Lawrence.

The big changes for the newcomers were in the format. 45-minute periods, with buzzers to tell you when it was time to move on. Seven periods plus cafeteria. A different teacher for every subject, or at least that was the idea. A modern gymnasium with stands for spectators. A real auditorium with a big stage. And a whole bunch of new kids: Falmouth had elementary schools in North Falmouth, East Falmouth and Teaticket that we in the center of town knew very little about, but their kids were joining us now in the big time. With that influx, there were well over 200 seventh graders, which number was divided up into seven classes, each of which was known by a number. The brainiest kids were in 7-4. The next smartest class was 7-1, then 7-2, and so on down the line to 7-7, with that jump at 7-4. I'm sure this system was cooked up so that a kid's class's numerical designation wouldn't too obviously reflect the intellectual capacity within, but it was crudely and ineffectively done, and it fooled nobody.

My first class on my first day was shop. Walking in there really nailed it home that we were in the major leagues now. It was a huge room full of workbenches, stationary tools, racks of lumber, cabinets full of hand tools, bright fluorescent lights overhead, rows of skylights, dust-collecting ducts all around and loads of room to move. Off to the right was a well-equipped print shop, with racks and racks of various styles of type, printing machines of many functions, drawers loaded with implements for setting up a page, and a potent aroma of ink even though nothing had been used for ten weeks. Print shop was what we did for the first marking period. It was fun, but even at the time it was pretty well understood that the old printing press and the skills required to use it to print words on paper were approaching obsolescence. After 500 years of movable type, the business/publication inventors were beginning to find easier ways to get the same results. While the boys were learning how to operate a printing press, the girls were in the home economics room, learning how to make their own clothes.

A marked increase in ethnic diversity accompanied the arrival of the kids from the east part of town. There was a sizable Cape Verdean population in Falmouth, many of whom went back generations and most of whom lived in or around Teaticket. They were, essentially, of African descent, but their ancestors arrived here not by force, but as seafarers, fishermen or farmers. I would hesitate to say that, as an ethnic group, they were full partners in the community. Many Cape Verdeans achieved notable success in school or in their professions, but their race was dark of skin and therefore not like ours. A great many Portugese lived in East Falmouth, where they had begun arriving many years ago primarily as farmers but had moved on into every facet of life in town, including its politics. Some traced their roots back to mainland Portugal, many more to the Azores. Falmouth in general, and the schools in particular, did have something of a melting pot effect, but there were divisions.

Part of the anticipation of moving up to the big school was being in a different classroom every period, and having a different teacher for every subject. It didn't quite work out that way. This year and next, Barbara D. Buchanan was to be an important and unavoidable fixture in my life. She was short, somewhat aged, even-tempered and a very competent teacher. If I'd had her for one subject, one period a day, we likely would have gotten along fine. But I was in her room for English, and reading, and social studies, and a full-period study hall each and every day. I was also in there for a half period after lunch, and all too often, I was there after school with a roomful of other penitent boys. Miss Buchanan wanted to educate her pupils and she wanted to understand them, but more than anything else, she wanted to straighten out the boys. And who can blame her? Boys at 12 and 13 wear their immaturity on their sleeves. The problem was, her primary weapon of persuasion – keeping you after school if you stepped out of line – was applied with alarming frequency and often with little discernible reason. It bred considerable resentment, especially among those like myself who didn't take well to authority, and it had very little impact on the malfeasors' behavior.

Steve Troynak and I were chatting in the hall outside of Miss Buchanan's room one day in May. We looked up and saw her approaching with that stern gait and downturned mouth that telegraphed: We can't have this going on around here. She faced Steve from close quarters, leaned her head back and queried: Young man, why are you wearing a sweater on a warm day in May? Steve replied with complete calm: Oh, I guess I just like this sweater. I'm comfortable in it. Said Miss B: Well I think you should come by my room after school and think about whether you should wear a sweater on a nice day like this. Of course, I couldn't resist: Miss Buchanan, can't he wear a sweater if he wants to? Her very predictable response: Tommy, I'd like to see you after school so we can talk about contradicting your teachers. We stood in stunned silence as she turned and walked back to her room. Being 12 years old, we were preoccupied with our own rage and frustration, not the least bit cognizant of how she was feeling. Now, after having dealt with kids for years and observed other adults dealing with them, I think I know how she was feeling: satisfied, and sure that she'd just done something to make us better people, and the world a better place.

Miss Buchanan could rest assured that any resentment engendered in the wayward boys by her intolerance of their behavior would not get out of hand, because there was a harsher and less desirable punishment she held in reserve for the real bad actors. If worse came to worst, she had the option of sending you down to the junior high principal, Henry Frank, whose office was in a former storage room down the hall. Mr. Frank was a husky, rugged man of about 60 who'd played a little NFL in its early days and didn't believe in coddling kids. It was rumored, or should I say known, that if a boy was accused of something truly objectionable, he'd lay a hand on him. He talked big, and loud, and came across as something of a blowhard, but I think he probably knew what he was doing as a principal. As a disciplinarian, he was old school and not ashamed of it, nor called to task on account of it. Almost any kid who raised his ire could count on getting it worse at home. I was never one of them.

Miss Buchanan was very capable of being pleased, even amused by the behavior of her miscreant pupils. She wasn't out to get us, she just wanted us to behave differently than we usually did. When we expressed ourselves in ways that didn't rankle her, she could get a kick out of it. One of the few times I saw her really laugh out loud was one day when she was asking me not to do something I was doing; of what it was I have no recollection. I told her: Donnie told me to do it. She asked of me, as all teachers and parents have asked of Falmouth kids since the Bourne Bridge was finished in 1934: If Donnie told you to jump off the Bourne Bridge, would you do it? To which I answered: I always do whatever Donnie tells me to do. And she laughed. She laughed in a way that the cool teachers sometimes laughed, with the mouth wide open and the head back and the shoulders shaking and, for just a moment, a cessation of control. She did it rarely, but she could do it.

Donnie was Donnie Bumpus, who lived in Waquoit, at the far east end of Falmouth, and spent his earlier years at the East Falmouth School. His father was a steeplejack, his mother the postmistress at the Waquoit office. Donnie had wavy red hair, alert bulbous eyes, and a deliberate manner of speech and movement that signaled an unusual degree of self-awareness. His sense of the absurd, and his ability to express it humorously, struck me as soon as we started to know each other. But friendships take time, and my personal jury was still out on Donnie until our class and others went over to the big book sale that fall. The gym at the Hall School, which was structurally sound again after a year of repairs, was filled with books for kids from the early readers through the high school. I wasn't sure whether we were expected to buy the books or just be elevated by having so many of them around us, but they walked a crowd of us over there and the gym was filled with books and 7th-graders browsing among them. After we'd been there a while, Donnie sidled over to me and asked: "So…seen any s-e-x?" I pondered him and his query a moment and replied, "Over in the art section, one of the book covers shows a painting of a woman with a bare boob." "Ooh, I missed that. Thanks." And off he went to the art section. Donnie and I had a great many moments of mutual understanding ahead of us, but that one got us started.

Not all of my time in school was spent in Miss Buchanan's room. Mr. Buck taught science, though without any lab facilities available to him, everything was straight from the book. He was a pretty loose guy with a lot to say about things that kids our age were dealing with that had nothing to do with science. His classroom fostered a certain degree of anticipation: yes, we'll go through the text, but something else is going to happen here, and what will it be? He had the unique habit of picking up an eraser from the chalkboard and firing it at the desk of a kid whose attention was elsewhere. He rarely missed. On October 31, he talked to us about whatever we might have in mind to do that evening: "Now listen, I don't want to be a wet blanket, but..." followed by a discussion of the consequences of misbehavior on Halloween. He knew what was on our minds and wasn't afraid to address it. Our math teacher, Connie Flood, was of similar mien. She was a very good teacher, maintained total control of the class, yet knew how to manage, and didn't feel threatened by, those moments when the kids in the class asserted themselves or their ideas. Those among us who valued the chance to be heard, and taken seriously, by the head of the classroom, couldn't help wondering: Why can't they all be like that?

My interests in the game of basketball and in getting out of the house led me that winter to attend a number of home games of the high school boys' basketball team. I specify the boys' team because there was a girls' team, but they played a very different version of the game then – an emasculated one, as it were – and received little notice. The boys' team enjoyed that happy combination of a serendipitous crop of tough, skilled players, one of whom was very tall, a generally competent coach who clicked with this particular group, and great fan support. The gym seated about 800, and as the season went on and the team won most of its games, it became increasingly difficult to find a seat. The uproar in that gym as a close game – as many were – wound its way to conclusion was absolutely deafening. When it got down to the last minute, the outcome still to be determined, a timely basket by Mike Finnell or a slick steal by Ralph Jonas was enough to raise them to the level of gods in my eyes, and those of my fellow spectators. The tall player was Mike Lopes, a slightly awkward, gangly but determined junior who knew how to play hard. I don't know how far that 1962 team got in the state tournament. Over the course of the next year, Mike

Lopes filled out his frame and developed an extraordinary athleticism that led to greater glory in '63.

I sang in the kids' choir at the St. Barnabas Episcopal Church for at least a couple of years. My family was never very regular about attending church. In Elkton, there was a church of some denomination just around the corner from our house, so we went there from time to time, often enough to befriend the pastor and his family, the Leswings. They had two boys, Chris and Jamie, who matched up agewise with Eric and me, so we were in their home a lot more often than their house of worship. In Falmouth, we had a similarly noncommittal connection with St. Barnabas, but at some point I was directed to the choir, so I became a regular there for a time. I had a fairly good voice and was chosen to solo at least a couple of times, but none of us was given any actual voice instruction. At our weekly practice, we just sang the hymns over and over under the assumption that the more we did it, the better we'd get. The part of choir membership that bordered on the enjoyable was the ritual of putting on the robes in the little choir room off to the side, and filing over to the choir pews at the edge of the altar. Showtime! There was a lot of highly ornate woodwork, arched doorways with wrought iron hardware, leaded glass windows, little nooks and crannies all around the church that appealed to me. There was a Sunday School after service with several kids my age, which I attended frequently but never took seriously. A year or two later, I was in a confirmation class and must have had a confirmation ceremony, since that was the whole point of the class, but it didn't impress itself upon me. About that time, my voice started to get hoarse and crack a lot, so I quit the choir and didn't attend another worship service anywhere for 35 years. I got no argument from my parents.

If either of my parents harbored a wish that one of their sons would follow in either of their footsteps, they did a good job of keeping it from us. I came to find out much later that when Dad was about my age, he was a member of the boys' choir at St. James's Church on Madison Avenue. He and Grandpa went to an enormous amount of trouble to get there from Port Washington for practices and services. I gather that Dad had a pretty fine voice and that this was an accomplished choir. If ever there was an occasion for Dad to break his vow of silence about his youth and relate his experiences to mine, or give me pointers, or just reminisce, you'd think this would be the time. Nope, not a word.

Other than our joint participation in family excursions, Eric and I never did much together. We were two years apart in age, but that could certainly have been overcome if we had shared interests or attitudes, but we didn't. Eric had a considerably restrained demeanor, or as we might put it now, he didn't always appear comfortable in his own skin. Yet he was very good at getting people organized to accomplish rather creative objectives. When he was in eighth grade, he and a few friends started putting out an unsanctioned newspaper, The Lawrence Broadcaster. It had some gossip, some reviews, some news about goings-on in the school as seen through the eyes of 8th-graders that would be of interest to 8th-graders. As such, there was always material that might not cast the school or its staff in the best light. It was a big hit. Miss Buchanan tried to have it banned from the premises. I don't recall what came of that, but I did admire the effort that was put into its publication. There was no mimeograph machine available, or perhaps even invented yet, so production was done by typing up a page on special paper, laying it face down on a slab of some gelatinous substance to create a reverse image, then pressing blank pages, one at a time, onto the bed of gelatin to create a printed page. Gutenberg would have been impressed, but it was quite a laborious process for a 20th century publication.

Eric was pretty poor at sports, but quite popular and an outstanding student. I may have been told one too many times – never by my parents – that he left me big shoes to fill, because I did gradually grow into an attitude towards schoolwork that if I wasn't very interested in the assignment, I wasn't going to knock myself out to do a good job on it. I withdrew from a competition that wasn't there in the first place. Or, I might have gone that way under any circumstances. As soon as I get the chance to do it over again, I'll find out and let you know. One indicator of my relationship with Eric came out in a game in the side yard, when Mark Denman and I were playing football against Kenny Ingram and Eric. If 2-on-2 football sounds a little meager, remember that this was on Scranton Avenue. One of them kicked off to us, the ball came to me, I fumbled it as I started to run, and I shouted "SHIT!" I well recall the flush of unwarranted embarrassment that came over me. I cussed around my friends and they cussed around me. Eric's friends surely cussed around him and I'm sure he cussed right back, but Eric and I didn't cuss around each other. Go figure. We started cussing around each other after we'd left home, when we were able to meet on different terms, and we've been cussing ever since, but never at each other.

Our parents were unalterably conscientious about their jobs. Dad's title at the Enterprise was associate editor, which meant he dealt with some of everything that came into and passed through the newsroom. He wrote up some of the news stories, took some of the pictures, did some of the editing and proofreading and reported on some of the town's regularly scheduled committee meetings. He was on the job from 8 to 5, five days a week, plus Saturday mornings and Monday and Thursday evenings. I don't believe he ever called in sick, even in the rare event that he was. He allotted himself a full hour for lunch, during which he made a fast meal of leftovers, then lay down on the couch and perused the New York Times until five minutes before one, when he went back to the office. He was a creature of routine who recognized that, at least for himself, creativity and pleasure in his work grew out of freeing himself of any debate as to whether he wanted to do it, or when he would do it, or whether he was ready to go back after lunch. These matters were settled before the question could arise, which left him at liberty to focus upon the task before him. He approached his work with great reverence for Fact and Truth, as journalists were then expected to. Only with difficulty could he show patience towards people who twisted those paragons around to please themselves. I hope that his bias is an admirable curse, because I have it myself.

Mom went about her work with the boundless faith that all good teachers have, that her subject matter was relevant to her pupils' lives, accessible to them, and would interest and enrich them if it was presented to them in the right way. The right way began with loving the subject itself, and that she did. I'm sure, as a teacher of freshman English, she devoted a proper amount of time to grammar and vocabulary and spelling, but what she wanted was for them to be exposed to great literature, to talk about it, think about it and write about what they thought. She well knew that she was not creating a generation of highbrows, but she did feel that any kid anywhere would be a better person for knowing how Sidney Carton felt on his last ride. She was very good at engaging the little minds before her with the works of the great authors, old and new. She had her classes reading "Catcher in the Rye" when it was still banned in a lot of schools and libraries. She knew the world was messy, as many of her students' lives were messy, and she would not limit them to reading about orderly things. She spent most of her evenings writing up or correcting assignments at the dining room table, which was the only place in the house it could be done. She didn't much care for this gritty side of her trade, as was evidenced by her inability to stay focused on the task without frequent breaks for a smoke, a piece of candy, a glass of water or a few minutes of TV. She said we had our homework, and she had hers.

I sometimes wonder how transportation arrangements were made to work with just the one car. Eric and Mom had to be at school pretty early, so it may have been that Dad drove them there, then went on to the Enterprise. I know that a bus came by for the later junior high start, and I rode it some of the time, maybe every day. Dad had to have had the car during the day, because he always came home at noon, so how did Mom get back from school? The high school was a mile and a half from our house, so it was understood that the boys could walk, but I don't think Mom did. Well okay, so except for Mom's return from the school I've answered my own question, but I know that getting a second car was not a consideration, for financial and cultural reasons. Most families that didn't view themselves as highly prosperous would no more own two cars than they'd own two televisions. Even if there were a practical reason for it, it would look showy and pretentious, and most people had an aversion to that. It may be that the Greatest feature of the Greatest Generation was that most of them didn't want to show off their success, such as it was, to their neighbors.

The summer passed without a lot to remember. I still had my paper route, I mowed a few neighbors' lawns, I went to the beach a lot and spent some time every weekend on the Swash with my family. Approaching my teen years, I was beginning to adopt a sullen and resentful attitude towards my parents. I'm sure that if I'd ever said to them, "I really don't want to go out in the boat today. I'd rather stay here and do something else", they would have been agreeable, perhaps even relieved, as I often did whatever I could to make sure my presence spoiled their day. But I felt that boating with them was expected of me, so along I went. I spent a lot of my other free days biking off to hang out with friends. Carl Soderland lived in Sippewissett, so we wound up at Wood Neck Beach from time to time. Mark Denman and I met up for Beebe's Woods, Mad Magazine, smoking or baseball cards. Ken Ketchum still lived in the Mill Road neighborhood and I sometimes went by to join in the high culture there. I never knew what would happen when I visited the Papps, but something always did. I was ten days too old to get in another year of Little League, which I regretted because I was becoming a decent player, but I still found myself in a pickup game once in a while.

I spent a fair number of my evenings listening to the New York Mets on the radio. This was the first year of expansion in the National League, and the Mets were brought into existence so that the greatest metropolis in the western hemisphere would have a franchise representing the Senior Circuit (when was the last time you heard that catchy moniker?). I never became a fan of the Mets, who started out in life as the worst team in baseball history, but I could pull in the station that broadcast them, so I was a frequent listener. Their primary play-by-play man was Howard Cosell, whose whiny voice and overwrought modes of expression annoyed the hell out of me, as they annoyed untold millions of football fans in later years, when Howard was the major domo of Monday Night Football. What really irked me about him was that he wasn't always nice to Ralph Branca, his color man. Branca was a former Dodgers pitcher, remembered chiefly for giving up a shocking home run to Bobby Thompson in 1951 that won the pennant for the Giants. It was not an incident he liked talking about, but Howard Cosell reminded him of it frequently. As the Mets were playing their first year in the Polo Grounds, where The Shot Heard Round The World had been hit, he had numerous opportunities. In time, I came to understand that Howard Cosell was one of the giants of the broadcasting world, and one of its most insightful, broad-minded practitioners. He showed respect and appreciation for Muhammed Ali when most whites, especially in sports, saw Ali as an ignorant, mouthy troublemaker. But I never did like to listen to Howard.

A high point of the summer was a trip to the Barnstable County Fair, which at the time was held in Marstons Mills. My parents rarely made a fuss over birthdays, but for this one they told me to invite a couple of friends and they'd take us out there and pay for everything. So Carl Soderland and Chip Papp and I went on the rides, played the carney games and ate the junk food to our heart's content. Having in more recent years gone en famille to that same fair, now held in Falmouth's Hatchville, I'm aware of how the money can flow out of your wallet like water from a faucet, but Mom and Dad seemed to enjoy the event. I think it made them feel good to see me having fun. I'm sure we didn't interfere with anybody else's enjoyment on our evening at the fair, but I'm just as sure that we were silly and obnoxious, as there can be nobody more obnoxious than adolescent boys cutting up in public. Next time you run across same, keep in mind: they can't help it, they'll grow out of it, and they probably need it now.

* * *

Eric, me and friends on
the stairs at Mill Road

The Turkingtons in the 30's: Lisbeth (Bee), Fred Jr., Peter, Ola, Fred Sr.

They put us to reading early

Working, too

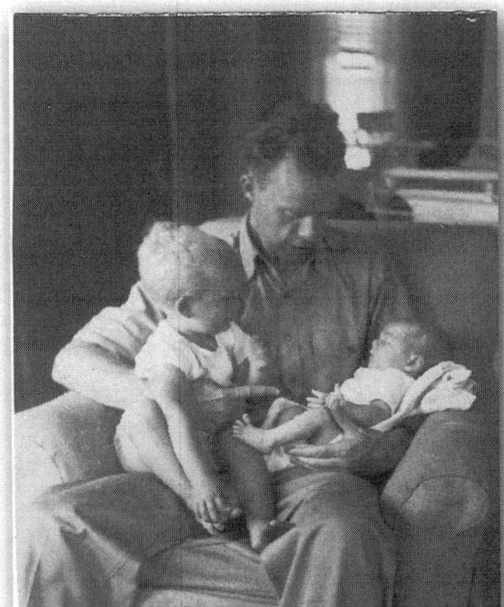

In the beginning

Dad was in the Reserves
and had a uniform

Mom kept us in raided rugs

The first home I remember

Mom always told me to pick
my nose whenever I felt like it

Miss MacIntosh was a good teacher to start out in school with

Cap'n Bob in
Chesapeake City

The Pickle was a starter boat

I wasn't afraid of Chief, I just look that way

The Swash was a no-frills vessel....

but it usually got us where we wanted to go

We found a use for the piles of scrap lumber in the barn in Seneca Falls

Mom made sure we were dressed well when we went out in Elkton

Going back to Lawrence for eighth grade offered none of the anticipation of starting school there for the first time. Already there was a sameness to having most of our classes on the bottom floor of the west wing and, wouldn't you know it, once again being assigned to Miss Buchanan's room for English, History, Social Studies, Study Hall and frequently Stay After School. Math class had a certain bounce, in part because it was held on the main floor, and because it was taught by Joe Bradley. He was the epitome of 1962 cool, an image that came and went quickly but was compelling while it lasted: slight stature, hair about two weeks past crewcut stage, large hornrimmed glasses and a breezy way of talking that made you feel you were being let in on the thoughts of someone who knew where it was at. Our nickname for him was J'Brad; he often taught his class while sitting on his desk, and if your work wasn't up to snuff he didn't feel the need to give you a heart-to-heart talk, or find something in your work that was good, as if that ameliorated the part that was bad, he just told you what you'd done wrong, graded you accordingly and moved on. What a concept! His signature expression was, "Y'see? Y'follow me?," spoken in a tone that conveyed command of the subject matter and, more importantly, was fun to imitate.

Back in Miss Buchanan's class, there was still a lot of straightening out to be done with the boys. I think we'd grown sufficiently accustomed to her ways to avoid committing the obvious stay-after-school offenses, but you just never knew what was going to provoke her displeasure. She told everyone to come in with a joke to tell one day, and one by one we went around the room and everybody told their joke. She got up at one point and left the room. We suspected that sometimes when she did this, it was to go to the head office and listen in on the intercom in hopes of catching some boy in the act of misbehaving, so we just went on with our jokes. Larry Ferreira was telling one about a farmer who couldn't tell his two horses apart. Miss Buchanan came in the door just as he got to the punch line: "The white one is six inches taller than the black one!" Miss Buchanan's face froze, she wagged her finger at Larry and said, "That kind of joke is not to be repeated in this classroom, Larry. I want you to come and see me after school." Larry's jaw dropped and his face turned red and he didn't know what to say. Or rather, he knew he'd better not say anything. We knew we'd better not either, and sat there in silent sympathy.

The history class was given an assignment to write a 10-page paper about some subject in American history. We were to pair up for this, so Donnie Bumpus and I got together and decided we'd write about the pioneers, the frontier explorers who preceded the settlers as white people moved west. Something happened to us as we started planning it. All we talked about at first were the goofy, inane things we could put into this paper, but we never got out of that mode. Without saying so, and without knowing why, we proceeded to treat the whole assignment as a joke. That wasn't the way things were supposed to be done in class 8-4, but that's what we did.

Looking for material, I came across a picture of a moose with a big rack of antlers. I cut it out, pasted it onto construction paper, and labeled it "A Bullmoose". Donnie saw it, found a picture of a moose without a rack, pasted it to construction paper and labeled it "A Lady Bullmoose". I came back with a picture of a chipmunk, similarly mounted: "A Chipmunk". That took care of three pages. My report on Davy Crockett started out very much like this: "Davy Crockett was born on the top of a mountain in Tennessee. Tennessee was considered by many to be the greenest state in America. Davy grew up with the woods all around him, so he got to know every tree. When he was three years old, he killed a bear." Those words will sound eerily familiar to anyone who ever saw the Disney movie about Davy Crockett. I wasn't worried that Miss Buchanan might see the connection. I figured she would. I wanted her to.

The project was meant to be a big deal, so a lot of class time was set aside for it. Most of the other kids spent that time writing papers, drawing maps, looking up material in the encyclopedia, working on the cover of their report: the sorts of things Donnie and I would normally be doing, but this project was special to us, and we spent most of our time just screwing around. Miss Buchanan kept watch over it all, and she didn't miss much, but we weren't disruptive, so she made no comment. We handed it in on time. A few days later they all got handed back. "Patsy and Donna, I really enjoyed reading this." "Very nice work, Arlton and David." And so on, until she was holding in her hand one last project. Pause for effect. "And I have something for you boys", as she placed it on Donnie's desk. She walked back to her desk and I looked across the room at Donnie. He made the sign of the D with his fingers, followed by his index finger held horizontally. Not the usual 8-4 grade, but at least we'd let her know. Let her know what? I'm still not sure.

We were still on split sessions at school, so I was usually riding the bus there, and often back. One curious sight I sometimes witnessed in the afternoon was small groups of high school boys wearing gym shorts and T-shirts, running on the roads. A lot of them seemed to be Cape Verdeans, and most of them were pretty thin. I asked somebody what was going on there and was told that they were members of the LHS cross country team, practicing. I didn't know much about running, but I knew that when you went very far, you got short of breath and tired, and it hurt. These guys looked like they were going pretty far. Can't be much fun if that's all they do. Looks like it's mostly for colored kids, anyway. Kind of interesting that they'd want to do it, though....

Pafford's bowling alley opened up for business about this time. It was set back from Main Street behind the Community Center, which was a dark green Victorian-era building, the function of which I never did figure out. That didn't much matter, because it was torn down a few years later to make room for a new Town Hall. Pafford's consisted of a bunch of candlepin bowling lanes and a pinball arcade. I did a little bit of bowling there in its early days, but found myself more drawn to the pinball machines. Mark Denman and I started hanging out there sometimes after school, intrigued by the challenge of the games and by the natures of the older kids who seemed to be there all the time. They were high school kids of rebellious nature who, shall we say, had yet to find themselves. Some were borderline dropouts; some were merely bored. Some – the greasers – wore their hair a la Elvis, with a coif in the front and a duck's-ass in the back. Some affected the James Dean look and posture. All of them were choosing to blow their afternoons playing the 'chines, watching others play the 'chines, or hanging out, smoking and shooting the breeze with others of similar ambition. To any solid citizen, they would be regarded as the detritus of their generation. To Mark and me, they were a dirty window looking out into someplace beyond the walls we felt closing in around us.

There was a certain kick to being a young, clean-cut, motivated kid choosing to spend time in the company of fringe characters at the bowling alley after school. Neither Mark nor I saw them as role models; au contraire, we may have used the example they set as indicators of the direction you head in if you turn your back on everything, to help us get a fix on the values that would keep us from straying too far from the straight and narrow. We heard a lot of talk there about the sort of conflicts and woes that high school rejects face, and we heard a lot of very coarse language spoken quite conversationally. If I got a good ball going on one of the machines, it could be very inspiring to hear from over my shoulder, "Hey, the kid's a bitch on this machine, man!" If three balls in a row dropped right down between one of the big kid's flippers: "What is this shit?" There was one little ditty that Mark heard a couple of times and recited to me, which I wish I could remember because I thought it was hilarious at the time. Its last line was, "You shoulda seen that motherfucker do the bunny hop". If I ever see Mark again, I'm going to ask him to repeat it if he can. We didn't walk out of there and start talking in that vein among our higher-echelon friends at school. But if you want to make sensible judgments about where you stand in the eternal tension between the refined and the profane, the only way to get a 3-D image is to see them both.

Alternatively, you can profit from the experience of others by heeding the considered advice of your elders. Yeah, right.

We weren't always very good drawing our own boundaries with clarity. A couple of times that fall, I found myself hanging around with Chip Papp and Lannie Anderson, looking for something to do on a weekend afternoon. Lannie – Alan, properly – was a really nice kid, son of an Air Force lifer, who lived near the school. We were shooting baskets on the paved courts outside the school when Chip suggested we go on in and mess around. But we couldn't get in, we pointed out, as the school was locked up. That's all right, Chip knew a way in. One of the cellar sash in the equipment room next to the locker room wasn't locked, so by crawling down into the window well and squeezing through the open sash, we could drop to the floor and be in the building. From there, we could, and did, shoot baskets in the gym, eat desserts from the cafeteria fridge, prance around on the auditorium stage and race up and down the hallways with nobody to interfere. It wasn't a bad way to spend part of a vacant afternoon. When we'd had enough, we walked out the front doors, bold as brass.

The wide world and all its tensions and terrors intruded on us that fall, and by "us" I mean everybody in the world, when some of our spy planes discovered that the Soviet Union was setting up nuclear missile installations in Cuba. I'd always been made aware of the Soviets as rivals at best, enemies at worst, and understood that they thought their system was best for all concerned, while we knew ours was. Everybody knew that we had thousands of nuclear warheads sitting on the tips of missiles aimed at each other, and that a ground war between us would probably lead quickly to a nuclear exchange, which would be a catastrophe for life on earth, even for people with fallout shelters. But the fears of that happening were a back-of-the-mind sort of thing until this Cuba business started playing out. It went on for days and was heavily covered by the TV news departments. I clearly recall Adlai Stevenson, at the UN, asking the Soviet delegate (was it Gromyko?) whether he'd admit to placing missiles on Cuban soil. "YES or NO? You don't have to wait for the translation." That was the closest thing to humor that the episode had to offer, as we were coping with the image of Soviet ships carrying nuclear weapons steaming towards Cuba, and U.S. warships going out to blockade the island. This was about as direct as a confrontation can be, the sort of thing that starts wars, and it was happening in real time before our very eyes.

I've spoken of the pointless preparations my folks, and many others, took to increase our chances of survival in the event of nuclear war, but the fact is, this was regarded by most aware people as a very real possibility. There were TV specials that enacted what might happen if the bombs were dropped. There were movies and books; it was a real element of Cold War culture. I don't know how often you have to have a certain nightmare before it can be labeled recurrent, but I had plenty of dreams of mushroom clouds appearing in the distance, accompanied by the sinking feeling that it's all over now, and I don't think I was any more sensitive to that fear than the next kid. Grownups being grownups, a lot of the older folks determined that they would do something about it, so there were cans of Spam and bottles of water in the basement, or underground shelters for those who could afford them. But there was nothing anyone could do but hope the people in Washington and Moscow who held sway over the arsenals would have the wits to figure out a way to avoid deploying them. Which, to the relief of all, JFK and Khrushchev were able to do this time. It was presented to us at the time as a triumph of U.S. resolve over Soviet cowardliness, but it came out years later that some sort of deal was struck involving U.S. missile installations in Turkey. All the better. Making deals beats playing chicken any day.

Having gained some familiarity with the game of basketball, I decided to go out for the junior high team that winter. I knew I wouldn't be one of the better players, but being in the 8th grade, I figured I wouldn't be the worst. Frank Towle (pr. Tole) was our appointed coach. In very few respects was Frank Towle like any of our other teachers. He was the shop teacher, so his attire of baggy gray pants, crumpled canvas shirt, work boots and crew-neck T-shirt with hair sprouting out at the neck were easily explained. What set him apart were his size, countenance and demeanor. He was tall and husky, with hands the size of ski gloves and covered with hair. He had a deeply furrowed face with awesome jowls and extended lips that gave him a distinctly simian appearance. He truly looked more like an anthropologist's image of Primitive Man than a junior high teacher. Our nickname for him was Animal. His voice was gravelly, hoarse and loud, which gave the impression that he was impatient at some times, angry at others. When he had something to say, he got right in your face, waved his arms around and really let you have it. He was at heart a very decent man, and I never knew him to be abusive, but it was impossible not to be afraid of him. He undoubtedly had some big, tough, older kids in his classes who he could control only by being as big, tough and ready to fight as they were.

At this point in my life, I was actually fairly tall for my age. I had my biggest growth spurt at 12 and 13 and probably wasn't too far from my adult height when I joined the team. I was also modestly athletic and probably had the tools to be a decent ballplayer, but I didn't know what I was doing out there, which is a major shortcoming in a team sport. Mr. Towle was really not the one to enlighten me. He had coached, I heard, at the University of Vermont many years before, but the game had changed since then. We spent a lot of time practicing two-handed set shots and primitive give-and-go's. The day before our first game, Mr. Towle told us we were going to get in line and practice one-dribble uncontested layups. Miss one, and you go sit down. Last one left is team captain. Well, I was just fine with uncontested layups, and before I knew it I was team captain. The next day, I went out on the floor before tipoff to meet with the Tabor Academy captain and the refs. I looked over at the bench where sat Paul Ingram, Dave Swain, Steve Paltz, Robbie Pena, Jack Carreiro and others far more skilled than I, and I thought, this is crazy, just crazy. I don't think I did too much to hurt our effort in the game, but I did little to help, and thereafter was not a starter and not captain, and deservedly so.

We usually practiced at night, since there were high school boys' and girls' varsity and JV teams with priority, and just the one gym. On many of those nights, I was greatly annoyed by the presence of a high jump pit, crossbar and standards set up near the seats. Mike Lopes, the fully-blossomed star of the high school team, was there practicing high jumping under the guidance of an energetic science teacher and track coach, name of Mr. Kalperis. Time and time again, Mike would leap up to clear the bar, and time and time again he'd knock it off, causing a disturbing CLANG to resound through the gym. Why is he doing this? He's the star of the basketball team, who cares how high he can jump over a bar? Well, I guess he did, and Mr. Kalperis did, and there they were, night after night, bothering me. A more pleasing interlude occurred one afternoon, when Bob Cousy showed up at the school. Why Bob Cousy came to our school in the final year of his storied NBA career I can't imagine, but Joe Allietta and Earl Mills were escorting him around, and our team was practicing on the floor, so we got to go and greet him. On the floor with the Celtics on TV, he looked like a pretty average-sized man, if not a bit on the small side. He was not. He was a big man, and a gentleman, and meeting him was an honor.

I must not have been too dreadful at the game, because for two or three years at the end of the season I found myself playing for a team of classmates in a tournament or two, and I wouldn't have been on the team if somebody hadn't asked me to be. These tournaments were pretty casual affairs, but once we got on the floor we took it seriously. I wasn't one of the better players, but I was an adequate fill-in. We played in some very offbeat venues. Towns that were slow to react to the influx of new pupils were, by the early 60's, scrambling around trying to find places to let all these kids pursue their activities, such as attending class. At least a couple of times we played on the stage of the old Barnstable High School auditorium. The stage! With a basketball net at either end! We had a game or two on an outdoor court in February, and in gyms that were very dark, on heavily rippled floors. None of this bothered us at the time, and it doesn't bother me now, but it serves as one indicator of how standards have changed.

My most exciting connection with basketball that winter was following the fortunes of the LHS boys. They had a pretty good supporting cast for Mike Lopes, who was a tower of strength and talent. They packed the gym for every game and they won them all, usually with plenty of room to spare. They won the two-game Principal's Tournament, sort of a Cape Cod championship just before the state tourney. Mike scored 51 in the final. This was high school basketball, eight-minute quarters. They headed into the Class D state tournament with their first game against last-seeded Harwich, a diminutive school from down-Cape who they'd trashed earlier. I listened to the game on the radio, and this time it was a different story. Our guys shot poorly, passed erratically and couldn't hold onto the ball. I was in agony. What is the MATTER with our guys? Richie Rose kept making great shots and passes for Harwich, and the lead kept going back and forth right up to the last seconds. Our guys finally took it, 44-42. I attended the rest of the tournament games, where order was restored to the universe. Thousands of Falmouth folk were in Boston Garden for the final, where the team beat Westwood, 59-50, to finish up at 22-0. Mike scored 40.

It wasn't Mike's first visit to the Garden that winter. The state high school track meet was held there a few weeks earlier, and he figured prominently in that, too. I was only dimly aware of this at the time, but he set the Class D high jump record at 6 feet, 3 inches. This was before the flop style came along, a time when a jump of 7 feet would almost assure you of a spot on the podium at the Olympics. His record stood for quite a few years. He also ran second in the high hurdles, and LHS won the state meet. Did I care? I did not.

My parents signed me up that winter for one of the weirdest activities I ever got involved in. What made it so peculiar wasn't the activity itself – ballroom dancing, it was – but the idea that its instruction could successfully be muscled into Falmouth culture in general, and junior high culture in particular. The instructors were a debonair middle-aged couple who, I would guess, made a living of setting up ballroom dancing courses for highly resistant youth in the backwaters of America. The man wore a tuxedo, did all the talking and looked and moved like Maurice Chevalier. The woman wore an evening gown and looked like Barbie with breasts and a shit-eating grin pasted to her face. The kids were mostly just normal Falmouth middle schoolers whose parents felt their own lives would have been better if they'd ever learned ballroom dancing and wanted to save their kids from that vacancy in their futures. Some of the kids were from wealthy families and were bound for prep schools and loftier destinations where ballroom dancing fluency might prove to be an asset. The classes met one evening a week in the clubhouse of the Woods Hole Golf Club, probably the most elegant setting available for hire in town. The parents sat around at tables ringing the room while their kids tried to learn the steps. I don't remember a single thing they tried to teach me about dancing; it's quite likely that I could have said that a week after the whole thing was over. It just was not a good fit, either for that decade or for the generation that was growing up in it.

There was one episode in the ballroom dancing course that puzzled me at the time, and has since stood out as a good example of adults' failure to comprehend the minds of their youthful charges. One of the scheduled classes fell on the evening of the LHS basketball team's final game in Boston Garden. There were a few girls missing from the clubhouse that night, and a great many boys. The following week, Maurice gave us all a bit of a dressing-down for our failure to appear, and warned us of consequences if it happened again. Now, it could be that nobody warned him that there was going to be a conflict that night that would draw many of us away from his class, but you'd think he could have made the best of it and figured rightly that this wasn't going to keep happening. You'd also think that he'd realize he had no leverage with us whatsoever. But no, he took it pretty hard and decided to berate us for our absence. At that time, it seemed to me that he could have given us a little credit for suiting ourselves up and proceeding uncomplainingly to his dance class week after week, and been a bit more understanding about a once-in-a-lifetime event that superceded it. Now that I look back on it, I feel exactly the same. You can demand a lot from kids, especially when their parents are on board with it. But you've got to recognize the limits.

I was still a flute player, and as such was expected to be a member of the school band. This band was coming off the headiest days it had ever known. Participation had been up for a few years, which led to a lot of fund-raising, new uniforms for the entire band and color guard, entry into and frequent winning of awards in marching band competitions, and at its peak, a trip to Miami to march in the Orange Bowl parade. Eric, a trumpeter, was on that trip. There weren't a whole lot of bowl games in existence then, and the Orange Bowl was a big one, so not only the game but the parade the night before was on TV. A lot of Falmouth folk proudly turned on their sets to see it, including 3/4 of the Turkingtons. Our band was one of scores, maybe hundreds, but they looked pretty sharp to us, playing the theme from "Peter Gunn" as they passed the reviewing stand. Eric came back from the trip with a miniature orange tree the size of a geranium. He still has it in his house. It's grown to about four feet high and produces a crop of hackysack-sized oranges every year. It's about 55 years old. Tough genes in that little orange tree.

I began to join in band activity during the summer, whether just before or after 8th grade I don't recall, maybe both. They practiced during the summer because that's when there was call for them to appear at big outdoor events. I was given the music, practiced it and had no problem performing it with the band. One sign of my scrub status was that I didn't get assigned a uniform for appearances, some of which I was asked to attend. Everyone else had on their full maroon-and white regalia, and there I was in black pants, white shirt and bowtie. Being a newbie, I wasn't bothered by this, but it gave me a sense of conspicuousness that wasn't wholly comfortable. I did get the pleasure, along with everyone else, of shaking Governor John Volpe's hand at the Barnstable County Fairgrounds. I also had the displeasure of marching in some big parade in Hyannis, the closest thing on the Cape to an urban center, and really screwing up. There came a time in the parade when we stopped marching and broke up into a carefully choreographed pattern of swirls and eddies that would have looked very clever to a viewer high overhead. We had often practiced this maneuver, but evidently not enough for me. Everybody was marching and turning this way and that and the moment came when I realized I was totally lost. When the others all fell back into rank and file I was able to see where I was supposed to be, and I was nowhere near it. So I marched around taking right faces and left faces in my white shirt and black pants, trying to act like nothing was wrong but knowing the whole band was waiting impatiently for me to get back to my spot, which I got to eventually. This incident alone was not enough to cause me to lose interest in becoming a full-fledged band member, but that did happen in time, as other interests intervened.

I was beginning to listen to music on the radio with increasing interest. The only station playing kids' music that could regularly be drawn in from Falmouth was WPRO in Providence. This was an AM station, and when I say kids' music, I mean Top 40. The only requirement to get air play was that the song sell a lot of 45 RPM records. Tune in, and you might hear Chubby Checker, or Tony Bennett, or The Singing Nun, whoever had the hits at the moment got the play. Youth music was wretched, for the most part. Novelty songs were popular, as much as anything because they offered a break from the featherweight schmaltz that most of the studios were selling, though even in the novelty genre, a guy like Ray Stevens could sneak in with something off the wall and on the mark. There were a few artists like Gene Pitney and Leslie Gore who adhered to the theme of teenage romance, but angled in on it in an offbeat way that provoked reflection. Bob Dylan was known about even in the hinterlands, primarily because Peter, Paul and Mary were singing his songs, and anecdotes of the beat/folkie lifestyle were passed about. I was fortunate to have an older brother who might put an early Dylan LP on the hi-fi, so I got a taste of his work fairly early on. My ear was geared toward more melodic sounds, and I was trying too hard to be normal to be drawn to Dylan's disaffected air. I found him interesting, but he didn't get me in the gut yet.

I haven't listened to the radio very often in some years, but there'll be times when I do that I'll hear a song that I may have heard a dozen or so times in 1962 and have neither heard nor thought about since. I will know all the words before I hear them, I'll anticipate the saxophone interlude and know just when the violins come in. There is something about the adolescent brain that opens up the memory bank to music while shutting the doors to the mundane assignments of day-to-day life. I keep this in mind when the latest digital music device gets activated the moment my kids get in the car. It really is a lot to ask them to engage in conversation when there is music to be heard, and I keep my demands limited. I sometimes think that I may become the last human on earth who can sing all the words to The Elusive Butterfly or My Boyfriend's Back or untold numbers of other songs more than 50 years after last hearing them and with no reminders of them in all that time. But I probably won't be; I'm sure there are many other old-timers with the same affliction.

Being, or feeling, normal was becoming increasingly difficult. Society was moving faster than I could keep up with, from boys doing things with boys and girls doing things with girls, to boys and girls doing things together. This seemed to have happened while I wasn't watching. My interest in girls was far outpacing my comfort level in interacting with them. Putting myself out there – the act of sitting down next to a girl I liked and engaging in conversation – was so fraught with the threat of rejection and subsequent humiliation that I steered myself away from it. It wasn't all that much of a threshold to cross over, but there was too much mystery to it, and I balked, then and for a long time thereafter. I don't think it was solely a lack of self-confidence that held me up. I was able to speak to a group when I had to, or sing or play to an audience, but for those sorts of things I could prepare, and know what was going to happen. I didn't have the boldness to go where I didn't know what to expect. Maybe it should have been an easy step, but once I excused myself from it, my defenses fed on themselves and stayed with me.

My withdrawal from the social scene was neither total nor immediate. I went to a junior high dance in the gym one evening that spring. Like everyone else, I was dressed up. I danced once or twice, then got to talking with Mark Denman and Chip Papp. Either Mark or Chip could have suggested this, but we decided to hitchhike down to Woods Hole and drop in on John Christian, a classmate who lived near the Coast Guard station. Hitchhiking was not regarded as the perilous activity then that it is now. So we left the dance, hitched to Woods Hole and found John at home alone. We yakked for a while, then asked John if he had any cigarettes, thinking it'd be nice to go down to the ferry docks and have a smoke. John found his aunt's smokes, grabbed four and we headed out.

Arriving at the docks, we found ourselves without matches. No problem, said John, we can go in the Leeside and Hank'll give us a pack of matches. The Leeside was a bar overlooking the Steamship Authority; Hank Jonah was proprietor and barkeep. Into the Leeside we went. Hank was at the bar while maybe half a dozen Coast Guardsmen – known as Coasties – sat quietly drinking at the tables. Everybody glowered at us, and who wouldn't have? Three young kids in ties and sport jackets along with a local kid, walking into a skuzzy bar on a dead Saturday night? This was highly inappropriate. John asked Hank for some matches, and Hank said, No, John, and I think you boys better leave right now. So we turned to go. I was the last to file out, and as I got to the door, the next-to-last guy turned around, cupped his hands to his mouth and shouted "SUCK DICK!" From behind me as I raced out onto the sidewalk I heard, "LET'S GET 'EM!"

We split up and headed out of there as fast as we could. Behind me, I could hear a bunch of men running and shouting. "YOU LITTLE BASTARDS!" I ducked into an alleyway by the Landfall restaurant, from where a few moments later I heard Mark shouting, "They got me, guys! Come on back!" Well, of course we had to, so we all stood in the middle of Luscombe Avenue getting an angry dressing-down from a bunch of half-drunk Coasties. What they really wanted was the kid who shouted that insult at them, but we told them that Glen Pierce did it and got away. Glen Pierce was about the least likely kid on earth to shout an expletive at a crowd of drunken sailors, but it's the name we gave them and they seemed satisfied. Fortunately, none among them was counting noses. They were in no mood to rough up a foursome of clean-cut young boys, so they told us sternly not to show our faces in there again until we were 21. We promised we wouldn't, and had a few laughs with them before they went back to their drinking. Chip and Mark and I hitched back then and got to the dance before it was over. We attracted a little attention, but not enough to spark the curiosity of the chaperones, so it wound up being a zero-trouble incident.

I tried out for the junior high baseball team that spring, once again on the premise that being a big 8th-grader would enhance my chances of making the team and playing. The coach was Robert W. Morris. He was a likable, energetic teacher of about 40 whose classroom was across the hall from Miss Buchanan's, and whose attitude towards his pupils was miles separate. For reasons I never thought about then, he worked a few evenings a week at The Sandbar, a lunch counter/convenience store on Main Street. Sometimes when I had dinner at Mark's house or he at mine, we dropped in there afterwards to knock down a soda and shoot the breeze. You could do that with Mr. Morris. He seemed to retain enough memory of his own youth to know that as soon as you start trying to tell kids where it's at or what they ought to do, they're going to shut you right out. We didn't hang out there for wisdom or advice. We just thought it was pretty cool to be able to chitchat with one of the teachers, away from school, on somewhat equal footing. We often asked ourselves why it had to be that he never was assigned the most academically promising junior high pupils. Maybe he was an ineffective teacher, not to be entrusted with the best students. More likely it was a seniority thing.

Our baseball practices were held at the Falmouth Heights ballfield, due to a lack of space on the grounds of the school. It was a pretty nice place to play, right next to the beach, and not so far away from school that we couldn't get there on our bicycles. I was getting bigger and stronger and was pretty good out in the field, both in terms of making the plays and of knowing what was going on. Hitting still was an issue. I just did not have a knack for it and was going to need to swing at a lot of pitches to start getting a real feel for it. This didn't happen. From what I'd seen of youth baseball before and have seen since, this is an extremely common fault in many programs. The coach observes that there are some kids who go to bat with confidence and often get results, and he figures, those are my hitters. He sees other kids who are tentative or gunshy and figures, those kids can't hit. This is an understandable conclusion, but it overlooks the potential benefits of repetition. It is also a conclusion that is often reached very early in the process of assembling a team.

My moments of glory were few and far between during our preseason practices. One that has endured came during an intrasquad scrimmage when, as was customary, I was playing left field. Billy McNeil, who was an outstanding athlete and really good guy but who moved away shortly after, ripped a liner down the third base line. I raced over to cut it off before it headed for the street, and backhanded it on a bounce with my back to second base. I spun around, saw Billy heading for second, reared back and fired that ball harder than I'd ever thrown one in my life. It went on a line to Lanny Anderson, who was straddling second base with his glove a foot above the bag. He never had to move his glove; my throw slammed right into it an instant before Billy's sliding foot did. Out. Making the play felt very good, and I heard some commentary about it from Mr. Morris. There you are, coach, I thought. I knew I was on the cusp for selection to the team, but I figured I'd just given him reason to want to have me around.

Wrong. Next day, I was deep in the outfield playing catch with the other cuspians while the talented kids took batting practice. A day or two later, the cuts were made and I was among them. Mr. Morris told me I'd be the first to get a uniform if one of the chosen ones quit or got hurt; all I had to do was keep coming to practice and maybe help him out at the games. Nah, I loved baseball and wanted to play, but I wasn't the hanger-on type. I heard talk that the high school's spring track coach didn't mind at all if junior high kids came to the workouts and meets, and I toyed a bit with the idea, but I didn't have any buddies doing that and our split sessions meant I'd be an hour or more late for every practice. Mainly, it was the buddies thing. And I didn't want to show up to start a new sport because I'd failed at the last one. I spent the rest of the spring either walking home after school or finding something unproductive to do with other uninvolved kids, who still constituted a large majority.

I made something of an art of walking home. I didn't need to go much further than a mile, but there were many ways to negotiate it, and it could easily use up a good part of what was left of the afternoon. I often chose to stop by the Sandbar or Smitty's to buy a pack or two of baseball cards, which still held my interest. Once on Main Street, I might be moved to stop in at Harvey's Hardware to look over the offerings there in bicycles or sports equipment. Getting home via the streets would have meant a series of right and left turns, but it was more interesting to go through people's yards, and doing so gave me the feeling that I was shortening the distance. I did this without a thought that anybody would mind. Sometimes the chosen route would oblige me to hop over a picket fence or pass within a few feet of someone's living room window, but little did I care. I just wasn't looking at the world through the eyes of a homeowner, never mind one who tends the lawn diligently or has a strong sense of privacy. A couple of times, I was accosted by older ladies who told me unpleasantly not to cut through their yards again, which I agreed not to do. The extent of my reaction to these encounters was: well, I guess I'd better stay out of that crabby woman's yard. There are other ways to get home.

A fair dose of angst was by now beginning to affect my view of life and myself. Self-consciousness is a terrible weight to be carrying around, and it was upon me. There are so many immutable facts of life that conspire to make an emotional mess of us in our adolescence. I'd about had it with being told what to do all the time, but there was yet no letup in the determination of the adults in my life to keep making their demands. I was beginning to ache to make my own decisions and go my own way, but I had next to no experience to guide me in any particular direction. I'd outgrown most of my toys, but I was still too silly to focus on anything serious. Silly? Mark Denman was a participant in the youth group in his (Congregational) church, and I started joining in. We met once a week with the pastor and Mrs. Hampton, whose daughter Dale was in the group. The idea was to strengthen our faith, plan activities, do good works, talk about the Bible and that kind of thing. But Mark and I felt we were participating in a sham exercise in good-boy building, and with that attitude, our being there was not productive, for us or the group. The slightest touch of irony or pomposity in the meeting sent us off into laughing fits over which we had no control. We tried to suppress it, but we simply could not. It all just seemed too ludicrous. So there were the adults trying to tell us something or lead a discussion of some kind, and there were Mark and I, sitting in our chairs, faces buried in our hands, trying in vain to hold the giggling back for minutes at a time. They must have hated us.

Relationships with girls, or the lack of relationships and cluelessness about how to forge them, were becoming a source of real strain. There were a relatively few boys who were at least able to give the appearance of being comfortable with girls. I admired them for that, and envied them, because I wanted that comfort for myself and didn't have it. At this point, it was more the cool, pretty girls who were at issue, in part because they were the ones who were at ease with the boys, even the misanthropes like myself. I could engage in some classroom banter with them, and feel cheered and warm about it, but where do you go from there? What's the protocol? I hadn't the faintest idea, and if somebody I respected had sat me down and told me, I probably wouldn't have listened. I sometimes think that Miss Buchanan's antipathy towards boys stemmed from an uneasy, but accurate feeling that what we really wanted in life was to engage in sexual activity with the nice, innocent girls in our classes. She was right, but most of us, certainly including me, were no more likely to attain that goal than we were to make our first million before high school. The hormones had been kicking in for a while now, but the savoir faire needed to meld these new feelings into intergender relations was not.

Sex was very much on the minds of we adolescent boys, but in the school and most homes a strictly forbidden or studiously avoided topic. Not a classroom word was ever spoken of it, or gender relations in general, until high school, when once a year all the boys were herded into the auditorium to get a 40-minute lecture from a doctor. It was hard, of course, to study biology without learning a little something about sperm and ovum and zygotes and such, but it was always entirely disembodied. Some of the parents, so I'm told, made an effort to clue their kids in on the birds and the bees, but it was usually in a very clinical way that might have explained the mechanics but did nothing to clarify the mysteries of sexual urgency. The rest of them must have just figured we'd learn about these things in good time, as they evidently did.

My summer passed about like the previous couple had, except that there was even less variety than before. I was too old for Little League and not good enough for Babe Ruth, if that level even existed in Falmouth at the time. I wasn't old enough to work anywhere or ambitious enough to line up a bunch of lawns to mow, and my days as a paper carrier were well past. My parents weren't prosperous enough to pack me off to summer camp. The one activity I did get signed up for was at the Woods Hole School of Science, which was run at the elementary school there in the village famed for ocean research. My course at the science school was marine biology, and I enjoyed it. Our class of about 20 kids spent most of our weekday mornings poking around marine estuaries, beaches and rocky shores looking at the flora and fauna of the coastline. We did some dissecting in the classroom and got familiar with microscopes and formaldehyde. Our teachers were grad students who were in Woods Hole for the summer, teaching at the school some and doing research the rest of the time. Most of the kids enrolled at the school were summer kids, though I carpooled in every morning with Janet Hampton and some other townie I've forgotten.

Our route to Woods Hole brought us down Quisset Road, which went by some fine old homes overlooking Buzzards Bay and Quisset Harbor. One of them was known as the Pink Castle, so named because of its color and architectural features: arches, cone-topped towers, graceful dormers and the like. Unlike practically every other house on the Cape, it was sided in stucco rather than weathered cedar shingles. Its elaborate wood trim was painted dark blue. The place was truly one of a kind. A Mrs. Webster summered there – most of the finest homes in town were unoccupied nine months of the year – and maintained an extensive rose garden that the public could walk around in. She kept a little parking lot for visitors just below the property. I went there a couple of times with Nano, and I ogled the castle and some of the other edifices along the road every time we drove by. Some time after Mrs. Webster died, the castle was torn down, leaving one of the most spectacular homesites in creation, which everybody who was aware of the place figured would soon have one or a few more modest, but highly marketable houses built on it. But that didn't happen for a very long time. It remained for many years a large vacant lot, available during the winter months to locals who could ramble over the lawn and down to the beach below, knowing they weren't supposed to be there and that there was nobody around to blow the whistle on them. Finally, a few years ago, the spell was broken and somebody built a jarring contemporary structure on that little slice of heaven.

My intense interest in the world of major league baseball was waning by now. As I was no longer active in the game, it was getting to be more than a stretch to fantasize about being a famous baseball star. But I still followed the season, through the box scores in the New York Times (the Turkingtons' daily of choice) and

Red Sox TV broadcasts on WBZ. Curt Gowdy was the principal play-by-play man, or maybe their only one. He was the Walter Cronkite of sports announcers: with a pleasantly modulated voice that conveyed gravitas, a determination to tell it like it was, and an ability to stay on an even keel no matter what was unfolding before him, he made the viewer feel that the game was worthy of attention, even though the team he worked for still stunk. Ted Williams was long gone in 1964. Carl Yastrzemski wasn't yet at the top of his game. Dick Radatz was a thrilling relief pitcher to watch, but he didn't stay that way for long. In its pursuit of talent, either by trade or player development, the organization continually sought out run-producing sluggers, with little consideration given to defense, pitching, or nonwhite players. Watching the team was usually unrewarding, yet not a bad way to kill a couple of hours on a summer afternoon. One regular highlight was the Narragansett Beer commercials. They were animated and hilarious, featuring spoofs of identifiable celebrities or caricatures of common types, imaginatively created and cleverly delivered. As with the game broadcast, the product fell short of the marketing:

> Hi, neighbor! Have a Gansett! Give this lager beer a chance, it has that straight-from-the-barrel taste, in bottle, can, on tap it's great.
> Yes, Gansett's got the flayayvor, Narragansett flayayvor,
> Gansett's light, but not too light. Straight from the barrel taste, that's right!
> That's Gansett!

* * *

Going back to school after Labor Day presented a few changes, none of them breathtaking. Now that the Morse pond school was finished and the junior high was housed there, we freshmen were the littlest kids in the school again. Miss Buchanan was no longer part of the picture, most of my classes were up on the main floor, and with the split sessions a thing of the past, we were all on the same schedule. Other than that, it was the same drill. One slightly curious wrinkle in my schedule was that my English teacher was Mrs. Robichaud and not Mrs. Turkington. Mom taught the most talented class, and under normal circumstances I would have been in it. There was never any discussion about this situation with me. I'm guessing that whatever talk there was about whether I ought to be in Mom's class centered on the consideration that I was getting to be a pretty sour kid a lot of the time at home and might not have the maturity to handle a period every day sitting in my mother's classroom. They were probably right, and it's likely we avoided a situation that could have led to considerable friction. Or maybe not. What is odd is that I was never a part of the conversation, especially since being kept out of the more demanding class in one subject led to scheduling conflicts that caused the same thing to happen in one or two others.

The boys had a new gym teacher. Up until this year, I think Earl Mills was the gym teacher and the director of athletics. The school was growing, the interscholastic sports programs were expanding, and LHS needed a new head football coach. With all these things coming together, Paul Maguire came on as the boys' gym teacher and football coach. We were not used to people like Paul Maguire. He was a firm believer in regimentation, unwavering discipline and obedience to authority. Had he been a little less soft-spoken, he would have been the complete stereotype of the Marine drill sergeant, which I was told he once was. He wasn't terribly big or fit, but in demeanor was every bit the military man. There were to be no more cutoffs and baggy T-shirts in gym class; we were to be dressed alike, in official school-issue maroon gym shorts and T-shirts with the LHS emblem (a clipper ship) on the chest. We lined up in rank and file while attendance was taken. We played a lot fewer games and did a lot more drills and strengthening exercises. We didn't talk out of turn, or we'd find Paul Maguire right there in our faces.

I got used to all this fairly quickly. After all, it was only three times a week and it was a break from sitting at a desk. Not everybody took that look on the bright side. I heard stories of harassment of Maguire at his home, at night, from rebellious kids driving by, shouting and throwing things. Personally, I recognized the need to restrain my wiseass tendencies and we got along all right. When we were doing situps, I tried my best to do as many as I could in the time allotted. When we were climbing the ropes, I pulled myself up as hard and fast as I could. Maguire had respect for that. At one point, we were going through a series of fitness tests that included a maneuver on the parallel bars. You stood between the bars, jumped up, grabbed the bars with your hands and tried to push yourself the rest of the way up. It was entirely a pass/fail exam. My turn came, and I got about 2/3 of the way up, lost my grip, dropped down and slammed my underarms into the bars on the way. The whole class groaned, because they could tell it really hurt. Maguire motioned for me to move on. I asked if I could try it again. He gestured as if to say, go ahead. So again I jumped up, grabbed the bars, got 3/4 of the way up, and dropped down again with the same result. Groans from the class. One last try? "Be my guest". So again, jump up, hands on bars, upward push, strain, strain, and my arms were straight and I passed the test. I dropped down with my arms pulled in and walked past Maguire as he made a mark in his book. "You've got balls, Turkington", he said, loud enough for the class to hear.

The academic program in the high school was two-pronged for the most part. There was the college-bound course, and there was the home- or work-bound course. Some kids complicated things by choosing to mix art or music into their curricula, and adjustments had to be made for them. For most of us, it was pretty straightforward. The first science course was General Science, followed in annual order by Biology, Chemistry and Physics. I'm not sure where math started, but it went no further than Advanced Math until my senior year, when Calculus was offered for the first time, much to my detriment. Those headed to competitive colleges had to have a foreign language on their resume and could choose Spanish or French. World Cultures I introduced us to the history of civilization, II did more of the same the following year, followed by US History and Contemporary Issues. Freshmen took English I, sophomores English II and so on. Tracking based on presumed learning ability was how classes (mine graduated 221) were broken up, which made perfect sense to everybody, since it'd always been done that way.

There was very little talk at home, and even less consideration in my mind, on the subject of what other activities I might get involved in beyond the obligatory classroom work. With no unpleasant memories of the soccer I played at the Armory in the 6th grade, I had a vague sense that I might want to try the game a little more seriously, but I didn't feel the urge strongly enough to show up at the early practices, choosing instead to walk home and hang around and do nothing. Eric was an untalented junior on the team, which was in the early years of its existence, as was true in most high schools across the land. I don't remember whether Eric's participation was viewed as a plus or minus by me, but the first two weeks of school went by and I hadn't gotten up the gumption to go and sign up. We uncharacteristically spoke to the subject over dinner one evening. Dad asked me if I didn't feel it was time to start playing soccer, and I said I just hadn't really felt like doing it. Mom said there was also the cross-country team, and the coach there was a really nice guy. I must have looked like I was listening, because Dad followed up: "It'd be a great conditioner for basketball". I thought a moment about all those skinny kids running out on the roads, and said I thought I'd go out for soccer on Monday. I had no interest in doing something that looked weird. Still, that "great conditioner" remark stuck with me, while puzzling me. Conditioner? Running around? What exactly is he talking about?

The following Monday, I headed down to the locker room after school let out with the intention of joining the soccer team. The football team had its own field house and facilities at Fuller Field, about a mile from the school, so the after-school activity in the main locker room consisted solely of soccer kids getting ready for practice. Fred Toran was the first head coach of LHS soccer, and was to remain in that post for years and years. I came to know Fred pretty well in my adulthood, and am happy to report that he was to become a congenial, laid-back fellow who laughed easily and enjoyed people. In September of 1963, he was lacking in patience and seemingly easily pained. On this afternoon, he was gadding about the locker room, commanding his players to get dressed and out on the field, scolding them for using rough language, complaining about their messy lockers, and in all appearing and sounding the picture of frustration. His players were solemnly pulling on their jocks and cleats and shorts, and it just didn't feel like quite the time to talk to Mr. Toran.

So I headed out through a passage that led past a little locker room near the entrance. I saw Geoff Cahoon leaning in the doorway with his arms folded. Geoff was a short, slight Woods Hole kid who I didn't know very well, but had hung out with a few times. As in all circumstances where one isn't sure of oneself, I was glad to see a familiar face. I said Hi, stood next to him and looked in. There were about 15 guys in the locker room in the process of getting into running clothes. There was hilarity in the air, radiating from two sources: Joe Rezendes, a lanky Cape Verdean senior who I soon learned was captain and top runner on the team; and the coach, Jim Kalperis, who was still in tie and jacket, holding a cigar and pointing it at Ray Costa as he said something amusing about him. Everybody was talking over everybody else, and they were all laughing. They were about to go out and run a long way on a hot September afternoon, and they were laughing, having fun.

"What are you doing here, Geoff?"
"I'm gonna sign up for cross country".
"Is that this team?"
"Yeah."
"So am I."

Moments later, Kalpy – for that is how he was known by all and addressed by everyone who established himself as a serious member of his running teams – noticed us and approached us as if we were two hotly recruited transfers from another school. He was so glad to have us on the team, and we looked like born distance runners, and all we had to do was get into our gym clothes and we'd get started. That was the extent of our signing up. There was no concern over the fact that we were two weeks late, either in the introduction or in the workout assigned to us. We changed up, joined the team outside for a few minutes of calisthenics and headed over to the starting line of the LHS 2.6 mile cross-country course, which was mostly on roads that led us far from the school. We all stood at the line, Kalpy said Go and off we went. I stayed with the other freshmen for a few hundred yards, but it felt pretty easy, so I passed a few of them. As I went by Everett Costa, I heard him say, "That kid's gonna be hurtin'." Nah, this wasn't hard. But a quarter mile later, just to be safe, I decided to ease up a little. Everett, then Mark Buguey, then the other freshmen went by me and pulled away. I slowed up a little more, then more. A little past the halfway point I could still see them, but barely, and Geoff caught up to me. We walked a little, ran a little, walked and ran the rest of the way. We weren't being lazy, we just simply couldn't keep running. It hurt too much. When we got back to the school at last, Kalpy was there at the finish, cheering us on. The rest of the team was already in the showers.

I'm not going to recount every day of my running career, but my first week made an indelible impression upon me and I summarize it here, not only because I still can but also because there may be lessons to be gleaned from its progression. Day 2 in cross country was a repeat of Day 1, except I felt stiff and sore right from the start and fell way behind right away. Geoff and I teamed up again, only this time there was more walking and less running. I got home afterwards somehow, but I must not have walked there, because I was so terribly sore. I sat down on the couch in the living room and could barely propel myself to the dinner table. Nothing I'd ever done had ever made me ache like this.

On Day 3, we all went up to D.W. Field Park in Brockton, an hour away. That's where the league meet was to be held later in the season and Kalpy, ever vigilant for any gambit that would give his team an edge, thought we should familiarize ourselves with it. It says something about the level of sophistication of running sports coaches and organizers in 1963 that, here in this park with its golf course and trails and dirt roads, the designated course was a 2.4 mile loop on a paved road. I was still feeling sore, but ambulatory, and this time felt a trace of strength in my legs. Geoff wasn't around, so I was alone, but I stayed in sight of the slowest other freshmen all the way to the end. I didn't want to lose them, and knew if I stopped to walk I would, so I kept running: pretty slowly, with my feet slamming into the pavement sending shock waves all the way up my legs with every footfall, but I kept running. Nobody took notice but me.

Thursday, Day 4, was an easy day because we were going to have our first race of the season at Old Rochester on Friday. All we did was run the warmup course, which was a loop of a bit over a mile on the roads that started and finished at the school. I reminded myself that nobody was trying very hard, but I couldn't help feeling some gratification that a lot of the soreness was gone, there was a touch of lift in my feet, and I was keeping up with the other slow kids. So I wasn't overcome with dread when we drove out to Old Rochester on Day 5. I figured I'd be at the back, but I thought I could keep myself from being all alone and way behind. The dread crept in when we gathered at the line for the junior varsity race. The OR kids all looked pretty big, and experienced, where most of us were doing this for the first time. Their coach said to them just before we lined up, "If you guys get shut out today, I'll never talk to you again." Much laughter from the OR runners. Our hearts were in our toes, and there was nowhere to hide. We went to the line, the gun went off, and a bunch of big, strong OR kids led us out on the course.

The course was mostly level and on the grounds of the school. I was in the back, but I felt fairly good and went out thinking I could keep up with my slowest teammates. Early on, I felt myself slip into a near-trance in which I was very dimly aware of my environment but keenly focused on the rhythm and energy of my running. After all the miseries early in the week, this was almost painless. The only element in my surroundings noticeable to me was that I was passing other kids: first, my slowest teammates, then the slowest opponents, then the middling runners. I wasn't flying past anybody, but I just kept picking them off one by one. The trance started to leave me a while later when I became acutely aware of three things: we were not far from the finish line; it was requiring much effort to keep running, as I was very low on air; and the next runner just ahead of me was Everett Costa. We were close enough to the finish for me to hear Kalpy shout: "That's TURKINGTON!" Up ahead of Everett was fellow freshman Mark Buguey, and ahead of Mark were sophomores Danny Costa and Eddie Santiago, and there was nobody else. We finished in that order. Shutout.

I staggered across the line a couple of strides behind Everett and for the only time in my running career, I hadn't the strength to stay on my feet. On the grass, I was gasping, begging for air and flopping around like a fish on the dock. Earl Mills, who drove half the team to the meet, was looking at me and laughing, and when Earl Mills laughed, he gave it his all. "I KNEW you could run! I KNEW you could run!" I'd never felt so close to dying, and I don't know if I'd ever felt better. At that point, without knowing it at the time, I was on the hook. All it was going to take to reel me in was an understanding and enthusiastic coach, which I already had, and a lively, enjoyable group of peers, who were already there and would grow in number.

It says a lot about the seismic shift in my focus induced by becoming a runner that I don't remember much of anything about most of my classes. As previously mentioned, Mrs. Robichaud was my English teacher. We read books, but I can't remember which ones. We wrote papers, I'm sure, and worked on grammar and spelling and what have you, but it has all slipped my mind. Whatever I did in science class was similarly forgettable, right down to not knowing who my teacher was. Math may have been Joe Bradley, whom I've cited as my 8th-grade teacher, but I could be off by a year. Maybe it was Miss Flood then? Somebody help me out here. All of my math teachers made distinct impressions on me, mostly for the better, but matching up the teacher and the year is less than automatic.

Sidney Roberts was the teacher of World Cultures I, a course in which we studied the history of the world and which would be followed a year later by World Cultures II, where we did more of the same, also under the direction of Mr. Roberts. He was a slightly gruff but kindly old gentleman with massive jowels, a wispy shock of hair that would not stay down, and a withered arm that I was told was the result of polio. He was often referenced by the less kindly among us as "Hookarm". He could take hold of your shoulder with that bad arm just as firmly as with the other, a technique he put to use frequently to rouse slumbering students. He had a deep, gravelly voice that defined monotony and induced somnolence regularly. He had some interesting things to say if you could stay awake for them, but it was a struggle. Our book was written many years before and had been used in that class for a long, long time. It had no photographs in it, just illustrations slightly more elaborate than those little sketches that accompany the definitions in Webster's Dictionary. I thought of it as the style of textbook that kids learned from in the 30's, and they may well have read from these very ones.

I had four different French teachers during my time at LHS, and three of them were beautiful, vivacious women. Anna Boido was there my freshman year. She had ink-black hair waving up over her shoulders and dark, alert eyes that could flash with amusement or anger or both at once. She had the happy faculty of being able to be friends with her students without letting anyone take advantage of that. She was a fan of the Red Sox, and especially of Vern Stephens, whose days with the team were long past. Any French teacher who knew about any ballplayer I wasn't familiar with, and who was cheerful and beautiful besides, was all right with me. Miss Boido probably would have been a pretty effective instructor if she'd had better material to deal with. She took her teaching seriously, but not many of her charges were anxious to learn French.

I've always felt that people who have a real interest in learning another language, and who have compartments in their minds where they can file away what they learn for later retrieval, must be approaching the discipline in a way that is beyond my ken. Most subject matter reveals to the student new information about the world, explanations of phenomena that you may or may not have been curious about, but which expose you, either through documentation, experimentation, observation or explication, to aspects of reality that you didn't know about before. Learning a foreign language doesn't quite do that. The French people know just what we know and they say just the same things we say, they just say it in a very different way, and you're here to learn what that way is. What have you learned when you've mastered the language? Not much, really, you've just learned how to express yourself in a new, but entirely parallel, way. This is not to minimize the value of being able to communicate with the French, or the reflective elements that can accrue from discovering aspects of another culture, but it just seems that the learning of another language is qualitatively different from the learning of almost anything else. It is by no means a poor expenditure of time, but it requires a different approach, one that forever remained beyond my reach.

My family acquired a new member during this, my freshman year. It was the first year of LHS's participation in the American Field Service (AFS) program, which matched up kids from around the world with stateside families for a year's immersion in Earth's dominant culture. The Turkingtons were the chosen ones to be Falmouth's first host family. How that came about was surprising and possibly instructive. The fledgling local AFS committee got its ducks in a row and late in the previous school year announced that they'd be accepting applications from any families that might wish to take in a foreign student for a year. Mom told me later about what transpired when she approached the group to tell them of our interest. According to her, she was told, Well, you know, the Burwells are under consideration. And Mom told them, Yes, well the Turkingtons would like to be as well (there may have been others, I don't know). So they very kindly told her that they'd be happy to take our application and they much appreciated our interest. The Burwells were a very fine family with lots of money and a grand old beachfront home whose kids went to public schools and who had a son, David, in Eric's class. He was smart, athletic, affable and widely respected. Dr. Burwell was, well, a doctor, and Mrs. Burwell was a pretty, kindly woman who was active in community affairs. A little while later, the regional AFS people did their screening, which included a lengthy visit and interview at our humble abode, and lo and behold, they decided we'd be the best match for Falmouth's first foreign exchange student.

Neils Lierow arrived late in the summer and was a most excellent ambassador for Germany, if only because of the myths about Germans that he exploded. Fred Toran, the LHS soccer coach, was very excited to meet him because he was pretty sure that European kids spend all their free time playing soccer and develop expertise that would jump-start his team. Sorry, Fred. Neils was an agreeable, slight, inquisitive fellow with delicate features and no experience or interest in athletics of any kind. He joined the soccer team for the sake of good sportsmanship and to cement the brotherly bond with Eric. Poor Fred, now he had TWO players he couldn't put in until the game was out of reach. If I hadn't moseyed on down to the cross country locker room that day, there might have been three from the same house! Neils got along well with everybody, but his circle of friends consisted mostly of the worldly kids in the class. Having already finished high school (or gymnasium, I think they called it), and that in Germany, no less, he was pretty far ahead of what his classmates were working on, so academic pressures never entered into his life in America.

I got along with Neils well enough except when I was determined to be grumpy. I was three years behind him in school and four years in age, so we didn't have a lot in common. One feature of his that didn't mean anything to me in those days when matters of sexual identity were dimly understood and never discussed was that he was quite effeminate. In looks, in voice, in body carriage, he was pretty clearly gay. I suspect such a trait was just as verboten in Germany in 1963 as it was here, so I imagine he forged ahead with his life and dealt with it as young people always had to, meaning try not to think about it and hope everything turns out okay. From snippets I heard about where he headed after his year here, I'd surmise that his smarts and good nature stood him in good stead. He and my parents corresponded regularly for decades after his year with us. For a time after university in Germany, he was a judge of some kind and seemingly always on vacation. Last I heard, he and his partner were running an inn in Burgundy in an old castle or something. Whatever it was, it didn't sound like a bad place to wind up.

He lived a pretty quiet life at 287 Scranton Avenue, as did the permanent residents. There were very few surprises in our home, and not a lot of coming and going. We all got up at the same time and had breakfast together, invariably eggs done in some way, breakfast meat, OJ and toast, with coffee for the parents. Then Dad went to The Enterprise and the schoolbound people went to LHS. How we all got there, I don't know. This may have been the year when the first VW, a '57, entered the picture, but I'm more than certain that Mom and Eric and Neils and I didn't go to school in it. Anyway, we all got there, Mom got home somehow after school let out, and the devoted athletes got home after our practices. There followed, at around 6, a period of sitting around in the living room with dinner cooking away in the kitchen while my parents drank a fairly stiff Manhattan and Mom orchestrated whatever conversation there was. It didn't require an alcoholic drink for Mom to become expansive, witty and emotive, but it did guarantee it. When she related a story or an incident that she found amusing or bemusing, she acted out the parts with grand gestures, voice changes and facial expressions that were truly entertaining, even to teenage boys. Quite often, a story got interrupted by smoke coming from the kitchen, something left too long on or in the stove. Mom was a pretty good cook for one who didn't care to spend much time preparing food, but she never learned how to be attentive, or how to prepare enough to satisfy her hungry sons.

Dinner was usually a quiet affair, perhaps because we'd already seen just about enough of each other and whatever was worth being told had been told. Coffee and dessert ended it. Everybody did something to help clean up, and then the evening lay before us. Mom usually spent some of it correcting papers or writing up plans at the dining room table. There was a certain amount of TV watching, but it wasn't excessive. Though the TV was six feet before Mom's eyes as she worked at the table, she didn't mind having it on, as it provided a distraction. On nights he wasn't working, Dad was sitting in the living room, reading books or The NY Times, where Mom joined him later over a glass of cheap red wine. For the boys, there was some homework, some reading, some TV, and that was it for another day.

* * *

After my breakthrough cross-country race at Old Rochester, I held a reasonably respected position as one of the best freshmen on the team, and one of the better JV's. I didn't really elevate that status over the course of the season, but I'm sure that's because everybody else was improving along with me. Mark Buguey was our best freshman, with Everett Costa and me close together a little bit behind Mark. Mark was one of a large brood of Bugueys who lived on Amvets Avenue. This was a cluster of maybe 30 or so identical Cape-style homes that were built to provide modest housing for returning soldiers and their families after WW II. A lot of kids I knew had lived there and moved on, but many were still there. Mark was gangly, talkative, highly amusing and an extremely thoughtful and caring kid. Our lives have continued to intersect. Everett was the younger brother of John "Mugsy" Costa, who was one of the stars on the state title team that preceded ours by a couple of years, and who was run down while changing a tire on the side of the road. Everett lived in the Teaticket/ Sandwich Road/ Brick Kiln Road part of town, where there were still some little farms, considerable acreage of scrub pine, and a lot of lowest-tier housing. Many of the town's Cape Verdean families lived here, not in squalor for the most part, but with very limited means. Everett and I had a pretty good rivalry going – I'd beat him on my good days, he'd beat me on his – and there were many times when we could talk things over and jake each other and do the things that friends do. There were also days when if I greeted him in the halls he'd say Shut up, Turkington, or I'll deck your ass, and something in his look told me that he meant it. I could say the same for Albert Barrows, another Cape Verdean freshman, also a tough runner, also a good guy to be around when he was right and scary when he wasn't.

The varsity team was pretty good, but not extremely good. Kalpy's teams had won state divisional titles in '62 and '63, but there'd been a lot of graduations, and at this point he was cobbling together a team out of disparate elements. The top guy was a senior, Joe Rezendes, who was one of the skinny colored kids I'd seen running around a year or two before. Joe could mock you, praise you, shame you and congratulate you, all in one sentence. He could talk serious or jive, cuckoo or rational without contradiction. He never ran out of things to say and it was always original, authentic, and usually amusing. He realized his place on the team and he took it to heart. He worked very hard, always without complaint. He'd been part of a glorious team, was now captain and leader of a second-echelon team, and he fully accepted his role. If I'd been a year or two further along and been able to train with him, I'd have seen him as a superb teammate and leader. As it was, he was just Up There with a status beyond my ability to visualize. If his classmate and co-captain, Ray Fike, hadn't had to deal with injuries all season, we would have had a couple of front-runners and likely been contenders for some championships. But Ray lost a lot of training time, and it cost us.

Geoff Cahoon, my way-in-the-back buddy my first fateful days on the team, got sick a couple of times and mildly injured a couple of times and never made much progress. Geoff was slight and lithe and had a fantastic stride, but didn't have the strength or the stamina to sustain it for long. He proved to be a cheerful, slightly goofy guy to be around, and I was glad he stayed with the team, but he just wasn't much of a distance runner. I had a pretty consistent season, but except for the big surprise I presented at Old Rochester, I had no extraordinary efforts. There were no statewide races for freshmen then, but if there had been, I'd guess I would have been towards the front of the main pack, but not near the leaders. Having first thought of the sport as a conditioner for basketball, which I figured I'd play again this winter, I changed my plan when Kalpy told me that the league was going to let kids run the two-mile in winter track for the first time. That's for me! I thought.

A bunch of us, and some incoming winter track aspirants, kept right on working out after the season ended. You could do things like this without a coach or adult around, just go down to the locker room after school, change up, run, come back, take a shower, get dressed and leave, totally unsupervised. It's a wonder we didn't cause all sorts of trouble. Some other freshmen were starting to join us: Salt Handy, Donnie Bumpus, Mark Denman and others were showing up. One nice, sunny November afternoon, we were out running the cross country course. Coming back down Gifford Street, we neared the Jones Road intersection where there was often a traffic officer we knew, a Cape Verdean woman whose name escapes me, stopping cars so that kids walking home from the Morse Pond School could cross. She was performing her duty there today, and as we went by her we could hear her crying. We asked if there was anything wrong. "Oh boys" she said, "our president's been shot."

I can't remember whether 11/22/63 was a Friday or whether any school was called off, but I spent considerable time in front of the TV for the next few days, along with an enormous number of other Americans. I saw Jack Ruby kill Lee Harvey Oswald, probably the first murder ever broadcast live. I absorbed all the dribs and drabs of information that came out, and watched the funeral procession in silence with my family. I felt appropriately dazed and sorrowful through all this, but I really had a hard time pinning down what my feelings were. There was simply no frame of reference to gauge what it all meant to me. There was this charming, intelligent, thoroughbred local boy who had a gracious, sophisticated wife and a couple of cute young kids. He seemed to be everything our parents and other mentors wanted us to be, though they knew we never would. He had the most important, demanding job in the world, and it looked like he had a pretty good grip on how he ought to do his work. JFK being president of the United States was a very important item in my life. Then one day he gets shot in the head. So that's all over now. Turn the page, kid. What the hell?

It wasn't unusual for the Turkingtons to be sitting in front of the tube watching the news; in fact, it was very much the norm. Chet Huntley and David Brinkley were the newscasters of choice every weekday evening at 6:30, was it? Maybe 6, maybe 7. So I was aware of turmoil in Southeast Asia, independence movements in Africa, racial conflict at home, the space race and America's many early failures in that sphere, national elections, all kinds of important things. Given that I lived in a house where the NY Times came in the door every day, and Newsweek, the New Yorker and Saturday Review of Books by subscription, I'd have been reasonably well-informed by osmosis alone. As it was, there were often items in the Huntley-Brinkley report that sparked enough interest in me to send me to the periodicals for further info. Only trouble is, there was not much discussion of these things in the family. It's hard to share thoughts on newsy topics without making judgments, especially for teenagers, and expressing a judgment would very often provoke the admonition from Dad that you really shouldn't say whatever you said without having all the facts. He was a newsman through and through, quite uneasy with partly-informed or poorly considered analysis. So who ever has all the facts? I sure didn't.

Interest in current events wasn't really fostered at school either. It's more or less understandable, expected even, that every teacher is going to focus on his or her subject matter. Since nobody had the assignment of presiding over discussions of world events, it didn't happen very often. There were teachers who'd stray from the syllabus when they sensed that the kids wanted to talk about something that was going on in the world, but it wasn't commonly done. And, not entirely coincidentally, there was not a lot of talk about the news among the kids on our own. I had some friends – they tended to be the scholarly ones – who I could be pretty sure would be up on whatever crisis was developing somewhere in the world, and a few who could, much to my surprise, tell me about some issue I hadn't heard of. I recollect a discussion with David Eisenberg about the perils of consuming dairy products. He was aware, as I was not, that testing nuclear bombs in the atmosphere, a practice pursued intensively by the US and USSR, was raining Strontium-90 down onto our cow pastures and grain fields and being passed on to our innards via milk and ice cream. When JFK was informed of this sobering fact – not by David Eisenberg - he negotiated a deal with Khrushchev for both countries to stop atmospheric nuclear testing.

Early in the new year, there started being some attention paid in the American popular media to a rock band called the Beatles that apparently was wildly popular in England. There was a photo in Life magazine of the band meeting the queen, and I thought they looked kind of goofy in their odd little suits and their soup-bowl haircuts, but I couldn't help being curious. What could be so new and different about their music that all their shows and all their records were selling like mad? More to the point, what was it about them that caused crowds of teenage girls to scream in ecstasy? There was probably more buildup on the Top 40 stations about their upcoming first release than I was aware of; reception wasn't a sure thing on my radio, and I wasn't a constant listener. Generally, at night I tuned in to 1010 WINS New York. I tended to hear the better music there, and Murray the K, the evening DJ, sounded like a character. One night I turned on the radio and came in in the middle of a song, and I knew right away, this has to be the Beatles. It was "I Want To Hold Your Hand", and indeed it was not like anything I had heard before.

I wasn't crazy about the Beatles then, much though I admired their proficiency and recognized their originality. I always had an aversion to the bandwagon effect, and there seemed to be an awful lot of hype attending them and their music. I didn't like the notion that I was supposed to be wild about them, so I managed to keep my enthusiasm under wraps. They certainly were more versatile as songwriters, musicians, singers, and producers of sound than any American band active at the time, with the arguable exception of the Beachboys. I made sure to be there when we and the nation gathered round to see them on Ed Sullivan, and I read commentary about them and bought their albums and memorized all of their songs (which was hard to avoid, since everything they put out got played ceaselessly on the radio for weeks). They were followed to our shores very shortly after their arrival by a whole slew of English groups of many different styles, some of whom – the Stones, the Animals – I was a little more able to sink my teeth into. They had a little more guts, a greater touch of badness. The contrast between the Beatles' and the Stones' debuts on the Sullivan show was graphic. The Beatles, in uniform suits, smiling and laughing and so cheerily wholesome. The Stones, dressed like ragdolls, scowling at the camera, moving about very little, looking like they wanted to be anyplace else but there.

Around this time, I made a snap decision that probably influenced my future path profoundly, though I didn't have the vision to recognize its import. I got a call one night from Arthur Perry, who was organizing a rock band. He asked me if I wanted to be in it. I pointed out to Arthur that I didn't play any instruments that a rock band could use, and he told me they'd have me on the keyboards. But I don't know how to play keyboards. That's all right, Arthur said, you can learn it. What he was looking for was personality. Feeling that I not only couldn't play keyboards but also didn't have much personality, I declined. He got his band together – I think they were named the Bol Jaggers (?), and they were fairly serious about their craft. I don't think they ever got beyond playing locally, but I know they were active at least four years later, because they played at my senior class banquet. Had I been feeling a little more self-confident the night Arthur called, I would have liked the idea and things would have gone from there. Speculating where they would have gone is a pointless exercise, but I would most certainly have been in a different orbit.

Winter track was at times an other-worldly experience. Like almost every other high school in the East, we didn't have an actual indoor-sized track to train on, so we did our track-type work (i.e., repeated intervals of a certain distance under the stopwatch) in the parking lot, which had a couple of small hills and where Kalpy had painted a series of dashed lines to approximate an oval of indeterminate distance. In very foul weather, we stayed in the school building. We found if we propped open the doors to the lobby of the gym to maximize the distance of one time around, we could get about 28 laps to the mile. Not really ideal distance training, but it was all we had. We also wedged open the firedoors in the longest corridor in the school downstairs, which gave us a straightaway of about 50 yards where we could do wind sprints to exhaustion. The hurdlers worked out there too, and made quite a racket. It was all very destructive to the doors, the floor and probably our lower legs, but it was something.

Our dual meets against other teams in the conference were run at the New Bedford Vocational School, where they had a real, official-sized board track set up on the playing field. It was made of wood sections bolted together, 11 laps to the mile and with banked turns. It was really a pretty good facility, except that it was outdoors. Since the meets were on weekdays, they couldn't get started much before 3:30, and since there was always a whole slate of dual meets going on, it was often quite dark by the time the last relay was run. And it was cold, of course, especially as it got dark. It was often below freezing and sometimes quite a bit below.

Transportation to and from New Bedford was provided by Russell Palmer's Falmouth Bus Company. These weren't schoolbusses, but they were by no means a step up from them: they were loud, gaseous and prone to breakage. True, they had bucket seats for 40 passengers, but there were about 60 on the team and we were packed in tight. Though there was no enforced pecking order for seating, it generally worked out that the varsity guys got the seats, upperclassmen JV's sat on the floor or the armrests, freshmen lay in the luggage racks overhead. With no means for bringing music along, the only way to drown out the engine and rattling windows was to talk, loudly, which everybody did for the whole hour's trip. Sometimes the freshmen came down from the luggage racks to crowd around a few sophisticated seniors to listen to talk about girls and cars and drinking. Sometimes the banter got rolling from various loci around the bus, or a monologue could erupt that Eddie Murphy might match on his best days. With the crowding, the smell of the gas fumes mixed with Hot Stuff (liniment), sweat and body odor from sixty hormone-juiced boys, the racket from the bus and so many voices raised in utter disunity, it was not an environment that would appeal to the fastidious. But it was intense, spirited and more real than anything I was accustomed to.

Having forsaken a mediocre basketball career to run the two-mile race in winter track, I wound up competing in just about everything except the two-mile. Kalpy was trying to find out whether any of his sizable freshman group was good for anything but the middle distances, so over the course of the season he had me in the hurdles and every race from the 300 to the mile. I had one race when for the first time I got the feeling of moving fast and running real hard. This was in a 600, where you sort of have to run fast and hard, but I knocked off a 1:27 (this was yards, not meters), set a freshman record and experienced a new dimension in racing. My best mile was 5:23, and I felt pretty good about that. Donnie Bumpus was a bit ahead of me in the 1000, as was Jorge Erol, a recent arrival from Germany, in the mile. With good health and steady training, Geoff Cahoon was starting to look a little bit like a runner in the 600 and 1000. Salt Handy had some decent mile runs. The real outlier was Greg Anderson, a Mashpee kid whose athletic reputation preceded him at Falmouth. Greg was both physically and emotionally more mature than most freshmen, and already not far behind the state's elite runners in the sprints. Greg broke his arm playing football in the fall and still had a big plaster cast on his forearm through the winter, which kept him from playing basketball. But he could run, fast, with it.

With all of my afternoons accounted for since September, I was largely a creature of routine by now. I either walked home from track practice or got a ride from Kalpy, who lived nearby. There was going to be about an hour before my parents assembled with their Manhattans and their three boys in the living room, and I usually spent some of that time watching TV. The networks must have had a hard time defining their audiences, such as they were, for that interval between the soap operas and the evening news, because there was some pretty peculiar programming. One show I tuned into a lot was the Rocky and Bullwinkle show. It consisted of maybe half a dozen cartoon shorts with some of the whackiest characters and sharpest satire on the tube. The animation was inspired, as was the variety from one short to another. I believe I could see an episode now and still be impressed. I can't say the same for Soupy Sales, who did a one-man studio production that held considerable appeal for me at the time. The format of the show was along the lines of Shari Lewis, whose presentation was sweet, charming and appropriate for the younger kids on Saturday morning, which is when she came on. Soupy Sales was on the zany side, and he gave the impression that he was just a small step from lunacy. His show was for people who'd stopped reading Mad magazine but still had a taste for its irreverent nuttiness.

Though I was never an eager participant in my family's half hour together in the living room as dinner cooked, neither did I withdraw from it. This surprises me, because everything

I remember about my frequently sullen and resentful attitude towards my parents suggests to me that I'd want nothing to do with this scene, but I hung in there. I suspect I was compliant enough to do what I felt was expected of me in this and other areas, but defiant enough to let it be known I didn't really want to. Conversation was the aim, and Mom assured there would be some of that, but it wasn't mandatory, or constant. I took the opportunity to read the day's papers and checked in on what was going on around me when it was of interest to me, meaning about me. All the while, I anticipated dinner, because I was always hungry, especially around 6:30 in the evening, which is when we sat down to eat.

I've said that Mom was a pretty competent cook, considering she didn't want or have the time to prepare something elaborate most days. When I consider some of the things that were put before us, I can't help thinking that people's eating habits from the Depression didn't fade away overnight. We had liver – beef and chicken liver – fairly often. Tripe, rarely, but we had it. Beef tongue. Cheeks and tongues, which were the cheap way of eating fish but were actually pretty good when prepared right. Brussels sprouts, parsnips. None of my kids have ever eaten or probably even seen most of these delicacies, and it's not because I have terrible memories of them but because their time has come and gone. There is that old cliché about every generation wanting to bring their kids up with a better life than they themselves experienced. A lot of my contemporaries have assured themselves of that progress by flooding their kids with material goods. Not I. When another dinner has come and gone, and I have once again not put on my kids' plates a slab of beef liver with a few sautéed onions on top, next to a spoonful of mashed turnips and a boiled potato, I have in some small way satisfied myself that, in this at least, my kids' lives are better than mine was.

There wasn't much extra space at 287 Scranton Avenue, but I always had my own room. When they learned that Neils would be joining us for the year, my parents got a carpenter over to take down a wall between my room and what I suppose was meant to be a sewing room – in 1926, homebuyers still wanted these – so that there'd be space enough for another bed. Eric and Neils shared the expanded room, I moved into Eric's room, and Mom and Dad stayed in the front bedroom, which was as small as the others but looked out over the harbor. Each room had a closet about three feet wide, two windows, one electrical outlet, a tall cast iron radiator and just enough wall space to squeeze in a bureau and a desk. There was very little open floor space left.

I can't recall what the bathroom was like when we moved in, but it had to have been pretty bad because one of the very few remodeling projects undertaken by my parents in 45 years in that house was to improve the bathroom. They had this done not long after we moved in. What we wound up with was a peculiar tub, nearly square, with a basin just large enough to soak in set diagonally across it. There was a shower on the wall, my first. This was coordinated with a boxy wall-hung sink and a standard toilet, with a new linoleum floor that resembled a Jackson Pollack work and never showed any sign of wear. The tub enclosure and the lower three feet of the scant wall space was tiled in 4" x 4" gray tiles. The upper wall space sported wallpaper, applied by Mom, that featured the signs of the zodiac. There was room enough to stand in there, but you could not take a full step in any direction without running into some fixture or the door. The remodel, such as it was, was probably done in 1959. I was last in that room in 2006 and except for some of the tiles and wallpaper parting ways with the wall, absolutely nothing about it had changed.

Ah, but there was another bathroom available to the Turkingtons and their guests. This one was just to the left of the back door and was somewhat less palatial than the upstairs bath. It contained a toilet, squeezed between the wall and the washing machine, and the tiniest little sink I've ever seen, wedged into the corner by the door. That sink was so small that with the faucets hanging out over the basin you really couldn't wash both hands at once, and just forget about the face. It and the faucets were, I am sure, original with the 1926 house and were still there and functioning in 2006, though dripping constantly. The washing machine was up to date, but there was no place for a dryer, so the clothes went out on the line. There was no heat in that little space, but with a short run of exterior wall it never got bitter cold. Still, it wasn't the spot you'd choose to sit down for a rest in the wintertime. Mom and Dad didn't entertain often, but folks would be over for dinner or a game of bridge once in a while, and there had to have been requests to use the bathroom. The options were two: get clear instructions to the upstairs bath, trudge up the hazardous, tightly winding stairway to the second floor, locate the bathroom and bob and weave through it to the toilet; or, head to the john by the back door that's easy to find but chilly and awkward to use. It didn't pay to be prissy if you needed to relieve yourself in the Turkingtons' unimproved antedepression house.

One lasting improvement of substance that was made around this time was an upgrade of the dining room table. For as long as I could remember, we'd eaten on a hollow-core flush door with luan veneer, the kind that you find used, as doors, in the very cheapest of cheap home construction. The door, or table, rested unfastened on two lengths of 2x4 with holes drilled in them to accommodate black steel rods that served as table legs, splayed out slightly to promote stability. It wasn't easy to get up from the table without kicking one of those legs, which caused the table to shake. A true kick would knock the leg out entirely, which knocked the table way out of whack. We lived with this setup for many years, in all our homes, through countless spills. At last, perhaps when my parents felt that we were settled here permanently, it was replaced with something better. The new table was Danish Modern in style – the happening fashion then – and had built-in leaves at either end that could be pulled out to seat a larger group. It stayed in that spot until Dad died in 2004, at which time it came to me, with whom it has served the next generation. It has its little dings and stains, but holds together and remains stable.

I kept working out between the winter and spring track seasons. Some of it was unsupervised training after school with other guys and some of it was on my own. By now, I was proceeding through life with the assumption that at some point during the day, I was going to put in some mileage. I wasn't extreme about it, nor highly imaginative; there was, in 1964, really no lore on the subject of distance training for high school freshmen. Everybody involved in it was flying by the seats of their pants, but it was intuitively clear to me that if I ran more, I'd get better at it. So I kept running.

The rewards were incremental and not always obvious. I did some of everything that spring season: every race from the 440 to the two-mile, the high hurdles, long jump, high jump, various relay distances, even threw the discus once or twice. One of my best days was at the state relays in Belmont. In a relay meet, you can dig pretty deep into the varsity roster, because there are a lot of events, and four kids participate in each one. Kalpy put our four best distance men into the distance medley relay, which they won, and went to the second-line guys for the two mile, or 4x880. Since Donnie Bumpus was tied up that weekend with the freshman class show, I made the cut. I still have a snapshot of our team: Ray Costa, Tom Vadala and Jim McHardie in LHS track uniform, plus me in gym shorts and a T-shirt. I was our leadoff runner, and I went to the line with a powerful sense of not belonging in this crowd. Seconds after the gun went off, I was dead last of about a dozen runners, and there I stayed for the first lap and well into the second. Then the trance came over me again. I don't think I speeded up at all, and split times confirmed this, but going up the backstretch I pulled out into the second lane and started passing runners. All the way up the straight and around the final turn, I kept passing runners until there was just one left, a kid from Lunenberg who I never caught. I handed us off in second place with a 2:14, which was an LHS freshman record until Donnie bettered it later in the season.

That snapshot of our relay team barely displays a scab on my chin that was a great source of embarrassment to me for much of the spring. I was never riddled with acne, but like most kids I had more of it than I would have asked for. Also like most kids, I dealt with the most prominent pimples by popping them in front of the mirror. I did this to a big one in the middle of my chin one day, but rather than diminishing, it scabbed over and started to grow. It got about as big as a dime, then stayed there for a couple of weeks before it slowly dried up and went away. I spent much of this period with my fingers held to my chin, as if deep in thought. I avoided face-to-face conversation with anybody and spent a lot of time flushed with shame. I think it may have been impetigo, but I never did anything to find out and nobody ever said anything to me about it. This included my parents. Even allowing for an often sullen, noncommunicative attitude on my part that may have made them reluctant to broach a sensitive subject, I find this a mite peculiar. It's all very fine not to feel you have to run interference for your kids all the time, but I had a glaringly obvious health issue, for God's sake. Never a word was spoken of it.

I ran the two-mile a few times, with a best of 11:16. I only ran the mile once but had a good one when Mark Buguey and I tied for first in 5:15 in a freshman meet in New Bedford. I suffered a great humiliation in a return meet on our track when Kalpy put me on the 4x110 relay team to test my sprinting skills. I was running second leg, lined up against a very tall, powerfully-built opponent who looked to be somewhat more than 14 years of age. Glenn Marshall ran first leg for us, and he was very quick and handed me a small lead. I took the baton and was rounding the turn when my opponent plowed into me from behind and sent me sprawling into the cinders. Then he threatened to compound my embarrassment by stopping, running back to me and offering his hand. "You okay, buddy? Can I help you up?" I waved him away and hissed, "Keep running!" That's all I needed, was to have a restart with the two of us standing next to each other. After the race, I was in the finish area and heard him explaining himself to his friends: "I didn't wanna run him over. I got the stick and turned to run and there he was! It was like he was standing still!". That was the end of my sprinting career. Strangely enough, I had some success in the high hurdles, where I broke the freshman record and ran in the state meet, where I was hugely underqualified but got snuck in by Kalpy because one of our better hurdlers was out. I performed abominably in my qualifying heat, and that was the end of my hurdling career.

One of our principal regional opponents was Dartmouth High, from over near New Bedford. Their running program was at something of a peak these days, but they'd been looking up at Falmouth a year or two before and were soon to be again. The head coach there was Al Porter, a gruff, high-volume man who we first thought of as a blowhard but developed some respect for as we gained familiarity with him and his athletes. What was really disconcerting about Dartmouth was that they had two freshmen, Ed Rossi and John Vieira, who were light-years ahead of any of our group. They ran in the same race most of the time and always seemed to finish together, not as a teamwork thing but because they pushed each other all the way to the line. I saw them run 4:40 in the state meet mile. I was told by Al Porter that they'd gone under 2:05 in the 880. Nobody on our team could do these things, freshman or otherwise. I didn't look forward at all to competing against them for the next three years.

Spring track got off to a slightly rocky start when Paul Maguire came on as assistant coach. It's not unusual for a high school's football coach to associate himself with the spring track team. It's a handy way of keeping an eye on next year's gridiron talent, making sure they're doing something to get stronger/faster, keeping them out of trouble and what have you. It did not go altogether smoothly at Falmouth, because Kalpy's and Maguire's ways of doing things were poles apart. With his soft-spoken but insistent personality, Maguire introduced a number of fundamental changes that didn't sit well at all with a lot of the team. One of his innovations was a very structured, disciplined approach to warm-ups. Everybody now had to be out on the field on time or face a penalty of some kind, lined up in rank and file to perform calisthenics. These were the time-honored series of jumping jacks, situps, pushups, leg stretches and other exercises that have been thoroughly and mistakenly discredited in the modern age, but everybody did them then. That completed, everybody ran down to Fuller Field, where the track was, about 3/4 mile away. We then lined up for isotonics, the latest thing in strength-building. At a far corner of the field, Maguire had arranged for the installation of a series of horizontal steel pipes anchored at assorted heights to wooden posts. The idea was that the kid would grip the pipe with both hands, and by pushing or pulling as hard as he could against that immovable object would develop some muscle or other.

With maybe eight stations and about 80 kids lined up waiting to use them, a lot of time was spent standing around. Talking to each other was allowed, but stepping out of line was not. It didn't take too many days of this for the discontent to set in. Among those guys who had a low tolerance for regimentation or who just really didn't like being told what to do – and some of Kalpy's best performers had always fit that description – it expressed itself in withdrawal from the team and the sport. Many more, especially the younger kids and the distance runners, just grumbled. "When the hell are we going to RUN?" With all the orderliness and pointless exercises, there really wasn't much time for that.

All of this came to a head a couple of weeks into the season. The team was lined up doing the calisthenics when Geoff Cahoon let loose with a funny sound he could make with his throat: it was deeply hoarse, it sounded like his larynx was rupturing, it was extremely loud and always good for a laugh. Maguire, strolling between the rows, came up behind Geoff and kicked him in the ass! He gave a little chuckle and kept on strolling. I was lined up right behind Geoff, but everybody saw it. So Geoff took a step or two towards Maguire and kicked HIM in the ass. I thought I was going to witness the football coach punch a kid out before a crowd of witnesses, but Maguire stayed under control. He did, however, bark at Geoff and ordered him to leave the team and never come back. So Geoff strode off towards the locker room, followed instantly by most of the freshmen and a lot of the rest of the team. Kalpy was a little ways away, saw all this happen and came running over, waving his arms and shouting. HOLD IT! HOLD IT! Let's talk this over! Who did the talking, I don't know, but in true Kalperis fashion, there were no repercussions, no lingering resentments, and no more time spent in rank, file, or line by the ones who had better things to do.

My peak moment of the season, in the 880 at the state relays, was made possible because Donnie Bumpus was in the freshman class show, which performed that same weekend. The show was one of those fundraising events that high school classes undertake in order to beef up the class treasury and, probably more to the point, because the adults in charge feel that doing this sort of thing is good for the kids. Donnie was hands down the outstanding performer in the class. Not that he had much competition, but he had an innate ability to take on a part and project himself to an audience with clarity and authenticity. This was a variety show, and Donnie was the interlocutor, kind of like Ed Sullivan except more a part of the action. I never saw the performance, but I recall some of it from being at a rehearsal or two. One of the show-stoppers was a skit by Carl Soderland and Chris Costa, whose routine mirrored a weekly performance by Jackie Gleason and Frankie Fontaine on

Gleason's TV show, wherein Joe the Bartender (in this case, Chris Costa) and Crazy Guggenheim (Carl) chat it up over a couple of drinks. Chris had the girth and voice of Jackie Gleason, and Carl nailed the Frankie Fontaine role, right down to the squashed fedora, frumpy clothes and tipsy, low-IQ reflections on life.

It strikes me odd that I haven't had anything to say about Carl Soderland until now, because we were pretty good friends in our adolescence. Carl was cheerful, smart, fairly good at sports, and an extremely thoughtful and well-behaved kid. He lived in Sippewisset, a part of town a few miles from my house, so it was a bit of an effort to get to his place, but I often did. He had Beebe's Woods close behind his house and Wood Neck Beach just up the road, so we never lacked for places to go. The one thing that made me feel alienated from Carl was that he did everything he was supposed to do. He wasn't self-righteous about himself, or judgmental of other kids, but he always stayed out of trouble and I don't know if he ever did anything that could get him in trouble. One day when we were about 11, we were at his house unattended and had gotten hold of a cigarette, which we smoked. After we put it out, he made a face and said, Don't you wish we hadn't done this? And I answered, Actually, I wish we had another cigarette. That was Carl, and me. As we moved into our teens, and I was overtaken by sociophobia and narrowed my focus down to running and girl avoidance, we didn't have much to do with each other. My highbrow friends and I sometimes referred to him as The Golden Boy, with less scorn than it probably sounds. Secretly, I wondered why I wasn't a little more like him, and I missed him.

This freshman show was not without some controversy in its conception, because for the first time in memory, it wasn't done with the performers in blackface. It had always been based on the minstrel show, with all the performers mimicking the presumed dialect and stereotyped ways of poor, ignorant black people. Here in the spring of 1964, the administration had come to the realization that making fun of Negroes not only was an insult to the Negroes, but probably wasn't teaching the white kids the values that they hoped we'd grow up with. And this was not a dim-witted, retrograde administration. Harry Merson, the superintendent, was a man of considerable vision and a member of the Baha'i faith, whose followers were well out in front of the rest of the world in their ideas about equality. Russell Marshall, our principal, was kindly, gentlemanly and as decent as they come. But they were both realists, and there was a presumption, even among those who may have been repulsed by overt expressions of racial hatred, that accommodations must be made to mainstream bigotry, just because they always had been. In 1964, through personal enlightenment that may have been provoked via conversations with some of their dark-skinned pupils' parents or by the civil rights movement's migration to the front pages, the mimicry of Negroes in the freshman play was ended. The 1964 freshman class show made fun of hillbillies.

A singular event in my personal growth came to pass late in the spring, on the night of the LHS senior prom. I was told some time in advance that I'd be alone in the house that evening, as Eric and Neils were planning to attend, and Mom and Dad were to go as chaperones. In anticipation of this freedom, I began the daily practice of pouring a little bit of cheap wine from my parents' gallon bottle into a smaller jar, which I kept hidden in the basement. I had never had more than a few sips of alcoholic beverage, at holiday dinners or while receiving Communion at church, and I was quite curious to know how it felt to get tipsy. By prom night, I had a pretty good stash of Gallo hidden away, and soon after the revelers went out I got into it. It wasn't long before I achieved tipsiness, and I kept right on going. At one point, I was high jumping onto the couch, wishing I had a crossbar because I felt like I was really getting up there. A bit later, it occurred to me that it'd be fun to run my 1.5 mile loop naked and barefoot in the dark. This is why we don't let 14-year-olds drink. I took off all my duds and went into the side yard to stretch. While I was there, the wind gusted up and I felt cold, and encountered second thoughts about this workout. I went back in, polished off the wine and tried some gin. I mixed it with some canned citrus to make it palatable. I know I didn't get sick, and I know I made it back to bed. I also know that I felt dreadful the next morning, and that nobody ever questioned me about my wild evening.

Spring track closed out its season a few weeks before the end of school, but some of the distance runners continued running every afternoon. During this time, Mark Buguey and I got to talking about running over the summer. Mark's large family had recently moved to Nye Road, which wasn't far from my place, and we thought it might build us up for next year to keep at it. We broached the subject to Kalpy, who as always would be heading up to his hometown of Old Orchard Beach, Maine, as soon as school let out. Our pitch to him was, if we ran every day and focused on the longer distance work, then come September, a 2 1/2 mile cross country race would feel like nothing! Kalpy considered this and agreed that it might be a good idea. Go to it, boys. It says a lot about the understanding of the physiology of endurance sports in 1964 that none of us were really sure that this course of action would make us better runners, or be good for us. But there was in

Mark and me some nascent awareness of the long-term benefits of regular conditioning, and with nothing much else going on in our lives, we decided we'd do it. Kalpy's approval of our aim was predictable: Sure! Go ahead and do it!

And so we did. It was mostly an evening thing, at least until the days started getting too short for it late in the summer. I've always reacted with some bemusement when I hear coaches or other sports-minded people affirm the importance of not eating for hours before exercising. Mark and I both sat down to dinner with our families every evening, then got up from the table and started getting ready to run. We varied our workouts as much as we could, but almost all of them in one way or another kept us running for half to three-quarters of an hour. We probably could have occasionally thrown in a really long, steady run, but we were pushing the envelope quite enough by totaling five to seven miles in a workout. And we didn't want to run slow. I never did like taking it easy just to get the miles in. Sometimes we ran in the soft sand at Surf Drive, sometimes in Beebe's Woods, sometimes on the track, often on the road, where we drew a lot of funny looks and some not-so-funny remarks. Running in public was just not done in 1964, and there were always a few people who needed to express their displeasure to us. I didn't mind; encountering rudeness satisfied my wish to be defiant, scorned for it, and know that I was onto something my belittlers just didn't understand.

We stuck to our regimen faithfully into July, when we heard about a road race coming up in Bourne, the next town north of Falmouth. Except for the Boston Marathon, I didn't know road races existed, and in fact they were uncommon. This one was a 20-kilometer event, which translates to 12.6 miles, which didn't scare us, but should have. The race and its 58 entrants started at high noon on a flaming hot July Sunday in Buzzards Bay on the mainland, went over the Bourne Bridge, followed County Road nearly to the Falmouth town line, then headed up along the shore road almost back to the Cape Cod Canal. I was wearing a standard V-neck T-shirt, cotton khakis cut just below the knee, sweatsocks and high-top Converse basketball sneakers. About four miles into the run, there was nobody else in sight, and I ran the rest of the course in solitude, but I ran it all. There was one water station along the way. Mark finished a few places and several minutes ahead of me. There was one college student in the race, so untrained that I beat him; all the rest were grown men, mostly in their 30's and 40's. Very few people out of school, and just about no women whatsoever, did any running, but those that did didn't screw around jogging. They were training for competition.

The race was sponsored by the VFW post in Bourne. They put on a righteous feed for everyone after it was over, and they had a couple of tables set up outside that were covered with merchandise prizes for the runners. This was more or less the standard way of rewarding the participants for a job well done. We visited the table in order of finish: the winner took his pick of the lot first, then on down the line. I walked away with a rather nice set of glassware. At the end of August, there was a 15k race in Dennis, down-Cape, that we also entered. With a cooler day, shorter distance, and another month of distance work behind us, Mark and I acquitted ourselves more honorably in that one. It was a very popular race, with about 80 entrants. Mark got away from me early, but I caught sight of him again over the last mile and finished only a couple of places behind him, 58th or so, in about 66 minutes.

At some point in midsummer, Mom asked me if Mark and I would like to go with her to visit her parents in Great Neck. The World's Fair was going on just a few miles from their place, the Mets' new ballpark was nearby, and except for our daily workout, we were both pretty bored with Falmouth, so off we went. It was a good time. We spent a couple of days at the World's Fair, which had exhibits and rides and foods and shows from, as you'd expect, all over the world. It's the sort of thing that isn't done any more. We went at least once to Jones Beach, where we could body surf and run for miles in the sand without turning around, neither of which we could do in Falmouth. We went to a Mets game at Shea Stadium. And we kept running, still as an after-dinner thing. That part of Nassau County was totally built out and had been for years, so in order to get any distance in we had to be pretty careful to take note of every turn. We were observant enough to get back every night before dark.

Until the night that we didn't. On that night, we went a little ways past where we'd been before, and when we headed back we missed a turn somewhere but didn't realize it for quite a while. Trusting in our sense of direction, we tried this turn and that until we realized we were utterly lost. What really brought that home to us was that as it got dark, we noticed groups of boys and young men hanging around on street corners or front porches, and they were all black. If there were any integrated neighborhoods in the New York suburbs, we certainly weren't in one of them. Two awkward, uptight white boys wandering around in T-shirts and cutoffs were very noticeable, and we drew some disapproving attention. Nobody threatened us, but we were made to know that we didn't belong there. Oh, what to do, what to do? We decided to knock on the door of one of the better-kept ranch homes, tell them our story and hope for the best. A burly black man answered and offered to let us come in and use the phone. There was a woman there too, and two girls a little younger than us. We found my grandparents' number in the phone book, told Papa the address we were at and said we'd wait for him. Nobody was very chatty, but the man did ask where my grandparents lived. I told him, and he shook his head and chuckled. You boys run a long way. After some silence, I asked if they'd like us to wait outside. No, he said, you better wait in here.

A while later, Papa pulled up with Mom. We thanked the family for their trouble and got in the back, most apologetically. Papa, who didn't speak often, spoke:

> "You two were lucky. There's a lot of bad niggers around here."
> "DAD!"
> "Well, I'm just saying…."
> "Those people were nice to us, Papa."
> "Well, I'm just saying…."

I'm not sure at just what time of year the 1964 Olympics were held, but I believe it was before I returned to LHS for my sophomore year. I followed the track events with considerable identification. The network doing the broadcast hadn't yet fully caught on to the idea that most of the viewing public was more interested in feature stories than athletic competition, so I didn't learn much about Bob Schul's home life or Henry Carr's childhood, but I got to see a lot of sports. Track and field has just about been excluded from wide-audience TV for a long time now, but anyone who thinks that the reason for that is that it's a dull sport to watch should download Billy Mills in the 10,000 or Bob Hayes on the anchor leg of the 4x100 relay in Tokyo, just to see what used to be available on the tube. Of special interest to me was seeing the New Zealander Peter Snell in the 800 and 1500, both of which he won. He was as much my idol in running as anybody, and not just because he was so good. His running form was a lot like mine was becoming, and he ran his better races the same way I ran mine. He had a methodical low-expression style, he kicked in to the finish from a long way out, and when he accelerated he hardly altered his appearance at all: his stride got a bit longer, his tempo a little quicker, it was like the song stayed the same but went from 33 RPM to maybe 35, then 38 as he pulled away. Actually, I ran just like him; he was just in better shape, that's all.

* * *

The new school year started with some new teachers, at least partly for the good. The ones that were new to me were, at the very least, memorable. Pat Moorman taught English, where I was back in the smarter kids' class. Todd Benton presided over math, which I believe was Geometry I. Much to my dismay, Anna Boido had moved on and been replaced by Mr. Longyear for French. Sid Roberts was back at it with World Cultures II, and Dennis Comolli taught the biology class.

Mr. Longyear was new, not just to me, but to the whole school and probably the town. Rumor had it that he was quite experienced as a private school teacher and had mentored the kids of some well-known diplomats and political celebs. He was a pale, delicate wisp of a man, but we all began the year with some trepidation when he informed us sternly that the work load would be very demanding and that after the first month, there would be nothing but French spoken in his classroom. Any French that any of us had spoken had been entirely by rote, so the thought of actually expressing ourselves in the language was sobering. I tried with all my might to pay attention and understand what was being said for those first few days, but then a book slid off Chip Papp's desk onto the floor, provoking a cry of "Ah, SHIT!" from Chip. Everybody froze. Mr. Longyear just kept on saying whatever he was saying. How could this be? He had to have heard it. He just ignored it.

The class's degeneration was incremental at first. Someone might turn around to ask a neighbor for a piece of paper. Someone might get up to sharpen their pencil without asking. A conversation might start up in the back of the class, leading within days to conversations going on all around the room. None of it fazed Mr. Longyear, who continued in his role as instructor despite a diminishing audience, with nary a nod to the distractions breaking out around him. There was an alcove in the back of the classroom with a few tables that had been used by art classes previously. We started seeing kids, cutting other classes, showing up in the room and sitting on those tables in the back, shooting the breeze with other miscreants who'd found the perfect place to hide. Someone threw a paper airplane across the room one day. It was answered by another, then another and another, and there was war.

The airplanes got bigger and more elaborate with time. One day, somebody made one out of poster board from the art closet. It had to be three feet long. Launched from the back of the room, it flew past Mr. Longyear's face, skipped across his desk and skidded to a stop between the feet of Harry S. Merson, the Superintendent of Schools, who was standing in the doorway with his hands on his hips and murder in his eyes. For the first time since the first days of class, the room was quiet. Mr. Longyear looked out across the classroom and shouted, "Who threw that?" Mr. Merson glared at us for a few moments longer, then left without saying a word. His quieting influence was effective but short-lived. Word was all around the school that there was a classroom down in the lower corridor where you could go any time you wanted. You could hang out there, listen to the radio, smoke, play cards, goof around with your friends AND NOTHING WOULD HAPPEN!

There was no homework, or if there was, it was forgotten as soon as it was assigned. There were no quizzes or exams. The majority of the enrolled members of the class, including myself, spent their time in the room getting other classes' homework done or pursuing other quiet activities. A few joined in the uproar, while a few sat in the front and paid attention to Mr. Longyear, who maintained the posture of a classroom instructor and spoke to those who would listen. When the first marking period was at an end, and it was time for the quarter's grades to be given out, he called us up, one by one, to discuss what we felt we had earned. I got an A-minus, as did the majority. The rest got A's, except for Bobby Olenick, who was not in attendance that day and received a C. This was far beyond being a clearly unsustainable situation, yet it went on until Christmas break. It's surprising to me now, and was then, that it continued for so long. The superintendent's office was directly overhead, and the volume in the classroom was that of a crowded cocktail party in its second hour. I imagine it isn't easy to remove a teacher on short notice, or to find a competent replacement.

Throughout this episode, I was well aware that I was in the middle of a bizarre circumstance unlike anything I'd experienced before or would again. And I was not without sympathy for Mr. Longyear, who did not appear to be in the best of health at the beginning of it all, and declined visibly as the weeks passed so discouragingly by. Though I had no burning desire to learn French, and usually tried to make good use of what was essentially free time, this was so clearly a train wreck of a situation that I felt a little dirty being associated with it. There's no question that if every member of the class had from Day One listened carefully, paid attention and studied hard, we would have had a very productive classroom. This is almost true by definition, and it could be that it's commonplace in high-end private schools that only enroll committed students. Well, it wasn't the case here, and wouldn't be in nearly any place that teenagers gather. There wasn't a single member of that class that anyone would consider a troublesome kid, but without authority from the front desk, things started to fall apart, and once the process began there was no stopping it.

After Christmas break, we were introduced to Madame Colton, and there was suddenly no question about who was the authority here. She was French by birth, accent and temperament: outspoken, lively and unrestrained. She was quite short, with wide, piercing eyes that never seemed to blink, her hair in a slightly disarrayed bun and abundant energy in her every move. She was maybe in her late 30's, and just could not have been sexier. Once she established herself as the boss, and determined that we weren't the bunch of rowdies that she no doubt came in suspecting us of being, she laughed a lot and allowed for a certain amount of repartee. I am sure that the kids who were capable of absorbing a lot of French did so under her tutelage, as she was all business when in teaching mode. I was not one of them, though I made enough progress to tell myself I was doing the best I could.

Patricia Moorman, my English teacher, was very much one of a kind. Craggy of feature and lean of build, she had an outsize personality and was the tallest woman, nay, even the tallest person in the school. Her nickname among the kids was Moose. She was close friends, or perhaps shared a home with, a secretarial teacher, Miss Ogden, who was the shortest. Together, they looked like Mutt and Jeff. Like most staff members in the English Department, Miss Moorman had an undisguised love of the language and its greatest classic works. Her personal predilection was for grammar and syntax. We spent quite a bit of time diagramming sentences in her classroom, and if there was within a kid the slightest potential interest in this highly analytic activity, as there was in me, Miss Moorman could kindle it. She could get very animated trying to get across to us the subtleties of a complicated sentence. Between diagramming sentences, grammar and punctuation, I'd guess two-thirds of our class time was spent learning how our language is supposed to be used.

We did read, as well. Much was made of the fact that this was the 400th anniversary of the birth of Shakespeare, and we undertook a thorough study of The Merchant Of Venice, among other works. What really distinguished Miss Moorman's class, aside from the total immersion in grammar, was her readiness to put the lesson aside and expound upon subjects unrelated to our work: prejudice, politics, human foibles, life's ironies. She didn't so much engender discussion as inform us of her views and passions. She did so with vigor, and then it was back to the lesson. She was a tough grader and not very understanding of excuses, but after many years at LHS she still got a kick out of the kids and didn't hide that fact. Like most of our teachers, she had her moments of cluelessness concerning the ways of 15-year-olds. I wonder if there are any teachers left who still instruct a roomful of silly boys that an abrupt exclamation is properly termed an "ejaculation". Not many, I bet. Together with my parents and a few others, she was on the team that left me with a great appreciation for proper, artful use of English, and low tolerance for those who care not to use it correctly. When I'm confronted with a professionally butchered piece of writing, as happens more and more frequently as I age, I can't help thinking or saying, This person just wasn't paying attention in English class. It's Miss Moorman's class I think of then.

For me and a select few other LHS boys, the most exciting feature of the new school year was the outset of the cross country season. We all figured the team would be pretty good, possibly very good. There wasn't much question that Tom Vadala and Ward Rainnie would be our top two runners; they were both among the 1963 team leaders and came into the season in good shape from summer training. Tom was a junior, a hard-working and ambitious guy in everything he did. He had no leg speed at all; in a sprint, he'd have been dead last among everyone on the team and most in the school. But he could take a hit, over and over, and in the endurance sports, that quality is of the essence. He was short, stocky and outrageously competitive. Ward was a senior and one of the bright lights of his class. Tall, handsome, personable and kindly, he started out in cross country as a conditioner for basketball, where he was one of the school's best players, but got hooked on distance running. Or maybe on being on Jim Kalperis's teams, it's hard to say which. For whatever reason, he sandwiched his basketball between the cross country and spring track seasons and was a standout in all of them.

The rest of the team was hard to assess. Ray Costa and Jim McHardie were seniors, returning varsity runners of reliable but not stellar talent. Eddie Santiago was our best JV in '63, now a junior. And then the sophomores. Mark and I had a good summer of running behind us and figured we'd be in the mix. We'd heard over the summer that Geoff Cahoon was working out, often with Vadala, and once practices started it was evident that he was no longer the weakling we'd seen as freshmen. Salt Handy suddenly was keeping up in a lot of the workouts. Kevin McDonald, a freshman, good guy and already a friend to many on the team, was with us. There were a few no-shows who were conspicuous by their absence. Donnie Bumpus, having showed us all up in the middle distance races the previous winter and spring, figured that cross country was a little long for him and not essential to his aims in the track seasons. And Everett Costa and Albert Barrows did not come out for the team. I suspect that as the era of minority-dominated teams faded into the past, they might have felt that this was just not the place for them to be any more. It might have been pointless, but it would have been easy, for me or Mark or somebody to get to those guys and tell them we really wanted to have them and their talents on the team. Doing so might have had no impact, but we'll never know because none of us did it. Not too many 15-year-olds think of these things.

Our first meet of the season was, again, at Old Rochester. I don't know why we ran on their course two years in a row, but it was the setting for my breakout race the year before, so that was fine with me. We didn't hear any talk from the opposing coach about what he'd do if his guys were shut out this time, which is a good thing, since we had nine runners in the varsity race and we all finished before the first OR kid did. Vadala and Rainnie got us off at a decent pace and gradually pulled away, leaving the rest of us running in what amounted to a pack. This was not intentional; any one of us would have happily left the others behind if he could have, but nobody was capable of doing so. I felt pretty strong, but had to stay focused because the pack never broke up or let up. Over the last half mile, there started to be a little spread as the ones with a little more strength left inched away from the wearier. I wound up in third place in 12:12, with the rest of the team all coming across within 15 seconds.

12:12!! an alert reader with cross country experience might say. How long was this course? I don't know, but it was indeed a lot shorter than high school races are now, and that was not unusual. There was considerable debate as to whether participation in strenuous activity, especially an endurance sport, would have harmful long-term effects for the boys who participated in it. There was no question about the girls: bad, bad, bad. When I went in to see Doc Tripp for the perfunctory annual physical at the start of the season, he asked me what sport I'd be in. Told, he scowled and shook his head and warned me, between drags on his cigarette, that if I did too much of this I'd get an oversized heart, and all the future cardiac problems that would come with it. And Doc Tripp was no fool; he was just repeating what a sizable body of the medical world held to be true. So the push to allow kids to run longer distances had many detractors, and the change came gradually. As for the length of the courses we ran, none of them were measured, many were entirely on the grounds of the school, and many of those that got off school grounds were mostly on the road, including our home course. We saw very few imaginative courses and never knew with accuracy how far we'd run.

I didn't consider my effort at OR to be a breakout race, except insofar as I went into it feeling I hadn't yet nailed down my bona fides as one of our leading runners, and here I was beating everybody except the two guys I had no hope of keeping up with. I felt pretty good, worked hard, used it all up, gave no quarter and all that, but the fact is a whole slew of my teammates poured across the line right behind me. To me, a breakthrough race is one where you feel strong and loose, work good and hard without straining for it, really bang on yourself when the pain comes at you, and come in with a result far better than you thought you were capable of. I did have one of those later in the season. New Bedford was one of the largest high schools in the state, and being located in southeastern Massachusetts, a frequent adversary. They had a savvy coach, a Mr. Sherman, and were always in contention for Class

A state titles in the running sports (we were Class D, based on the size of the school). They came to race us on our course late in the season, and there was talk about the importance of this meet for quite some time leading up to it. I was always anxious as race time drew near, and if I felt that my performance was critical, I could get very anxious. On this day, I was a basket case. One of the JV's tried to chat with me a few minutes before the race and I couldn't talk to him. I could barely breathe. He told me later I was pale as a ghost, and he wondered if I was even capable of running. I wasn't too sure myself.

But run I did, and after a little jostling at the start everything was smooth as silk. I had a good rhythm, fluid stride, I was keeping up with some pretty good runners and it was totally anesthetic. One might think, and it crossed my mind in that first mile, that if I was feeling so great maybe I should just blast up to the front of the race and really use it. Ah, but you have to maintain some sense of how much you've got left in the tank, and feeling good here isn't going to do much for me if I find myself with half a mile to go and nothing left to work with. So I pressed the pace but didn't force it, kept creeping up through the field and tried to stay on that aerobic edge, where I was using what I had but keeping enough in reserve to see me through to the end. With about 3/4 mile to go, I was heading down a straightaway on Gifford Street towards the coach's van, which was parked at the last checkpoint to observe the race before shooting back to the finish line as we looped around via Dillingham Avenue. I was right behind Ward Rainnie, who I had no business staying with based on all past performance, but there I was. And yet, as we neared the van, I heard everyone cheering for Ward and Ward alone. Here I was, running the best race of my life, and all I heard was Come on, Ward! This was no place to be proud, but I figured I'd give them something to cheer for, so I swung past Ward and started after the next NB guy, Tony Esteves. And everyone shouted like mad. They hadn't seen me! Ward was a big guy, and I was tight behind him, and they didn't know I was there. Now Bobby Olenick was doing windmills in the middle of the street and Kalpy was screeching and other JV's were cheering and I guess I let them know who was on his game today.

Of course, the reckoning came. I caught up to Esteves, but he responded and I didn't have it in me to match him. I still felt strong, but I was locking up and getting low on air. Just as we started up the last little hill before the finish line, Ward went steaming past me. I just had the breath to say Go get him Ward, and he did. Vadala won the race in a new course record, then came two NB kids, then Ward, then Esteves, then me. A lot of highly-ranked runners from strong teams had raced on that course in recent years, and the course record as of that morning was 13:43. I ran 13:53, was followed by a number of teammates who set personal records that day, and we tied New Bedford, 28-28. This was a big one. We went up against a championship team from Class A with all their horses in the race, and we were equal to them.

All of this was a lot more engrossing than anything that was happening in some of my classrooms. One particularly moribund class was math (algebra? geometry? What did the college-bound sophomores take in 1965?). The teacher there was not named Mr. Benton, but I'll call him that. He was a one-man argument for the abolition of tenure. His home was just down Lakeview Avenue from LHS, so he could be seen walking up the drive every morning just before opening bell: brisk stride, erect posture, shoulders back, chin up, arms swinging freely, hands empty. Similarly unburdened, he strode off in the afternoon as the final echoes of the last bell faded. His pedagogic style was strictly hands-off. On his blackboard were written the chapter and section in the textbook that was to be mastered that day, and the problems at the end of the section that constituted the homework. At the beginning of every class, each student passed his homework to the kid sitting behind him, and that's how the homework got graded. Mr. Benton picked up all the graded homework, then retired to a student desk in the back of the room, where he kept a stack of magazines for his reading pleasure while the class pored over their textbooks.

To my good fortune, most of the material came easily to me, so I was generally able to absorb the assignment and get the homework done in class. Early in the year, I came across something that wasn't clear to me, and went to Mr. Benton for help. He took the book from me, held it up with one hand, tapped the cover with the back of his other hand and said, "It's all in there, boy. It's all in there". From time to time, he stood before the class to talk about something of interest to himself. Occasionally, he touched upon his minimalist teaching style. One time: "Does a bricklayer bring his bricks home with him? Of course not! So why should I bring the tools of my trade home with me?" At this point, my wiseass inclination got the better of me: "Mr. Benton, maybe you should have been a bricklayer!" I got a stern look from him for that, but there was never any fear of being kept after school by him. He was always the first one out the door.

My biology teacher was Dennis Comolli, who compensated for coming up a little short in the charisma department with kindliness and good humor. It wasn't hard to get him sidetracked from the subject, especially by entering in on a discussion of sports, but he knew what he was supposed to be doing and he stayed on task pretty well. I was a grateful receiver of his generosity of spirit one day when we were taking a test. I knew I wasn't at all prepared for the exam, so I did something I almost never did: I cheated. I wrote down on a crib sheet some of the terms and definitions I'd failed to memorize, put it on my seat, sat down on it and peered down between my thighs when I needed an answer I knew would be there. At one point, I looked up and Mr. Comolli was staring right at me. Gulp. Just before the end of class, he walked around and planted himself behind me. The buzzer sounded, everybody got up and I had to too. So I swiped that crib sheet off the chair, stuck it into my stack of books and tried to act like nothing was wrong. He never said a thing. He could have nailed me and felt very righteous about it. Or, if he wanted me never to even think about cheating on one of his tests again, he could do just what he did. Thanks, Mr. Comolli, it worked.

World Cultures II was very, very much like World Cultures I. Go back to the tales of my freshman year for a description of the course, the book, the atmosphere in the classroom and the teacher, Mr. Roberts. I did my part to liven things up in there one day. Our desks were basically a frame of chrome-plated steel piping with a solid wood top hooked to it, and a sculpted plywood seat. The top was about an inch thick and spacious. There was a section of the frame a few inches off the floor that served as a footrest. With the feet on it, there were a few inches of clearance between the knees and the bottom of the desktop. In an effort to build up my calves and Achilles tendons and to survive the boredom of the class, I often stuck a few books on my knees so they'd press against the desktop. Now I was ready to perform some of Mr. Maguire's isotonics. I could push just as hard as I wanted with my legs, and except for a few soft grunts out of me, there was no way for anyone to know I was doing it. So I did it a lot. Well, eventually, my poor old desktop couldn't take any more of this, and when it broke, it broke with a CRACK that elicited screams from half of the dozing class. It truly sounded like the report of a rifle. With all those pounds per square inch suddenly released, my books went flying through the air and landed a couple of rows away. Mr. Roberts was probably the only person in the class who wasn't holding his hand to his heart in the aftermath. His gaze rolled over to me and he asked if everything was okay. I told him yes, but for some reason my desktop just broke in two. Well, go sit in another one, he said.

Aside from my masterpiece in the New Bedford meet, I had no other supreme efforts during the cross-country season. On a good day, I was third man on the team; on a bad day, sixth or seventh. We were a well-balanced team that pushed each other pretty hard and could give anybody a race, but we didn't quite have the talent to make it to the top tier. Geoff Cahoon and I were at a similar level of achievement. With the both of us being blond, and thin, and sophomores, and becoming good friends, we were starting to find ourselves being associated with each other by our teammates and by opponents who we saw with any frequency. We shared an embarrassing episode at the league meet at the Bristol Agricultural school near the end of the season. There were two divisions, both with varsity and JV teams, so four races in all. We saw that we had plenty of time before our race was called, so we wandered away from the starting area to check out the school's livestock. We were walking around the pens of sheep and goats when we saw a race lining up in the distance. We got a little closer to see the start, then realized that our teammates were standing there waving at us. We raced a few hundred yards to get to the line, and the gun went off just as we got there. So we ran the race in sweatsuits and basketball sneakers and did pretty badly. Our team, being in the small school division, won anyway, but you never want to perform poorly for whatever reason. It was the first time I got caught being mistaken about a race's start time, and I wish it had been the last.

I finished up the season pretty well in the Class D state meet at Franklin Park in Boston. I finished 34th, which sounds like it's a ways back, but this is the state meet, and everybody who's any good is there. I felt loose and strong and came in as our third man, just ahead of Jim McHardie. What was disconcerting was that when I was moving through the chute, which is where the officials send you as soon as you finish so that you keep your place, I saw Tom Vadala crawling on his hands and knees just a few places ahead of me. You'd expect to see Tom among the leaders. He had a rare ability to push himself right to his limit and stay there without breaking down, but once in a while he took on a little too much, and he did on this day. His guts got so low on air that they locked up on him, so there he was on all fours with the dry heaves just ahead of me in the chute. Still and all, we finished third out of about 35 teams, but not close to first.

One happy development of the season was the degree of commitment and sense of unity that was developing among the underclassmen, meaning the sophomores plus Kevin McDonald. Nobody was too surprised that Mark Buguey and I jumped up to varsity status; we were respectably talented as freshmen, trained steady over the summer and went at team workouts in earnest. Geoff Cahoon came along quicker than one would have thought, given that he was a ways behind the previous year and didn't always seem to take running or anything else as seriously as high achievement requires. We weren't far into this season before it became evident that he was serious about his running. Kevin had jumped in on some JV workouts when he was in 8th grade, so we knew he'd be competitive and a good guy to have on the team. One sophomore classmate seemed to be materializing out of nowhere. That was Arlton Handy.

Arlton's nickname, "Salty", was bestowed upon him inadvertently by me when we were in the fifth grade. Shortly after school let out one day, I was among a bunch of kids walking up Shore Street on the way home. Arlton was on the opposite sidewalk and the Wesslings' dog was trotting alongside him. I heard a couple of kids shouting "Salty! Hey, Salty!" in the direction of that kid who I recognized from my class, so I figured that was his name, so that was what I called him from then on. By the time I realized I was mistaken - Salty was the dog – the name had taken hold all over, and Arlton Handy was universally known as Salty for the rest of his days in Falmouth.

Though I hold fast here to my vow to report my recollections with neither burnish nor embellishment, I can't help but suspect that certain parts of my history take on a different look when they continue to reveal themselves at later times. Any insights into Salt Handy that I express here have been subject to the influence of subsequent events, as Salt and I have crossed paths periodically throughout our lives. As a runner at LHS, I don't think he ever got the credit or the appreciation from his teammates that his performance warranted. Some of that may have been because he started out a little later than the rest of us, and came along a little more slowly, so we got it into our heads that Salt was doing pretty well, but he wasn't as good as us. Once people get something into their heads, it's awfully hard to chase it out. It was also in Salt's nature to be somewhat more the observer than the participant, and I'm drawing very fine lines here, but he had a highly analytic view of the world that bordered on the esoteric and suggested that he was standing off just a bit, that he wasn't all in. What do you have to do to convince your teammates that you're all in? Well, for one thing, you have to work as they do and compete as they do, and Salt did that. The other thing you have to do is give them the impression that you're all in, and that he didn't do.

This perceived lack of commitment can be a real drawback in the team sports, especially if the coach shares in the perception. Most coaches at all levels are, by definition, average, and the average coach makes his task easier by drawing conclusions about his athletes quickly, and usually irrevocably. I encountered this in my own experiences with youth sports, have seen it repeated in those of my children, have discussed it before and probably will again. One of the wholesome features of the running sports is that the stopwatch tells no lies; if someone gets to the finish line before somebody else, there's really no way to skew the result to fit neatly with one's preconceptions of the individuals involved. It's undeniable that the one who gets there first is the faster runner. As the season progressed, Salt kept getting there a little bit sooner, and we who thought ourselves to be more accomplished noticed that we didn't have to look too far over our shoulders in our workouts to see Salt chasing us. He was without doubt a junior varsity runner, but by the end of the season he was a very good one.

Halloween came shortly before the season ended, and I was not yet finished with Halloween. I was beyond wearing a costume and trick-or-treating, but the evening still provided an excuse to get out of the house and roam around the streets in the dark. I met up on Shore Street with Wayne Copeland, who was a stocky little guy a year behind me who I knew from baseball and the beach and who was fun to be with. We ran into a couple of girls from his class who I knew vaguely, one of whom was named Brenda. The four of us strolled around a while, gradually separating into two pairs, Brenda with me. She was nice-looking and had a lot to say and I felt comfortable with her in a way I hadn't with a girl before. This was nice. We held hands and I gallantly walked her home when it started getting late.

What next? I had no idea, and I wasn't in the habit of asking anybody for advice about anything. I had enough wit to know that this is the sort of thing that a relationship can begin with, but not enough to know how to develop it. I did start calling her at night on a frequent basis. I could handle that; if I said something dumb or acted weird in some way, nobody would see it or know it. Fear of being regarded as uncool or clueless was a chronic paralyzing force in my life, and not at all a good attitude to take into a friendship, especially if there was a possibility of romance in it. Worse yet, I was pretty sure that nobody else was as self-conscious as I, which lent to my view of myself as abnormal and led me to assume that no self-respecting girl would want to have much to do with me. Poor Brenda. Where she might have thought that our Halloween surprise was a good start, she couldn't know that it represented the very outer limit of my comfort zone at the time.

There was a semi-formal dance for the freshmen and sophomores coming up in a few weeks, and by semi-formal I don't mean tie and sport jacket, I mean gowns for the girls and suits for the boys. Who plans these things? How many boys have a suit hanging in their closet? Not I, that's for sure, but it hadn't been that long since I'd attended a dance or two and had a decent time, so I invited Brenda, she said yes, and I told my parents I needed a suit, and they said okay. Mom brought me to Issokson's, the only menswear store in town, where I got fitted up for a costly set of duds and started feeling that I was headed into something for which I was unprepared and with which I could not connect. There were few enough sets of circumstances where I felt I could comfortably be myself, and this was clearly not going to be one of them.

But the big night came, Dad dropped Brenda and me off at the gym, and I bombed. I probably danced a few times, since that was the excuse for the whole wretched affair, but I found myself unable to connect with anybody or anything there. I would hope, these many years later, that I didn't appear to be as uptight and alienated as I felt, but I probably did. I was too old to put on a demeanor of silliness, not mature enough to be suave (the common term then for how the cool kids acted), too short on self-confidence to go with the flow in any way. None of this had anything to do with Brenda, who realized she was out with a stiff for the evening but was very patient about it. To top it off, we were invited to a party at a mutual friend's house afterwards where there was a chance that I might find some kind of groove, but I declined. I just wanted to get the hell out of that scene and put it as far behind me as I could, as soon as I could. What a lousy date I was.

One unfortunate corollary of putting my social disaster behind me was that I locked myself into making sure that it wouldn't happen again. The surest way to avoid similar failure and embarrassment was to keep out of situations where I might experience them anew. That meant a self-imposed ban on social gatherings that I adhered to for a good deal of the rest of my time in high school. In school, I was okay, enjoyed the comraderie of many kids of both genders; no problems with running into friends doing homework at the library; chance group encounters on the street or anywhere else were fine with me. But when it came to any events that existed for the sake of socializing, I counted myself out rather than deal with the fear of not knowing how to act. Of course, those are the very events where most kids have a good time, and I did miss out on a lot of good times. But I must have felt it was worth it to keep myself protected. I say "must have" because there was certainly nothing calculated or remotely deliberate about this. Assuming a position of avoidance of potentially uncomfortable situations seldom has a rational basis or is recognized with any clarity by the avoider.

If there was any upside to my withdrawal from extracurricular society, it could be that I threw myself ever more earnestly into my progress as a runner, that being the activity that seemed to be working well for me and that I could influence. I asked for and received a set of Sears barbells for Christmas, with which I hoped to build up some of the body parts that go into running but don't get strengthened much by running only. I set them up in the storage room in the basement that was to serve as our fallout shelter. I kept a log of which exercises I was doing, how much weight, how many repetitions. Who knows if it made any difference? It didn't add appreciably to my dimensions or the definition of my muscles, but a look at my log confirmed that with time, I was able to lift greater weight more times than when I started, so I felt I was getting somewhere.

The aim, of course, was to become a faster runner. I was beginning to find that almost no matter how much of a workout we put in after school, I was fully recovered by evening. I was still sore, of course – that never went away – but I no longer felt tired out or weakened a few hours after getting home. Kalpy was considerate enough of his team not to talk a whole lot about the star runners he'd had a couple of years before we came along, but when he did, he related how Jimmy Barrows would rap on the Sharpe brothers' window before daybreak to get them out to run the roads of East Falmouth. How often Jimmy did this I can't say, but the idea was planted in my head and had a certain appeal. It was the time of day that got me; I just couldn't, and never did, get excited about arising early enough to get a workout in before breakfast. But there were the evenings. I wasn't usually burdened with a lot of homework and there weren't many TV shows I cared to watch, so I could find the time then. I didn't get regular about it at first, and I didn't go very far. The loop of 287 to Queen Street to King Street to Clinton Avenue to 287 wasn't hard to handle, and as I regarded it simply as extra credit, I didn't get out there often at first. But it was the start of a unique, richly rewarding facet of my life.

* * *

We at the Turkingtons' observed the Thanksgiving and Christmas holidays in traditional but characteristically low-key manner. Our closest relatives, meaning my parents' siblings and their families, most conveniently all lived in Winchester, a suburb of Boston about two hours north of us. They were the Sunesons: Mom's younger sister Ginny, her husband Roy, and children Neil (one year behind me), John (two) and Karen (four). And the Hopkinses: Dad's older sister Bee (short for Lysbeth), her husband Bill, and children David (about eight years ahead of me), Jon (six), Kit (Three) and Libby (a year behind). There's some guesswork in that age business. The Sunesons, who lived in New Jersey when I was younger but moved to Winchester later, inhabited a nicely appointed ranch house in a hillside subdivision that screamed Postwar Development. The Hopkinses lived on a narrow little street of handsome Victorian homes just outside the center of town. When holiday festivities brought us to Winchester to commune with the relations, we divvied our time up between the two families and quickly grew accustomed to the scenery between the two homes, though I couldn't negotiate the drive now.

Nobody ever would have asked me, but if someone had, I don't think I could have given a clear answer to which family I most enjoyed visiting. The Sunesons were very much of slightly-upper-middle-class contemporary tastes and sensibilities. They were open, gregarious and casual. Neil and John were lively and unrestrained; Karen less so, as her lot as the youngest kid and only girl left her a bit of an outsider. She did the same things we boys did, but wasn't One Of Us. We all moved among the older folks, which included Mom's parents, but spent a lot of our time there playing outside or hanging out in the basement or the boys' room, depending on the weather, sledding conditions and time of day. Uncle Roy was a businessman of some kind, soft-spoken, amusing and to my eyes patient and tolerant of the antics of the kids. Aunt Ginny was a homemaker by trade, which was pretty much the norm in Falmouth and probably more so in Winchester. She'd gone to Oberlin and was clearly very smart, but seemed to have fully embraced the role of housewife and its accompanying concerns with appliances, housekeeping aids, her kids' activities and such. She was easily amused and, like her sister, expressed herself unrestrainedly with voice and gesture, and smoked a lot.

A change was evident in Mom when she found herself in the bosom of the family she grew up with, especially when not on her own turf. As patient as she was with practically everyone she met, as tolerant and understanding as she was of their personality quirks or cuckoo ideas, that is just how impatient and intolerant she was of her sister and mother. Her father didn't say much, so he didn't really enter in on this. But Mom was very quick to challenge Ginny's reasoning or Grandma's knowledge of the facts, or their memories, or their logic, even if the subject at hand was innocently bland, which it usually was. Her confrontational stance was never so harsh as to cause resentment or escalate into ill will, but it was definitely there, and it was the only time I ever saw it. This was my first look at a phenomenon that became clearer to me as I grew into adulthood. The dynamics that get shaped among people spending their formative years in close quarters with each other (read: families) can be difficult to alter in later years, though the circumstances that led to the creation of those dynamics are long in the past and possibly forgotten. Everybody knows they could use a fresh start, but nobody knows where to begin or wants to take the first step, so they just forge ahead with what they're accustomed to.

The Hopkinses were somewhat of a breed apart from any family I'd ever been familiar with. They were of refined but subdued tastes, wry humor and a restrained worldliness that always left me feeling that they were in some important way superior to me, if for no other reason than that they would never say or think they were. I believe they were pretty well off; it was hard to tell, because if they were, they didn't exhibit it in obvious ways. The kids were all well-behaved, bright, talented, motivated (Yale, Dartmouth, Yale, Mt. Holyoke), and ever ready to engage their bumpkin cousins from the Cape. Uncle Bill was a major operative in the White Fuel Company, which once had an immense neon sign depicting a gushing oil well visible from the grandstand at Fenway Park. For a while before we smartened up, Eric and I thought that Uncle Bill owned some oil wells, which assigned to him a mystique that he never quite lost. He was one of very few men to sport a mustache in those conformist times. He was tall, quick-witted and musical, as were his progeny. Aside from one time when he showed me the shop where he enjoyed working on old pendulum clocks, I don't think I ever had a one-on-one conversation with him. I had many with Aunt Bee, who was kindly, gracious, and always deeply curious about whatever her nephews were thinking and doing.

The first time I ever saw those itty-bitty Christmas lights that kept on lighting after one on the string had burned out was on the Hopkinses' tree. The first time I saw a Frisbee was when the Hopkinses brought one with them on a visit to Falmouth. There was a tiny little half-bath partway up the stairs to the second floor in their house. There was a little room apart from the home's mainstream to which the TV was consigned. The TV was a little one, and it was built into the wall. Very cool. If there was a football game being broadcast after whatever feast we were there for, we'd crowd into that little room to watch it for a while. Not many people were onto this yet, which was part of the pleasure. When we ate there, it would be turkey (Thanksgiving) or roast beef (Christmas). Bill stood at the end of the table and carved, while the plates went around getting loaded up with all the side dishes. When we all had a full plate before us, we took our first bite. I got a useful lesson in patience, and manners, from this. The kids got a small glass of wine with their dinner.

Though we very often devoted most of our Christmas Day to getting to Winchester and back, we observed many of the basic secular Christmas rituals. We bought a tree every year and took an evening to set it up and trim it out. At one time, we had several exquisite glass ornaments from Grandma's German heritage, but Jingles had a stiff tail and every now and then she'd wag it by the tree and break one of them. One of the reasons I was so impressed by the Hopkinses' tree lights was that we still had the big screw-in ones that caused the whole string to go out when one burned out. To get it going again, someone had to get a fresh bulb and replace them one by one until the string lit up again. For some years, I gladly shouldered that duty, but by my teens I let the lights burn out if they wanted to burn out. And why not? What did they have to do with me? Those bulbs burned hot, too. Every day, the tree got drier and the risk of fire greater, but we blithely went along admiring the pretty lights and avoiding tragedy by good fortune alone.

By Christmas Eve, we generally had a pretty good bunch of gifts strewn around under the tree. Many of them were books, but many were not, especially those for Mom, who denied herself little frivolities most of the time but was happy to receive them on Christmas, and happier still to have to unwrap a package to get to them. She LOVED opening presents. Every Christmas Eve, she proposed that we all open one gift, just as an appetizer. And we did. Then she reminded us we were leaving for Winchester the next morning, so we'd better open another. Soon we were saying, well no, but you go ahead. And she did. Mom knew how to be happy, but I don't think I ever saw her happier than when she was opening presents on Christmas Eve.

Winter track got under way early in December. Kalpy let me know at the outset that he had me figured as our principal miler. Vadala and McHardie were going to be in the two mile, Cahoon and Bumpus in the 600 and 1000, Ray Costa wherever he was needed, and Rainnie was playing basketball. That left me in the mile. What a grave responsibility, but I was feeling pretty well-conditioned and thought I'd be up for it. There were hardly any indoor track facilities available to high school runners anywhere, so we competed in some very peculiar venues. The Huntington Avenue YMCA had a big-time high school meet over the holidays. The track was shaped like a slightly ovate soup bowl, suspended by cables high above the gymnasium floor. It was some odd distance, like 12 3/4 laps to the mile. The railing against the inside lane was hip-high, so as you raced you had to avoid getting pushed, because it was a long way down to the floor. I felt pretty good in my race and almost broke 5 minutes even though the track wasn't conducive to fast times. We were in another big meet in the Fargo Building in South Boston, which I believe was an armory. The track there was marked out with masking tape on a flat, polished concrete floor that offered zero traction. I broke 5 minutes by a lot, but then we saw that the top runners were running incredibly fast times, too good to be true. The track was shorter than they said.

My first couple of league dual meets at the New Bedford Voke track brought me in at just over 5 minutes, so I'd established some consistency but was beginning to get irked by this 5-minute barrier. That's really not a very fast time for a high school miler, especially for Falmouth. And we had the big BAA (Boston Athletic Association) meet in Boston Garden coming up soon, and 5 minutes will get you eaten alive there, since everyone you're running against there is his team's #1 man. But I went with high hopes and considerable anxiety, which grew to near-disabling intensity when they clerked us in on the Garden floor and led us out to the track. I wasn't in one of the top-seeded heats, but everyone around me looked fit, strong and older than me. I got lined up in the second row, on the far outside, which meant my seed time was the slowest in the field. At the gun, I tried to move in, but there was no passage and I wound up in last place for the first lap. And the second. And the third, this in an 11-lap race. But I felt that I was moving along pretty well, and after a while I passed a kid. And then another, and another, and before too long there was no one left to pass. I was down on the floor in Boston Garden with thousands of people watching me leading the field in my mile race. I got passed near the end by Richie Stafford of Salem, who later became a friend, but I held on pretty well and kept the rest of the field behind me. 4:45.5.

There were two high school meets conducted in Boston Garden during the winter, not because we needed 13,909 seats to accommodate the fans, but because the track was already set up for a big-time meet later that evening that drew in many of the top athletes in the world. So we got to compete there in the BAA meet in mid-January and then the state meet two weeks later. A lot of the country's big arenas had the capacity to stage an indoor track meet. All it took was a whole lot of sections of wooden frame covered with a running surface of pine boards, requisite hardware for fastening them together into a banked, 160-yard oval, a place in the building to store it all, enough manpower to haul it out onto the ice and bolt it together, and a Saturday when the professional basketball and hockey teams were on the road. It wasn't a great running surface in the Garden – the boards bounced a lot, the sections weren't always tight together, and it made a racket besides – but it was as good as it got and it sure beat hell out of the YMCA or the Fargo Building. Just the trip up to downtown Boston was reason enough to go. To attend a signature event in our chosen sport in that shrine to big-time athletics was a grand experience. Getting the chance to compete there was a privilege, and I think we knew it at the time. The only downside was that the place was full of smoke, as thick as it got in the Turkingtons' living room except here you had to breathe intensely hard. You could drink all the water you wanted afterwards, but you'd still be coughing hours later.

My state meet effort was a tough one. I thought I might have a chance to place in the top five, but as soon as the race got started I knew this one was going to be hard work. Nothing was flowing, my feet felt hot and heavy, I had no spring and every stride was a conscious effort. But I kept my head in it, and towards the end of the race I found myself close behind a tall guy who was running in a shirt! I mean a collared, button-up, full-length dress shirt the likes of which can be worn with a tie and jacket. The rules governing proper uniform must have been pretty lax then, because they wouldn't let him on the track today. But I passed him on the last lap and crossed the line figuring, well I made the best out of a lousy day, and at least I caught that guy in the shirt.

I cooled off a bit and went up into the stands where the team was, and got a nice greeting: Nice going Turk, you got fifth place! What? Yeah, we got you in fifth place in 4:48! Hmmm, not so bad after all. So Donny and Geoff and Mark went with me down to the scorer's table to pick up my medal, where I was told it'd been picked up already. Huh? There must be some mistake. (Are there any words in the English language more promising of crushed expectations than those?) They showed me the official results: 5th place, Barber, Masconomet High School, 4:50.2. Some mistake, indeed. The fifth place judge missed me, that's what happened. I think that's the last time I cried in disappointment. You could say it should be enough just to know that I did it, but no, that's not enough. When it isn't recorded in the official results, its degree of actuality is severely diminished.

As a team, we didn't score near the top in our Division (Class D, assigned according to the size of the school). Dartmouth High won it. We had a very good dual meet team, because we had pretty good competitors in every event. We'd beat you with our numbers. But in the big meets, it's the stars who rack up the points, and we didn't have many. Bruce Mogardo could keep up with the best in the shot put, Greg Anderson in the 300, maybe Philip Rabesa in the dash, but otherwise we were second-tier. But we were coming along. Kalpy had a tidy stack of state titles in his back pocket already, and I know at this point he was saying, We're a year away.

The younger guys on the team believed him, set our sights and did our work accordingly.

Now, about Kalpy. Properly, James T. Kalperis. The fact that the name commonly used to refer to him and the one used to address him were one and the same is more telling than you might think because I don't believe that could be said of any other teacher or coach in those times. Some new kids, including myself at one time, might call him Mr. Kalperis, and there were a few ass-kissers who'd call him Coach, but to everyone else he was Kalpy. He bore considerable resemblance to Groucho Marx, from the hustling gait, bent slightly at the waist, to the mischievous dancing eyebrows to the ever-present cigar to the offhand commentary from the corner of the mouth to the vague but usually accurate sense you got when he talked to you, that you were being conned, you knew not how. He was an operator who saw more clearly than most that if everybody follows all the rules to the letter all the time, nothing worthwhile will ever happen. Kalpy was all about getting worthwhile things to happen by greasing the wheels of progress. Some years later, he was elevated to the role of assistant principal in charge of activities, an assignment that played to his special talents. It is often in the furtherance of student activities that bureaucracy, protocol or regulation stand in the way of initiative. Kalpy could find a way to get around the roadblocks.

Of course, he was not all things to all people. There were those who felt he came up a mite short in the teaching of science, which was his primary job description. He was probably an energetic, knowledgeable instructor, but he could be distracted with ease. Many is the time that I'd wander off from a study hall or a lunch break or another class with a teammate or two to drop in on Kalpy. Seeing us at the door, he would assign someone to monitor the class while we all went into the adjoining audio-visual storage room to screw spikes into racing shoes or discuss the day's workout or plot strategy for the Dartmouth meet. There was a rare, enlivening mix of humor, gravity and intensity of purpose in dealing with Kalpy and participating on his teams. He became a coach of runners a year after the LHS cross country program was successfully begun under Don Joslin, who moved on after that inaugural 1960 season. The team then was made up largely of underprivileged black kids who so often went through four years of high school without ever tasting success in a school-related endeavor. The principal, Mr. Marshall, wanted to see the program continue after Joslin left, and presciently recognized Kalpy as a good man to take it over, so he asked him if he would, and he did. Kalpy knew nothing about distance running when he took over the cross country team, and nothing about track events when he subsequently took over the track teams, but he started winning state titles right away.

As a coach, he did not take an authoritarian stance, to put it mildly. I don't believe he ever took attendance. Why bother? Attendance was not required. He never said you had to be there; he established an atmosphere that made you want to be there. He never made his athletes do the work; he made them want to do the work. What a difference. It wasn't possible to rebel against the requirements of team membership or the demands of the coach, because there weren't any. If a kid had the wish and the work ethic to want to be good at what he did, Kalpy was there to help him however he could. If it should prove annoying to an 8th-grade basketball player that Kalpy was in the gym at night working with his best high jumper, so be it. He gave people a whole lot of leeway and encouraged an atmosphere in which every kid felt he could be himself and achieve respect for it, first from the coach, and by extension from his teammates. He was a master at reading an individual and figuring out what he was in it for, and this applied to the adult world as well as the track team. He aimed for the heart, and his aim was true. That's what it takes to grease the wheels. In later years, when he was dealing with a broader spectrum than sports, people often came to him asking for something. His first inclination was to see to it that they got it. If that couldn't be done, he'd try to persuade them that they really didn't want it. If that failed, he'd convince them that they already had it! It didn't often need to go further than that.

I got home from practice on April 15 and took to shooting baskets in the driveway. I was aware of the significance of that date for the college-bound seniors, as there'd been some anticipation discussed at the dinner table. Somehow, all the selective colleges were able to time the mailing of their admissions decisions so that all the applicants in the country got their decisions in the mail on that day, and not a day sooner or later. Mom came out to tell me that Eric was not delighted with the news. He had applied to a modest number of very hoity-toity schools, but got the fat envelope from only one, that being the University of Pennsylvania. No slouch of a school, Penn. But Eric's grades were near the top of his class, he was a National Merit finalist and class president, he'd shown every sign of having imagination and leadership qualities, and he'd hoped for a little more show of enthusiasm from the various admissions offices. When he pulled into the drive in the Volkswagen a little later, I tried with some awkwardness to congratulate him on his success with Penn, which he accepted with little expression. It was not common with me to care about someone else's feelings, nor to make an effort to salve the ones that hurt. This time, at least, I knew this was not about me.

Shooting baskets in the driveway had for some time been my default activity when there was not much else to do, ever since I'd reached an age where I needed to have some sense of purpose in killing time. It probably started out being an effort to make myself a better basketball player, but that aim was largely behind me now and I was still doing it. The setup, installed by Dad at the lower edge of the garage roof, was pretty well executed for a man without carpentry skills or power tools. I have both, and have done it a couple of times, and it's not a snap job. The backboard at 287 was decent-sized and fairly rigid; the rim was substantial, firmly fastened and stayed that way for a long time. Good work, Dad, sorry I took till now to tell you so. The floor surface left something to be desired, as it was a gravel driveway onto which Dad tossed a load of clamshells as a binder when he had them. So there were a couple of ruts where the car's tires always went, and then there was lumpy grass on the right side, and six months of the year the Swash was up on blocks preventing any long attempts. But late in the afternoon, it was either shoot baskets or watch Bullwinkle or Soupy Sales, which offered an even lesser degree of self-improvement.

I mention the Volkswagen. A lot of kids of driving age had cars, and most of them acquired them in one of two ways: they withdrew from practically all extracurricular activities so they could get a job to pay for the car, or they had well-to-do parents who bought them a car. There were a few, and Eric was one, whose parents didn't have a lot to spare but recognized that their kid really needed a car so they bought one, though not a costly one. This Volkswagen was not costly, or spiffy in any way. It was a pale blue 1957 model, at a time when no motor vehicles could reasonably be expected to last eight years or 80,000 miles without major repairs. It got Eric around reliably through his senior year and into the summer, when he and Ray Rodriguez were coming back from Boston on Route 3, caught a gust of wind, flipped the car and wrecked it. I found out about this when I came into the house to find Eric and Ray and my parents sitting in the living room. Mom and Dad didn't seem to be angry or even very unhappy about this turn of events, which surprised me at the time, though I understand now what was on their minds: the car is totaled, but my son isn't hurt. I know exactly how they felt. Exactly.

Spring track started towards the middle of March, a time on the Cape when it's usually cloudy, often cold and drizzly, and almost always very windy. I have two distinct images of spring track. Early in the season: bad. Late in the season: good. I didn't compete in the first few races because I got a C+ in biology and Mom and Dad wouldn't let me race until Mr. Comolli assured them that my work had improved. This was the only time that my parents applied the carrot-and-stick approach to my activities. I can't fault them now and didn't then; I really was slacking off in that course. So I missed the first few meets, but once I was back I felt generally pretty good and seemed to run a 4:48 every time in the mile. Good conditions, 4:48. Bad conditions, 4:48. Felt good, 4:48. Didn't feel so good, 4:48. I again ran the leadoff leg in the 2-mile relay at the Belmont Relays, my breakout race the year before, this time in 2:08 and didn't feel very happy with it. The D-Y Invitational had a freshman-sophomore division, where I won the mile in 4:46.7, and that one pleased me, if only because it broke the 4:48 routine.

The state Class D meet was held at White stadium in the Roxbury section of Boston. There was a golf course adjacent to the stadium where the state cross-country championships were run in the fall, and the Franklin Park Zoo was right nearby. Over the years, I got to know that little corner of the city pretty well. White Stadium was where I'd so ill-advisedly and incompetently raced in the 120-yard high hurdles the year before. Now I was a full-fledged miler who had some idea of what this was about and, consequently, grew terribly uptight as race time neared. Feeling that I really didn't belong near the back of the pack, I was determined to run with the crowd from the start, and I did. There was a sizable lead bunch of 8 or 10 runners that didn't break up until the second half, and only gradually then. I hung onto that bunch and thought when heading into the last lap that with a decent kick I could get a scoring position, but I never found it. I kept moving well and came in at 4:40, but I just wasn't strong enough to run any faster. I finished seventh, and considering that I'd knocked several seconds off my best time I was content with that. I was also content with knowing that Ed Rossi was somewhere behind me. Among the other sophomores, Geoff and Donnie both ran the 880 in the neighborhood of 2:05, well off the lead pace but not far out of the scoring. Greg Anderson placed in the long jump and the 220. Earlier in the season, there were some freshmen who were making noise in a number of events, though they weren't state meet material yet. As already noted by Kalpy, we were a year away.

* * *

The womenfolk at the Hopkins home: Bee, Libby, Mom and Nano

And the menfolk: Dad, Grandpa, Kit, Uncle Bill, me, Jon and Eric

Mom and Papa Hedner visit the Webster gardens in Quisset

Old folks: Eric and Margaret Hedner and Mrs. Suneson. Young Sunesons: John, Neil and Karen

I shared the driveway with
the Swash and the Lancer

Uniform shortage for our two-mile relay team: Ray Costa, Tom Vadala and Jim McHardie

Mr. Earl Mills, Physical Education Supervisor.

Earl Mills was chief of school sports and the Wampanoag tribe

We got into road races when we could find them

(Staff Photo by Joe Sherman)

Giving Falmouth some vital points in the mile run yesterday is Tom Turkington (136), who crosses the finish line in 4 minutes, 28 seconds for second place behind Malden Catholic's Tom Dempsey, foreground. Further back is Clipper Arlton Handy, whose 4.32 timing give him fifth place. Both clockings were personal bests for the two Falmouth stars.

Top test-taking talent at LHS: Ken Ketchum, Linda Bennett, Mark Denman

Editors of the school newspaper view the latest in newsprint technology. Pat Ortins was our ace photographer

expected to compete are this year. are not recorded.

TOM TURKINGTON GREG ANDERSON GEOFF CAHOON

V.I.P.'s Head Track Team

The winter captains display some of our team's hardware

Early in a race with Kevin McDonald, Mark Buguey, Victor Almeida and opponents

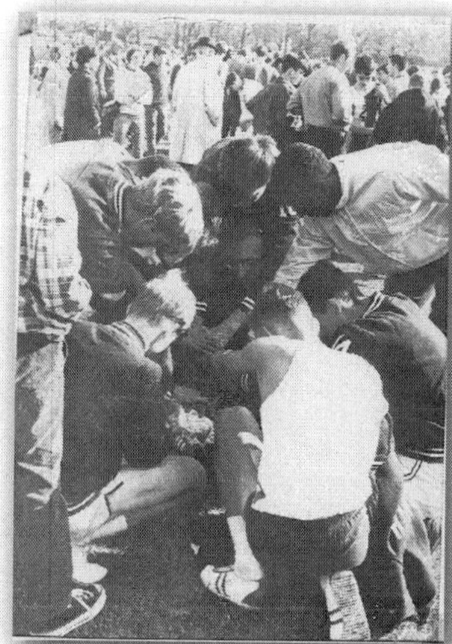

Kalpy shares his thoughts at the '66 state meet

CLASS C CHAMPIONS — Lawrence High cross-country team which added another state championship trophy to their school's collection. From left: Peter Bingham, Don Bumpus, Kevin McDonald, Geoff Cahoon, Arlton Handy, Tom Turkington, Mark Bingham and Coach Kalperis.

Tom Turkington and Arlton Handy often took lead.

Long before there was a Falmouth Road Race, there were Falmouth kids, like Salt and me, running around Nobska Point

I almost didn't get to run in the state meet because of a conflict with my job. Yes, a real job. I was taken on as a busboy at The Pancake Man, a seasonal restaurant located at the traffic-heavy Falmouth Heights corner, where stores and offices and eateries and gas stations were sprouting like weeds. I think I got the job because Kalpy was a friend of Gardner Lewis, who managed and possibly owned the business. The place had just opened for the season and the state meet was on Memorial Day weekend, so we arranged my schedule so I'd be off that day. Trouble is, the meet got postponed a day at the last minute, maybe because of a storm, so it took some special dispensation for me to get the next day off too, but Gardner granted it.

The Pancake Man did a whole lot of business. Eating there wasn't a bad deal; the seating and the atmosphere were a cut above hash-house standard, and the food was pretty good and not too costly. Breakfast was served from 7 till 2, then dinner from 5 to 8. The breakfast menu covered a lot of ground. You could get plain pancakes, or blueberry, strawberry, pineapple, banana, raspberry, blackberry or apple pancakes, and I think I've missed a couple. Waffles. Pigs in blankets (sausages wrapped in pancakes). Silver dollar pancakes. Cheese blintzes. Home fries. Hash browns. Ham, bacon, sausage patties, sausage links, hash. Eggs scrambled or fried. Omelettes, I think. Big servings of all of the above. Several kinds of juice. Cereal. There was usually a waiting line at the door when it opened at 7, and the place was full all day. Full, and hectic up front, bordering on chaos back in the kitchen. Things were a little more mellow for dinner in the evening, but it still crowded up and stayed that way. I'm sure there was more on the menu than grilled steak but that's all that comes to mind. Charlie Haynes worked the grill and kept things from getting too serious.

The job of the busboys was to get those tables turned over as quickly as possible by clearing everything off them and wiping down the tops just as soon as the customers have gotten up to leave, if not sooner. We pushed around carts with three shelves that held large plastic bins for depositing the debris from the tables, which we brought back to the kitchen when full, there to toss the trash in cans and sort the dishes on racks for the dishwashers to deal with. I wanted to do a good job, so I was quite careful and thorough in carrying out my duties, gentle with the dishes, polite and considerate of the customers, far too much so on both counts. There were usually three busboys on duty during the day, one or two at night. The first couple of weeks I was there, I got a strong sense that nobody liked working with me because too much of the work fell on their shoulders. One night I was sweeping the floor long after closing, the place deserted except for me puttering around with the broom and Gardner Lewis doing paper work near the register. As I walked by, he said, "You're going to have to speed up, Tom." What? I pointed out that Mike Childs was on with me that night but had left a long time ago, and that's why I was still there so late. "I told Mike to go home. He'd already done more than half of the cleanup." Gardner was being nice enough about it, but he was letting me know.

Not by conscious decision, but via evolution of my sense of what needed to be done out on the floor, my ways changed. Working alongside Freddie, a husky, somewhat older fellow who came in to bus on madhouse weekend mornings, contributed a lot to my change in perspective. Freddie didn't play it cute with the dishes or with the customers at the next table who might catch a splash or two from his heavy-handed clearing. If there wasn't room to push his cart over to an emptying table, Freddie just picked up his bin and toted it over like a waiter with a tray, holding it up with one hand while loading it with the other. He took no pains to do it discreetly. If a cluster of people stood in his way, he muscled through them: "Watch it, Mac." When he swept up after closing, he didn't pull the chairs out so he could get everything under the table, he just whipped that broom around and made short work of it. His efforts were highly respected by the staff and valued by management, and mine got more and more so as time went on. Dave Trow was a college-age busboy from Revere with parallel streaks of meanness and friendliness. He was my personal bete noire through my early days on the job, but his acknowledgment of my rising status as a co-worker did more than anything else to make me feel at home there.

Landing a summer job wasn't hard for a Falmouth kid. The town was swamped with tourists and summer residents from mid-June through Labor Day, and there was a constant labor shortage. Great numbers of college-aged kids moved in for a summer of independence and high times, but most of them took jobs at the young people's drinking/dancing establishments that were popping up all over, especially in Falmouth Heights. Under-21's who summered there with their families weren't usually interested in spending their vacation time working, so that left lots of service jobs available for Falmouth teens. Probably half of the waitresses at the Pancake Man were girls I knew from school. Boys worked as dishwashers, busboys and cooks.

It wasn't a bad place to work, once you demonstrated some utility. I got paid 85 cents an hour, plus the busboys split 15% of the waitresses' tips. They outnumbered us at least three to one, so I'd get about half what a waitress got in tips, which wasn't bad. It was hard earned. One of the busboys' chores was to take the garbage cans out the back door when they got filled up. To do that, they had to be brought down the rear stairs to a walk-out door. Filled with garbage, they were too heavy to pick up, and the only way to get them to the back door was to drag them down the stairs. The stairs could get very slick with garbage spillage, and the cans could start to slide faster than the hauler could take the stairs. More than once, I lost control of the can, it overturned and left me standing knee-deep in garbage. I always reeked of food waste when I got home, but on those days I smelled really rank.

On days that I worked the early shift, I had time to get to the beach in the late afternoon and get my run in after dinner, sometimes with Mark (who washed dishes at the Pancake Man), sometimes on my own. When I worked the late shift, I tried to run in the morning, but I didn't then and never did grow fond of working out early in the day. Dress code for busboys was white shirt, black pants and leather dress shoes. Many is the time I closed down the Pancake Man and ran home in my busboy outfit by way of Palmer Avenue and Elm Road, for the sake of the mileage, in my dress shoes. It strikes me odd now that I should have been so unconcerned about looking goofy running the streets in full dress when I was so self-conscious about appearing abnormal in any other respect. I was running down Queen Street one night – not in my busboy duds, but in shorts and t-shirt – when a couple of police in a cruiser pulled alongside and queried me:

"Hey fella, where you running to?"
"Um…I'm just running to get in shape. I live right over on Scranton Avenue."

"Get in shape for what?"
"Well, I'm on the track team at Lawrence."
"Oh, you're running track?"
(Hesitation) "Yeah, I'm running track."
(Turns to his partner) "He's just running track! Well, keep it up, kid. A lady called in and said there was a boy running around the streets in his underwear."

I'm pretty sure it was during this summer when "Like A Rolling Stone" got frequent radio play and sold a lot of records. I was somewhat acquainted with a good part of Dylan's portfolio through hearing Eric play his LP's on the hi-fi, and there'd always been certain of his images that struck me, but this was the first time he got hold of me with a complete song. Some of the newfound appeal could have been because backing himself up so artfully with an electric band was more the kind of sound I wanted to hear, but mostly I think I was starting to grow into it. The lyrics didn't have to be completely accessible to me or tied to the topic of teenage yearnings to make their impact. There was also something very independent about releasing a song of such length that the deejays had to play it as two separate releases. It was like playing a joke on Top 40 radio. What really clinched it for me was that one day I was standing outside the Dairy Queen when Donnie Bumpus pulled up in his Rambler with the song playing loud (Donnie, living way out in Waquoit, got his license and a car at the first opportunity). When I went to greet him, he pointed to the radio and said, "Dylan, man, he's really got it."

Donnie came out for the 1965 cross-country season, having seen some of his teammates move past him during our sophomore track seasons and attributing our superior progress to the mileage base we built up during the fall. We all went into this season with some anticipation, in part because he was with us and otherwise because everybody we were counting on had run steadily all summer. It was clear from Day One that Tom Vadala would be holding his place as our front-runner, but Geoff Cahoon and I looked to be not far behind him, with Donnie, Salt Handy, Kevin McDonald and Mark Buguey close behind us. There was a good crop of junior varsity runners assembling, but the top seven, which is the number of runners who go to the line in a varsity race, appeared to be set early in the season and stayed that way.

There were a few complicated dynamics that entered in here at both ends of the team. Vadala just wasn't one of the group in the same way that everybody else was. He was our only senior; he was determined not to let anyone get by him, in practice or in competition; and there was an indefinable touch of earnestness in his approach to the sport that the rest of us did not share. We all got along well, he was not excluded, we counted heavily on him and couldn't do anything but admire his ability to push himself to the max at all times. But he was a separate entity. At the other end of the order, Mark was doing everything he could to be in the middle of the mix, but he wasn't quite getting there. He had some minor but nagging injuries, got sick a couple of times and lost some training time, and surely had many days when he was right there with anybody. But in general, he was a step behind. This hurt us all, because Mark was the psychic soul of the group and his heart was into what we were doing as much as anybody's. And yet, and yet… it wasn't very often that anybody eased up during one of Mark's weaker workouts so that he could keep up. It doesn't work that way, and he wouldn't have wanted us to.

Our competitive schedule was pretty much the same every year. We ran dual meets against the teams in our conference, then in the Catholic Memorial Invitational in Franklin Park towards the middle of October. Then in the all-conference meet a week or two later, then in the State class D meet early in November. Most of the dual meets were pretty easy, but this year Dartmouth was in our division, and we knew they'd be tough. They had the aforementioned Vieira and Rossi, who were juniors now with Jim King, who was a lot like me in that he wasn't supremely talented, but was in killer shape and relentless in a race. They had Jim Hodgson, who was a star half-miler. When they came to run us, I had one of those days that make you wish for a do-over; I went out close behind the leaders, but struggled to do it and lost ground over the second half. Rossi went by me, then King, then a couple of our guys, then Hodgson. Coming up the last hill, I found another gear and flew the last 80 yards, didn't even feel my feet touch the ground, and nipped Hodgson at the line. I'm always scornful of kids who stagger through a race and then come in with a glorious sprint – where was that when we needed it? – but if it's all you have to offer on a given day, it's better than nothing. We won the meet without much help from me.

We had another dual meet a little later that was out of the conference. Randolph was a legendary team from up near Boston. They had never, ever lost a dual meet. They won the New Englands by a wide margin in '64 and were destined to do so again in '65. Art Dulong was either the best runner in the country or very close to it. Mike Burke was Class C champion in the mile, Elliot Stevens in the 880. Jim Hunter was second in the two-mile only because Dulong was first. And there wasn't much dropoff after that; everyone on that team had championship credentials. They came to Falmouth because Kalpy was friends with their coach, John Pistone, and wanted us to race against the best. As we started to warm up, a big shiny charter bus with huge tinted windows pulled up. No school bus for this team. Seven runners and Pistone got out. No scrubs for this race. We met, chatted a bit, everybody warmed up and went to the line, whereupon the Randolph crew blew us away. Vadala kept up with them, but nobody else dared to. They were running too fast. At the 3/4 mile checkpoint, there was a cluster of seven Randolph guys with Vadala hanging on, then a gap of about 80 yards, then the Falmouth team. We weren't even putting up a fight. Kalpy told us later that he'd never been so humiliated by the performance of one of his teams as he was at that moment.

A couple of very important lessons were learned that day, because we won that meet. We beat Randolph, and we beat 'em good. We beat them because we'd decided before the race that the only way to approach this competition was to throw our best race at them and see what happens. Run smart, run hard, just get to the finish line as soon as possible, stop the watch and hope it's good enough. Blowing ourselves out in the first mile wasn't going to do that for us. We also beat them because they fell victim to a phenomenon that holds true in any sport: if you're in the middle of a contest against a worthy opponent and you start thinking you've got it made, you're dead. A worthy opponent will not give up on you, and when they start to challenge you, you're going to have to adjust your attitude, which is a very hard thing to do during a race.

Gradually we gained on them, and a number of man-to-man battles developed. One of my most enduring images from many years in this sport has me racing down Gifford Street brushing elbows with Jim Hunter for what felt like hours, though it couldn't have been more than six or seven minutes. Our intensity of effort was off the charts, constant and unforgettable. Geoff strode past us going down the last hill, Hunter inched away from me going up towards the finish, I passed Mike Small around the corner of the school and we won. Art Dulong told me years later that their season got turned around that day. They came to realize, at Pistone's ardent urging, that the good teams weren't going to give anything away to them just because they were the exalted Randolph team. This was the sort of slap in the face that can chase away the over-confidence of a talented group. You're welcome, Mr. Pistone.

We had another intense dual meet after that, then a complete collapse, then a race that was just good enough. The dual meet was at New Bedford, where our performances were all good to excellent, but so were New Bedford's, and they edged us out in a tight one. I got a little bold that day: about the middle of the second mile, I'd pulled up to within 10 yards of NB's Lloyd Geggatt and Wayne Silveira, who were sharing the lead with Vadala. We were on the trails of Buttonwood Park on a clear, calm day, and I was feeling real good and thinking: If these guys don't speed up, I'm going to win this race. But they did, and I didn't, Geoff caught me near the end, so did John Neenan of NB, and we lost a noble effort.

Our performance a week later at the conference meet was by far our most ignoble effort of the season, and maybe of all time. Dartmouth was the principal competition among eight teams, but we'd beaten them earlier on a so-so day and figured, after our epic battles with the state's iron, we could handle them again with no trouble. We were wrong, oh so wrong. We stunk the place out, all of us, and Dartmouth beat us with ease. We were all there, uninjured and in good health, but running in that race was like one of those nightmares where you have to get someplace fast but just…can't…move…your…legs. Driving us back in the jitney, Kalpy had one of his extremely rare losses of composure. He told us bitterly that he was going to take all of the medals and trophies we'd won all season and send them to Dartmouth. They deserved them, we didn't. He went on for a while about the magnitude of our failure, then the bus lapsed into silence. "Satisfaction" was at the top of the charts about this time, in part because the guitar intro was easy to duplicate orally by clenching the teeth, curling the lips, and squeezing a high-pitched grunt through the nose. Kevin McDonald and Mark Buguey, sitting in the back, roused the somber jitney with a high-volume rendition of that intro, and we all erupted in laughter, Kalpy included. "I can't win with you guys", he said. "Just be ready next week, okay?"

"Next week" meant the state class meets in Franklin Park. Malden Catholic had a front-runner named Tom Dempsey who won practically every race he ran, and as far as we knew, they were the most accomplished rival in Class D. It was hard to scout your opponents back then, because there were so few meets that brought all the best teams together. With about 35 teams and 240 runners in the field, it's hard to gauge your pace or your position as the race develops; that sense of knowing where you are was something I needed, and I often found it hard to locate a comfort zone in the mass races. This one was typical. I went out onto the course in a position that seemed about where I ought to be – a little back of the leaders – but sustaining it was a struggle to which I was not equal. I gave ground grudgingly but constantly over the second half, wondering where my teammates were and fearing we were blowing another one. But with about a mile to go, Donnie and Kevin (!) drew up with me, offered a word of encouragement, and moved on. Just before the finish, Geoff went by. In the end: Vadala 5th, Bumpus 9th, McDonald 12th, Cahoon 16th, Turkington 17th, Handy 20th. Falmouth 59, Malden Catholic 63, nobody else close. State title.

It may by now have begun to seem somewhat dubious, if not tedious, that I can recall and recount so many times, places and scores from obscure cross-country and track meets that I was involved in so many years ago. There are a few reasons for my broad and presumably accurate recall of these meaningless statistics. For one thing, they were not at all meaningless at the time they occurred. They were, in fact, the handiest yardstick available for measuring the degree of progress gained from a great deal of dedicated work in this endeavor by me and my teammates, and therefore of great significance. Throughout this time, I was keeping a log/scrapbook of my performances and those of my team, so I relived them all briefly at the time I noted them in my log, or cut the article out of the newspaper, be it the Enterprise, the Cape Cod Times or the Boston Globe or Herald.

Another aide-memoire was that I wrote up many of the articles that went into the Enterprise. Dad had no objection to performing that duty and he often did, but if I wanted to be sure the account was going to be in the next edition, I often had to write it myself and give it to Dad, which deposited the results yet more deeply into my memory bank. As much as anything else, I suppose these statistics have stuck with me because I always had a head for retaining these sorts of things. I can't tell you why I know that Willie Mays batted .477 in the minor leagues before the Giants called him up in 1951, or that Hank Aaron hit 46 doubles, 7 triples, 39 homers and drove in 123 runs in 1959. I just do. And in case you're wondering, the license plate number on our 1963 Lancer was 492-472. Our home phone number was 548-1048. At the time I learned these things, they mattered to me, and they've stuck. I'll probably be on my deathbed with visions of that Perfect Night Workout when I was 17 and ran my 4.8 mile course in 27:04.

While all this running and competitive drama was going on, I continued to be a student in the junior class at Lawrence High. I wasn't setting the world on fire academically, but I was reasonably engaged for the most part. My schedule got a little quirky because the administration had decided it was about time to introduce calculus to the math curriculum. In order to proceed to calculus, it was considered obligatory to have taken a year of advanced math, which until then was as far as you could go at LHS. So that year's seniors were out, but there were seven or eight juniors who were considered talented enough in math to take the standard junior year, college-track math course (algebra II, was it?) and advanced math concurrently so as to be set up for calculus the following year. Their parents had to be on board with it, as it involved monkeying around with their schedules, and mine were. Nobody ever asked me if I was on board with it, but if they had I would have gone along. Of course, by filling up another period in the day with another math course, something had to give, and for me it was chemistry. Chemistry was taught by Irva Levine, who I'm told was a very capable instructor of chemistry but had always struck me as a rather impatient woman whom we referred to as Hatchetface, so missing out on a year in her classroom was okay with me.

Both math courses were taught by Jim Kinney, a stocky, voluble middle-aged man with great energy and a passion for mathematical concepts that he was singularly able to articulate and convey to his students. Imagine Edward Asner with a little more good cheer and you have Jim Kinney. He was the best math teacher I ever had and maybe the best teacher of any subject at any level. He was a grad of Dickinson College, where he'd played football, and was an assistant in the LHS program. One lasting image I have of him is the progression of his persona over the course of a 45-minute period. To start the class, he was cool and calm in his tie and jacket. As he got going on the lesson of the day, the tie would be loosened, the jacket removed, the sleeves rolled up, and before long he was breaking the sticks of chalk as he slammed them against the blackboard. How anyone could generate that enthusiasm for the subject at hand several times a day, day in and day out, is a marvelous mystery to me, but Mr. Kinney did, and I happily let myself go right along with it.

I associate Jim Kinney with a couple of ego boosts that came at a time when I was just beginning to have the sense that I was a worthwhile individual, and which no doubt contributed to that. This was an awkward, ill-defined process with no clear destination or arrival time, a three-steps-forward, two-steps-back kind of thing, but a little bit of confidence and the sense of self-worth that accompany it were creeping up on me. My unspoken achievement as one of a few juniors in a seniors' math class was definitely a check on the plus side of my status ledger, as was the fact that I absorbed the content as well as anybody there. When he was presenting us with the next step beyond some concept we'd been working on, and the time came for him to ask a question that could only be answered if you knew just what he was saying, his eyes would scan the silent class and linger on me for just a moment. If I knew the answer, I'd give a quick little nod, and he'd boom out,

"Mister Turkington, do you know?" No nod, no ask. There was also the time, probably a year earlier than this, when we came back from a winter track meet and passed by some coaches gathered in the gym. They asked how we did, and somebody mentioned that I'd won a race or set a class record or something, and Mr. Kinney congratulated me and told me that they were going to be looking for a good (some position on the football team) next fall. It was out of the question, of course, but I liked having it suggested to me. A good man, Mr. Kinney. He did a lot for me.

If I was beginning to acquire a reputation as one of the class's brightest students, and I think I was, it was because more of the academic challenges that were coming our way were ones that played to my strengths. There was the binary math program for selected juniors, where I was being instructed by a teacher who really knew how to explain things to me. There was an English class that focused on concepts that came readily to me, of which more later. There was no chemistry class to run aground on. And there was the beginning of the College Board standardized exams, where I discovered in myself a talent for picking the right answer out of five choices even when I wasn't sure which one it was. These tests were given and taken then for the same reason they are now: to give college admissions officers some way of sizing up their applicants and seeing how they did on the same test on the same day. First, there was the PSAT (preliminary scholastic aptitude test). That was early in the junior year. Then there was the SAT (obvious), which most college-bound hopefuls took later in the junior year and again early in the senior. There were the ACH's (achievement), which were meant to measure mastery of a given subject. And there was the National Merit test, just before or just after summer vacation, which was basically a rerun of the SAT's but offered commendatory titles for the high scorers and scholarships for the very highest.

These tests were given on Saturday mornings, usually in the cafeteria of a nearby high school, which in my case was Lawrence High. Anyone who was reckoning on applying to college took some of them, and those eyeing the very selective colleges took all of them. If this sounds like an awful lot of Saturday mornings spent filling out multiple-choice exams, I'll tender the observation that the past 50 years have not eased, but greatly intensified the process. Kids who are aiming high now often take them over and over again, hoping to get a jump on the competition. On top of that, they're taking Advanced Placement tests in hopes of making a better impression and of getting college credits for their high school learning. I never heard of anybody I knew actually taking and paying for a course to sharpen their test-taking skills. It's very common now, especially in high-intensity school systems where a lot of kids, and more importantly their parents, take the rat race seriously and get started on it early. Falmouth, in 1965-66, was not in that league, or world. I took the PSAT's in the fall. The results were given as if they were the SAT's, but without a zero at the end. I scored a 56 in verbal (covering all sorts of English language concepts and skills) and 68 in math. I knew these were not great scores, but I thought they were pretty good.

The winter track season came on with a measure of excitement because Lawrence High was now the proud possessor of an indoor track. Or I should say, it was an indoor track in all respects except for the fact that it was outdoors. But it was the standard indoor track oval size (160 yards, or 11 laps to the mile), its turns were banked, its lanes were marked, it had a six-lane straightaway appended to it, and its surface was an early, but very adequate, attempt at a lasting, weather-impervious material that accepted short track spikes and had a little bit of give. It was known commercially as Reslite. I believe that Kalpy managed to persuade the Reslite company that this would be the ideal place to install a track of their material at no cost. With Earl Mills an enthusiastic athletic director and a powerful record of success in the running sports as a talking point, Kalpy got the school committee to finance the grading and prep work, which was done in the fall. The track was installed just outside the gym and next to the parking lot where all our winter workouts had been done previously. This was better, far better. The finishing touch before the track was ready for use was painting the lines that marked the lanes. Kalpy got hold of some sort of device that was engineered to execute that task, and one fall afternoon he was doing it, with the help of some track guys, including me. At some point I must have been getting in the way, because Kalpy said, "Turkington, you're as good a leader as the man in the moon." My reply: "Well, everybody looks up to him, don't they?"

The christening of that track was the Falmouth Invitational, a popular event that Kalpy organized for Christmas week and had previously held on the parking lot track, with its hills and elliptical turns. I expected Ed Rossi to be the toughest competition in the mile, and he was; he got a pretty good lead on me, which I closed up somewhat towards the end but came about 15 yards short. I was fairly pleased with my effort on the suspended soupbowl YMCA track a week later, where I just missed placing in the top three, except that Rossi ran eight seconds faster in another heat and took first place.

I experienced an important epiphany in my race on the slick concrete floor of the Fargo Building at the South Boston Naval Annex. As was my custom, I started out in the pack and gradually worked my way up and took the lead with about a quarter mile to go. Then something happened that took me by surprise: as I accelerated, I found myself landing on the balls of my feet rather than my heels. It was a totally new feeling, and a good one, because it gave me just a wee bit more reach to my stride and a wee bit quicker turnover. Those two wee bits added up to discernibly more velocity, and I zoomed around those last two laps. Why, after running steadily for two and a half years, it should have taken until that day for me to get up off my heels, I can't say. I guess I just crossed some threshold of lower-leg strength, along with an adjusted body balance derived from moving at higher speeds, and it came to me. Except for the long training runs, that's how I ran for the rest of my days as a middle-distance runner.

With my workouts going well and no injuries or illnesses to impede me, I was nervously looking forward to the BAA meet in the Garden. It would be my first attempt at running with all the top milers in the state in one race. I knew I couldn't keep up with the truly elite guys, but I felt ready to be in the same field. When they called for the milers, I went down on the floor and found they'd assigned me to the second-seeded heat. What the hell? Kalpy came down and tried to get me switched, but it was no go, and when Kalpy can't talk his way into a desired end, you know he's up against a brick wall. So I went in the second heat, and early in the race I looked like I didn't belong in that crowd either. But we hadn't spread out much, and it didn't take too long to work my way up to the lead, which I took over with about a quarter mile to go. Then I let it rip. Seeded heat or not, the crowd takes note and makes a lot of noise when someone down on the track is blowing away the field. That's what I was doing, and I was hearing them. My time wasn't quite good enough to score overall, but it was good enough for some official to know that he should pay attention to Kalpy next time. 4:36.1: school record, Cape Cod record. I was happy with it.

We were back in the Garden two weeks later for the state meet. We were still a small school, still in Class D, which in the running sports at that time didn't signify much, if any, of a reduction in the quality of the competition. We went there with a team that could enter at least one guy in every event who could score (top five) on a good day, but except for Charley Johnson in the shot put and Greg Anderson in the 300, nobody was a sure thing. It was the kind of team that refuses to fill its coach with confidence. My own confidence was held in check by the presence in the mile of Tom Dempsey, who was nearly of state-record caliber, Ed Rossi of Dartmouth, and a few names whose accomplishments I was familiar with through meet results that used to get printed in the Boston papers. Salt Handy was in there too, and Salt and I battled it out fairly often, but I'd always been able to pull away from him and didn't view him as a rival.

Our race started out with me typically towards the back, but I moved up quickly and drew up behind Rossi early in the second half. Dempsey was far out in front, and I was pretty sure that everyone I'd put behind me was going to stay there, so I knew that either Rossi or I was going to take second place. I was never much for thinking or strategizing during a race, but a certain amount of that can't and shouldn't be avoided. I knew that Rossi had a faster sprint right at the end of a race than I did, so if I hoped to beat him I'd have to take him from a long way out. That's as complicated as I let it get. With three laps to go, I threw in a surge, went past and held it as close to the floor as I dared with 480 yards left. Al Porter, the Dartmouth coach, was in the seats next to the track in mid-straightaway. Al was known for possessing a voice like a fog-horn and little patience for athletes who failed to perform up to his expectations. Shortly after I passed his man, we heard that voice clearly: "ROSSI! DON'T LET HIM BY YOU!!!"

That was not the last we were to hear from Al Porter. 160 yards later, a lap and a half to go: "ROSSI! WHAT ARE YOU DOING? THAT'S TURKINGTON!!!" I heard him, but I was supremely centered on marshaling whatever forces I had left to carry me to the finish line. 160 yards later: "TEN MILES TOMORROW IF HE BEATS YOU, ROSSI! TEN MILES!!!" Around the last turn, just about to see the finish line, and there was too much noise to hear anything behind me, but my peripheral vision picked it up. There he was, creeping up on me. We were both going as fast as we could, and he was going just a trace faster. And what did I hear at this intensely critical moment? "Hey, Turkeytin". No kidding. I rarely had anything to say to anybody under any circumstances during a race, figuring I had better things to do with my breath. At the end of a tough race, when every muscle in my body is screaming for oxygen, I could no more say Hello than I could sing the national anthem. And here was my opponent, closing in on the finish of an epic battle, greeting me. We were in lockstep about eight strides from the line, and each of Rossi's strides was an inch longer than mine, and that's about how we finished up. I was there at 4:33.5. Salt was the next man in, at 4:42. Five points out of the mile for Falmouth, and we were on our way.

Others: Greg Anderson won the 300 by a lot; Charlie Johnson took second in the shot; we'd hoped Ken Luckraft might score in the high jump, then he went and won it; didn't expect much from Geoff, who'd lost considerable training time earlier in the season, but he took second in the 1000. We picked up a few more points here and there and won the state meet with room to spare.

The only downside of holding the big high school events in Boston Garden was that the big-time night meets for which the track got set up were in January. So there were still a few weeks left in the season, which actually ended with the conference meet on the New Bedford Vocational board track. Under decent weather conditions, it was a good facility, and on this day we had them. Dartmouth would be there, and Rossi of course. I was kind of hoping that Al Porter would switch his 1000 yard and mile entries around so I could try my luck against John Vieira, but he didn't. When our race came, Rossi and I put some daylight between us and the rest of the field right away, and entered into a re-run of the state meet. This time, rather than make my move with three laps to go and risk being overtaken at the finish, I waited until there were two to go to start kicking. I got right up on Rossi's shoulder and spent the next 320 yards waiting for him to falter just a little, but he held on and I never got by him. 4:34.8 winning time, me a yard back. We were flying those last two laps. Donnie told me later that he was warming up some distance away, looked over at the track when he heard all the shouting, and thought he was seeing a heat of the 300.

That winter track season was the most successful season of training and racing I put together in my four years running for LHS. I had some faster races ahead of me and some equally vital performances, but I had no bad days and a lot of very good ones in the winter of 1966. I never got sick, never got hurt, never missed a day and I answered the call every time it was made. I was a member of an enthusiastic group of hard workers who asked and needed a lot of me, and I never let them down. It was as close to an ideal set of circumstances as a high school athlete can hope to attain. It's tempting to say that I wish I'd realized all that at the time, but that would have led me to revel in it, and that might have kept it from happening.

* * *

Some of us were down in the locker room for a between-seasons workout one afternoon when a tall, mature-looking kid in tie and jacket showed up and asked if any of us knew Mr. Kalperis. We sure do, we said, and here he is now. The kid was Joe Rivers, he was the biggest name in running in Vermont, and his coach there was, of course, a friend of Kalpy's, and Joe was sending his greetings. Joe was in town as a member of the All-New England chorus, whose annual concert was being hosted by LHS that year. Kalpy asked him if he wanted to work out with Geoff and me, he said sure, we went out for a run, and when we got back Kalpy told Joe that the host family assignment for him and his singing buddy from Burlington had been changed. They were going to be staying at the Turkingtons'. Kalpy could operate very quickly when the situation called for it. They were good guests, and I was impressed with the preparations they made for the rehearsals and the concert. It was a lot like gearing up for a race, with greater emphasis on the larynx. Joe was the elite of the elite among New England distance runners. Evidently, he was in that class among its singers as well.

While all this important stuff was going on, I continued to be a student in the junior class at Lawrence High. I managed to miss out on chemistry, but the standard course of study for a college-bound student called for some kind of social studies course every year, and I have no recollection of what that course was for me that year. There was no World Cultures III, and American History came a year later, so what was the junior class doing, and under whose tutelage? It totally escapes me. French I remember, if only because Madame Colton was as lively and sexy as ever, and we started speaking a little bit of French in her class. I wasn't very good at it. There is a shifting of gears that has to take place when converting from English mode to a foreign language in conversation, and it didn't come smoothly to me, either then or in college. Oddly enough, I found that 30 or 40 years later, after not having read or spoken more than a few words of the language in all that time, I could clumsily but effectively communicate with real French people in their mother tongue. Things that often didn't come to me in the face of an exam or a conversation while in high school just popped into place while trying to make myself understood all those years later. I have some vague theories about why this should be the case.

My English instructor was Bill Fraher, a frustrated dramatist who lived in Yarmouth, about an hour's drive away on a good day, and was teaching high school English for the same reason that serious musicians who aren't quite good enough to make a living wage playing music teach it in school: he wasn't quite good enough to make it on the stage. Mr. Fraher had a fatalistic attitude towards his students' level of interest in his subject and a slightly cynical take on just about everything, though he was easily amused. His class was a comfortable one to be in. He was a very active classroom teacher, had a lot to say about the matters at hand and various peripheral topics besides, but his pronouncements came with the understanding that most of us wouldn't take much of an interest in any of this, but that's okay, I'll do my job and you do yours. One feature of his pedagogy was a booklet that everyone got that had many pages of vocabulary words of which we were assigned to learn about 40 each week. He explained, almost apologetically, that the verbal section of the SAT's contained many words to define, and that since most of us were going to take the SAT's, this would be of help to us. He was absolutely right; I ran across many of those words on the tests and nailed them all.

There was nowhere near the officially sanctioned dialogue about human sexuality then that there is now. In fact, there was none whatsoever. I was very hazily aware that males sometimes engaged in sexual activity with each other, and that this was at least frowned upon, or otherwise viewed as an abomination by anybody who cared to express their feelings about it. It was known to all that homosexual males exhibited certain characteristics as markers: they spoke with a lisp, they took mincing little steps rather than manly strides when they walked, they were fussy and gestured often with limp wrists. Bill Fraher had a little bit of all of these things in his persona, but not to the extent that would have been necessary for me to identify him as gay. And yet, he was. Not only that, but he demonstrated no attempt to concoct a cover story for his life. He spoke from time to time of John, whom he described as his roommate, and let it be known that there were no women in his history. None of this landed with me. This may sound terribly dated, but I really thought of Bill Fraher as my English teacher, one who tried to give us interesting assignments and seemed to have plenty of appreciation for my classroom production, and I never gave any thought to his sex life.

I gave a great deal of thought to my own sex life which, my being socially insecure and largely outside the world of female companionship, was still on the back burner and destined to remain there for some time more. I was getting more comfortable with girls, but well short of anything that might lead to physical excitement, much less sexual activity. This was becoming a bit hard to take, because I was hearing of more and more wild times from guys I knew who were going to parties and dance clubs and drinking and making it with the more precocious girls. This was before The Pill hit the scene, and I believe that most girls understood that if they truly wanted to avoid getting pregnant, the only sure way was not to engage in sexual intercourse. Since most girls were determined to remain virgin, at least for now, most boys shared that fate. But there were parties, and there was the A Go Go in Hyannis, and there was a joint on Falmouth's Main Street that featured music and dancing and no booze for high school kids, and even the unassuming guys I knew from track were going to these events and enjoying themselves, knowing full well that they weren't going to come anywhere near to getting laid. It all seemed so uncertain to me, fraught with the threat of feeling awkward and embarrassed, that I counted myself out. It was so much safer to lift my weights and go for a run.

I spent an occasional weekend night babysitting for the Kalperises. Tommy and Betty were still too young to leave home alone, so the track team was a good source of reliable, beholden sitters when Jim and Angel went out. I never talked about childsitting with anybody, and got no sense of the Kalperises' preferences, so I figured I was just there to preside over any disaster that might occur, and treated the gig accordingly. I read some, watched the TV some and pretty much just made sure the kids got up to bed when they were supposed to. I wasn't the only track guy who got the call. Mark lived just down the road and came over one evening to tend the kids. The way I heard it, Geoff stopped by to hang out with Mark, and after the kids went to bed they decided to sample some of Kalpy's liquor collection. They didn't know when to stop, and by the time the Kalperises got home the boys were pretty sloshed. I don't know if there were any troubling consequences, probably not, but I do recall thinking at the time that this was a little over the top. Of such incidents are our accommodations to alcohol formed.

Angel was a schoolteacher in Greece when Kalpy appeared in her town on an overseas trip to visit the old country, shortly after college. They met, fell in love, and a little while later she was in the U.S. and they were married. She was an extraordinarily gracious woman with striking, classic features who I made friends with right from the start. When I dropped in to talk track with Kalpy, she always joined us for some polite conversation at the kitchen table and offered me a cup of tea and some Greek pastry. I gathered that her family back home was educated, prosperous and cultured. I sometimes wondered how comfortable she ever became among the commoners in rude America, not that she would ever utter a derisive word about our ways. Mom told me that she witnessed a moment of anger in Angel once. My folks had returned from a trip to England, and Mom was relating to her how impressed she'd been with the display of the Elgin Marbles in the British Museum. "They STOLE them!" said Angel. This was years before doubts about the propriety of plundering classical art by the imperial powers had even crossed the radar screen of those who'd taken them, but it must have been a sore point with the Greeks. Angel and I were always glad to see each other, and I hope I helped make her feel at home here.

My aspirations for a basketball career were satisfactorily met through my association with the Speedsters, a Falmouth recreation league team assembled by Mark Buguey. The rec league had eight or ten teams and scheduled each team for a weeknight game every week at the Rec Center. I'd played for the Speedsters the year before, but this year Mark found a ringer in Dan Krynovich, who was a senior and a good ballplayer though not a track man, and signed up Carl

Soderland and another enthusiast or two, so we were pretty good. At the same time, some of the black guys had a similar team: disaffected ballplayers from the track team and a few good players from outside, who comprised a team they named the Soul Brothers. They won all their games and we won all our games, and the schedule called for us to meet near the end of the season. Apparently, there developed considerable interest in the game, because the venue was relocated from the Rec Center to the LHS gym. This was somebody's good idea, because a lot of spectators – 100? 200?- showed up. They saw a good game. Everybody played hard and clean, and the final score was in the high 70's, the Soul Brothers taking it by a few points.

My hometown had been known as a summer resort for the well-to-do since the late 1800's, but the year-round population began to swell in the postwar years and hasn't stopped yet. Forgive my rounded figures here, but these are from memory: there were 8000 residents of Falmouth when I was born; 13,000 when I entered fifth grade; 18,000 when I was away at college. When I lived there as a young adult, the open spaces between the town's several distinct villages were filling in with homes. When I go back now, it appears that most of the new homes are being built where existing ones have been torn down to make room for them. The new ones are much bigger, and sometimes but not always a good bit uglier. Most of the newer residences are single-family homes or high-end condos. Not a whole lot of apartment building yet that I've noticed, but I'm sure that will become the norm.

One indicator of the growth and modernization of Falmouth has been the evolution of the food stores. When I was little and we lived on Mill Road, the closest thing to a supermarket in town was the A&P on Main Street. It was right next to Town Hall, which was razed in the 60's to make way for a parking lot and a nice little park.

There were other food stores besides the A&P – S.S.Pierce sold specialty items and there was a butcher shop on Depot Avenue – but the A&P was about it for general food shopping. It was a little bit larger, though not nearly as neat and clean, as a standard convenience store today. There were maybe 4 or 5 aisles, half the width and one-third the length of what we're used to now. If you were over by the butcher shop, the smell all around was of meat getting old. By the checkout lines, they kept the coffee grinders, very large machines considering their simple function, and that whole end of the store smelled of ground-up 8 O'Clock coffee, which never got swept up. There was no dedicated parking lot, though there were spaces next to Town Hall and a paved lot between the store and Shiverick's Pond, next to the police station. My lingering impression of a trip to the A&P with Mom in my early years is one of having to deal with inconvenience: no place to park, hard walking on a badly ruptured sidewalk, difficulty opening the door, sticking wheels on the shopping cart, traffic jams throughout the store, piles of merchandise stacked in the way, long waits in the line....the reward was to watch, hear and smell the coffee grinder at work.

First National Stores was the first chain to offer shopping relief to the beleaguered Falmouth housewife. They opened up a snazzy new supermarket at the foot of Shore Street, either just before or just after we moved back to town. It had a parking lot and automatic doors, wide aisles and new carts, and sales and promotions. Of course, it was an instant success, which was noted by the Stop N Shop chain, which acted quickly, and radically: they got away from Main Street and onto some vacant acreage at the Heights corner, where they opened up a store that was bigger yet, and had a modernistic arched roof and a huge parking lot and a few other little stores attached and reachable by a covered walkway, and they called it Falmouth Plaza. Trying not to be outdone, but being outdone nonetheless, the A&P put up a spanking new store on a vacant lot just off Main Street. It was a whole lot bigger, cleaner and more amenable than their outworn old place, which became a stationery store, but not as much as the new Stop N Shop or the even bigger supermarket that was later to come to the Jones Road intersection. And most disastrous of all, the fools built it on Scranton Avenue! There it remained for decades, poorly managed, lightly patronized, constantly emblematic of the decline of the Great Atlantic and Pacific Tea Company.

Between the winter and spring track seasons, I entered a couple of road races. The first was on St. Patrick's Day, a 3-mile event organized by Kalpy that started at Falmouth Plaza, went down Main Street and returned via Lakeview Avenue. Most of the LHS distance men ran in it, and some of our rivals came from out of town, including Ed Norris, a nationally ranked 2-miler from Brockton, who won it by a healthy margin. There was a cute photo in The Enterprise of the leaders going by the Elizabeth Theatre, whose current film title was displayed on the marquee: The Great Race. I ran pretty hard, finished just behind Geoff and, for the first time, just ahead of Tom Vadala.

The other race I got into may not have been a smart one to enter, but I couldn't resist: it was the New England AAU 30-kilometer championship in New Bedford. Geoff and I never trained at anything longer than five or six miles, but we figured, if we can run six, we can surely run 18.6. Heedless of our faulty logic, we went ahead with it and took it seriously. There were about 50 in the race who spread out quite a bit as the miles went by. My lasting image is of me in the latter stages, all alone on a bleak March day in the canyons of the abandoned warehouses of New Bedford's underbelly, no people, no traffic, no sounds, looking for the next cardboard arrow stapled to a phone pole to keep me on the course. There was nobody in sight ahead of or behind me, my feet felt on fire and every footfall felt like my lower legs were getting slammed with a baseball bat. I'd have made a good case for those cynics who feel that distance runners are driven by masochism.

Though I slowed down, I kept pushing and ended it in about an hour and 58 minutes, about two minutes behind Geoff. When I finally got into a warm room and took my shoes off, I had blisters that I didn't know existed in nature. There were the longitudinal ones that ran the length of my soles, about an inch wide and a half inch high, and the golf-ball sized ones behind my big toes, all of them dense-packed with blood. I felt a certain degree of pride that I was able to keep myself going long and hard enough to bring such wreckage upon my feet, and in knowing that Rossi and Vieira were also in this race and came in way behind me, but I couldn't help wondering whether this was a wise thing to have done.

Regular track practices at Fuller Field started up right after that. Having popped my blisters, the only aftereffect of the 30k run was a certain deadness in my legs that subsided slowly. Our first meet was a scrimmage of sorts against three of the Boston schools in White Stadium, where the state meet would be held at the end of May. The athletic director of the Boston schools was Ed Grant, a supporter of the running sports and, like everybody else, a friend of Kalpy's, so they arranged a meet where we could gain some familiarity with the track. The city schools didn't offer much in the way of distance runners, though Boston English had a kid named Wayne Lucas who was pretty good, but he didn't factor into the mile race, where by the last lap it was just Salt and me again. I was about to pull away and run to victory as usual when Salt went by me, and he wasn't messing around. I was too perplexed to respond in a meaningful way, and spent the last lap trying to cut into his lead, but he just wouldn't slow down and I couldn't speed up. I wound up about 20 yards behind. I was happy for Salt, kind of, but reassured myself that it wasn't an important race, I was still recovering from the 30k, Salt had a great day, I was a little overconfident, things would be back to normal next time around.

It didn't happen that way. That race got into my head in some way that had an enormous impact on my running for a long time. I'd often had days when I felt awkward and tired and it showed in my running, but now I started having nothing but days like that. Every workout, every race, I'd be 100 yards into it thinking, Ah man, I feel like shit again! What had always come, if not easily, at least comfortably, to me felt now like a very tiring and unnatural act. Even my night runs were not exempt, though I kept doing them. The only way I could think of to get out of this slump was to work my way out of it. There was a spell in midseason when Kalpy had to pull me out of the group I always did my track intervals with, because I just couldn't keep up. In the dual meets, it was still usually Handy vs. Turkington in the mile, and my times weren't really very far off what I thought they ought to be, but in every race, we fought it out right to the finish, and Salt always prevailed. It took every bit of focus I could bring up, all my determination and tolerance of pain, just to challenge him. I felt day in and day out that I was running in soft sand, wearing mud boots, against the wind. It was a total psyche job, but I had no idea how to deal with it.

It wasn't something we talked about much, but I did sense that my teammates were pulling for me. I was a friend and teammate, after all, but besides that, there was the matter of the state meet coming up, one that we had every hope of winning if we gathered points from everyone who was capable of scoring. I was supposed to be one of those guys, and here I couldn't get out of my own way. The last meet before the state meet was called the Upper Cape Championships, which was held at Fuller Field and which we knew we'd win easily. As was customary, Salt and I were in the mile, we were well out in front halfway through the race, we were never separated by more than a stride or two and it was killing me just to keep up with him. We were about to start the gun lap and I was anticipating it with dread, knowing how painful and frustrating and ultimately unsuccessful it would be. The gun went off, Salt went by me and started pulling away, and I thought about what lay ahead and decided: Screw it. Let him go. Just finish the goddamn race.

A number of important things happened in the 3-second time frame after the gun fired for the fourth and final lap. Salt went by me and pulled away. I gave up trying to win the race. Earl Mills, officiating at the finish line, shouted "TURK! YOU'RE BOUNCING!". I had an out-of-body experience, dreamlike and unprecedented, in which for an instant I looked at myself and saw that, by God, I sure was bouncing. The clouds parted. The sun shone. The seas calmed. The planets aligned. The orchestral music cascaded down from the heavens, and I felt great. I pulled up on Salt's shoulder as we went around the turn, distrustful of this feeling of omnipotence that I hadn't had in so long. But it was real. I blasted up the back straight, around the final turn and into the finish, ahead by 40 yards. It was easy, so easy.

Now here's something about Kalpy and his approach to his athletes. All spring, after every disappointing effort, which means all of them, Kalpy would be right there with me as soon as I finished. I'd be 20 yards past the finish line, hunched over with my hands on my knees, gasping for air, and Kalpy would have his arm on my shoulders, trying to say something positive about the quality of my effort or my determination or the assurance that I'd get squared away soon. I don't know how much his words managed to cut through the discouragement, but I got used to a visit from him after every failure. On this day, I knew I'd crashed through a big barrier and part of me was so glad that at last Kalpy and I would have something good to exult about. But Kalpy wasn't around. He was over there with Salt. I understood completely, and was grateful for that man.

A few years ago, a bunch of us got together for a mini-reunion with Kalpy that ended up at Mark's house in East Falmouth. Mark's wife Patty screened a CD that was made from old home movies of some moments in track. At one point, I realized that some of the scenes were from this very meet. I was hoping to see that some of the mile had been filmed, but all that showed was the very finish, behind a bunch of people blocking the way, and it didn't show much. But then there was footage of me walking across the infield minutes after it was over. Kevin was with me, and we were chatting and smiling. Watching this video, I was seeing a smiling kid on the screen who had just won a difficult race and exorcized some demons that had been buggering him all season. This kid saw someone off-camera and expressed his joy with a modest shake of his fist. He was a handsome, happy young fellow who looked and acted like someone I would have liked to have known.

The state meet was held on a nice day a week later. It was sunny and warm, but without much humidity or wind. There'd been some recent rain, so the White Stadium track was in good shape. Like the indoor team, we had a lot of guys who might score points but few that we could be sure of. Canton High had a lot of good weight throwers and sprinters and looked like our strongest opponent. The mile field had one true elite runner, Tom Dempsey again, and a lot of good ones. Our race was scheduled about in the middle of the order of events, and in spite of my recovered confidence, the anxiety started kicking in early. LHS got a bunch of early points out of the javelin and high jump, but then we got stuck there, nothing happening for us while Canton kept getting closer. Kalpy, worried, caught up to Salt and me on the infield where we were getting clerked in. He told us he had a lot of confidence in us, that the team really needed some points about now, and he asked us how we felt. We were so uptight we couldn't talk to him. Really, we could not communicate verbally, everything came out in a stutter and didn't make any sense anyway. Kalpy managed to force a smile and a few words of encouragement, but he must have walked away shaking his head and hoping his field events guys would come through.

I often found there to be an inverse relation between the nerves I felt going into a race and the strength and calm that overcame me after it started. That happened on this day. The race was a process of attrition: a sizable pack headed out at a brisk, but not blazing, pace, and one by one, all but five of us dropped back. At the gun, the side-by-side leaders were Tom Donnelly, a powerful little guy from Bishop Feehan, and Dana Hill, a tall lanky guy from King Philip. Dempsey was a couple of strides behind them and Salt and I were together, just behind him. Dempsey was unbeatable and as he took over the lead I didn't give him any thought, but I aimed to catch those other two. I opened it up a little and pulled up behind them on the turn. They say you shouldn't pass on the turn - it adds distance – but I say when it's time to go, you better go, turn or no turn, so I went around them and headed into the back straight pretty sure that nobody was going to catch me from behind today. I rarely looked around me much when I raced; usually, my eyes were set about 10 feet in front of me. I always felt that watching the track speeding by beneath me helped me stay locked into my pace. Tired as I was getting at this point, I couldn't help noting that I'd never seen it go by so fast.

Then a pair of swiftly moving track shoes entered my field of vision. OMG, as we might say now. I was closing in on Tom Dempsey. I was entirely focused on putting distance between myself and my pursuers, not at all on what might be ahead of me. If I'd gone into the race with any reason to entertain the notion that I'd be close to the lead at the end of the last straightaway, I might have found the other gear I needed to challenge Dempsey. But as I've said, it's very hard to adjust your attitude during a race, especially towards the end. I didn't slow down, but I didn't find the inspiration to dig down any deeper than I already had. I crossed the line about four yards behind. 4:27.9. Salt was right behind Donnelly and Hill in 4:32. The rest of the field, Rossi included, was nowhere around. That was five points in the mile for Lawrence of Falmouth.

We won the meet with room to spare. Pat Bishop won the javelin, Ken Luckraft and Carl Gonsalves went 1-2 in the high jump, and Don McLane tied for first in the pole vault. Charley Johnson, Wayne Tavares, Greg Anderson and Geoff all scored points. It was a good day. The same cannot be said for our return to White

Stadium a week later for the All-Class meet. That one brings together everyone who scored in their division meet, so I was in the mile, in the seeded heat no less, matched up with all the best ones. I was never a factor, starting out in last place and staying there for quite a while before getting past a few tired-out guys towards the end. I wound up 10th in 4:34, a bit of a letdown after my breakthrough the week before. I'm not sure how everybody else did, but I do recall feeling that we were kind of a dead-ass team that day. We had our heroics in the Class D meet to console us, as well as the consideration that even though we weren't quite at this maximum level of competition, we were getting there.

This was my last season as a teammate of Charley Johnson, who was about to graduate. Charley was a larger-than-life figure who seemed to make it one of his many missions in life to make everyone in his path feel that they were important to him. He was of above average height and far above average mass, which he put to use as a star, star lineman in football and a shot putter and discus thrower on the track teams. He was one of eight (?) children of Tillie Johnson, who cleaned prosperous peoples' homes for a living and raised her brood in a little ranch house on Central Avenue, not the toniest address in town. Some of her kids met with more success than others, but they were all substantial and personable as can be. Charley liked to joke around as much as anyone, but he was essentially of very earnest nature. It wasn't unusual on our teams to fall into conversations about world affairs or social issues, and Charley was usually in the middle of them. When he started up a rendition of Curtis Mayfield's "Amen", the whole team joined in. Being a talented and determined student, a star athlete, a gigantic personality, and highly regarded by everyone who knew him, he was much sought-after by a great many fine colleges. He chose to attend Dartmouth, where the markers of success continued to come his way.

It's hard to know the appropriate place to offer my impressions of Earl Mills, because for me and for many years' worth of kids growing up in the Falmouth schools, he was a part of our lives for longer than anyone else in the system. I address him here because of his succinct and timely observation of my running form at the Upper Cape meet, which did me as much good in three words as anything anybody ever told me. I believe that Earl was director of physical education in all the Falmouth schools for some time, because even in elementary school we saw him around a lot. By the time I got to Lawrence, he was head of the phys ed department and director of athletics. High school sports activity was exploding as the Boomers came along, but Earl held both posts for years. He was a great believer in doing what worked and not feeling bound by precedent or protocol. He shared that with Kalpy, along with an oft-substantiated belief that kids can do great things if you give them plenty of room, an ability to speak directly to those kids, and a tendency to laugh like he really meant it. The two of them worked well together; they both saw potential in kids where a lot of other educators just saw trouble. We saw Earl Mills at a lot of our meets on the road.

He had other lives as well. He was head chef at the Coonamessett Inn, Falmouth's nearest approximation to fine dining at the time. How he managed to work that in with his demands at the school I can't imagine, but he did. He made it even tougher on himself in the 70's when he opened his own restaurant, The Flume, in Mashpee. There he served up, among many other treats, the best clam chowder, fried clams and Indian pudding I've ever had. By far. It was a ways off the beaten path, but it was a big success and stayed that way for as long as he ran it. He wrote at least a few books that I know of. One was about growing up in Mashpee as a member of the Wampanoag tribe, of which he became chief in his adulthood. One was a cookbook oriented towards native seafood recipes. One was about Wampanoag culture and aimed at kids. There were probably others. As chief of the tribe, he devoted himself to knowing and sustaining the traditional dress, dance, music, history and general culture of his people. He was a gifted athlete who displayed his skills with reluctance. Every once in a while, you'd see him climb the rope to the ceiling of the gym, or demonstrate some move on the gymnastics equipment, or take a few jump shots, and you knew you were seeing a rare talent. He had a chiseled physique that would put Charles Atlas to shame and a facial profile akin to New Hampshire's late lamented Old Man Of The Mountain.

We only know of people what we see of them, and how they treat us and those around us. The rest is hearsay, gossip or mystery. With that disclaimer, I can't help but say that Earl Mills was one of the most admirable people I ever met and had the good fortune to know. Same goes for Charlie Johnson. There simply aren't enough of their kind around.

There was one more race left in the spring track season, but it was only for four of us. The Knights of Columbus in Danvers sponsored a fairly big-time open meet in early June that attracted some high-level talent. Somehow, Kalpy and John Pistone, the Randolph coach, managed to get a distance medley relay race put on the schedule, and agreed that our two best configurations of runners would enter it. Pistone felt that his crew had a shot at the national record in the event, and with his two most talented runners about to graduate, this was their last chance at it. We were in there as sacrificial lambs to lend some legitimacy to the race – we knew we were good, but we weren't national record good – but also to see what kind of time we could put together at the peak of the season. When we got there, we found that we'd be running on an artificial surface for the first time, and that Pistone had pulled Art Dulong out of the relay in favor of the open mile, which he won in 4:04, the fastest high school time in America at that point. With him out of the relay, we thought we had a shot at it.

It turned out to be a hell of a race. Geoff ran the 880 leg against Elliot Stevens and came in a just few yards behind. Donnie ran the 440 against Gerry Spellman, went under 51 seconds but couldn't get by him. Salt started out trailing Tom Perakslis by those few yards, fought like a dog for 3/4 mile, and handed off to me virtually tied. Ours was the better handoff, so I started out a stride or two ahead of Bobby Jayes. And there we stayed. Jayes never went past me and never fell back. He was a loud breather, so I could locate him the whole way. He was right there. This was at night, there'd been some rain an hour earlier so the air had that nice, misty feel to it, and the track surface was hard, almost like pavement, so I was loving the conditions. I considered kicking just after the gun but figured I was in control of things, so I could wait. I figured wrong. Jayes shot past me in the middle of the back straight, and I chased him all the way in, but having lost the initiative I couldn't get it back. I ran a 4:31.2 but forgot my own cardinal rule: when it's time to go, you better go. Still, we ran 10:38.4, which was easily a new school record. I had occasion to be in the Falmouth field house in May 2014 and came across a display that had on it all the school track records. There's one from 1966. Distance medley relay. Still ours.

* * *

Just after the school year ended, I went with a few other Falmouth guys to Boys State. This was a week-long immersion in civics and politics that was sponsored by the American Legion and held at the UMass campus in Amherst, where we stayed in dorms and ate cafeteria food. What they did was break up all the participants into units that functioned as mock townships, so we met every day and elected officials and passed budgets and did other things that town governments do. There was a mass meeting in the cage (field house) every night, where we listened to speakers and made announcements and other things, I'm sure, but what comes most clearly to mind is the heat. It was a nice early summer week, but every day started warming up by midmorning and got hotter and hotter as the day went on, hitting a climax at night in the sweltering cage. We were divided up into two parties, so that at the end of the week we nominated candidates for statewide office, had rallies in the cage, listened to the hopefuls speak and grew surprisingly partisan, considering this was just a short-term sham exercise in electioneering. The losing gubernatorial candidate was Larry S. DiCara, whose party's rally featured all the delegates running around the cage shouting "LSD!, LSD!", and waving eponymous banners. Larry lost that one, but later was a lifer in Boston politics.

The Legion had a lot of other activities going on. One of them was a track meet, where who should appear but Dana Hill of the state meet mile. He and I ran, of course, the mile, led it all the way and tied for first at Dana's last-lap suggestion, seeing as how we were both citizens of T-1. I think he knew I had him. In all, there wasn't a lot of time for hanging around, but when there was, many of us did our hanging around at the student union, trying to get a feel for the life of a college student. The week was a little bit too summer-campish, a little too directed, a little too contrived and way too hot for me to get excited about it, but it was interesting and I made a few pretty good friends there. I wonder if it still happens. I can't imagine the American Legion today having the personnel, the funds or the energy to pull something like this together. I'd also suspect that attending it might not have the appeal it once did. My guess would be that a lot of the guys who would go in 1966 would now be more likely to spend a free week doing something that looks good on a college application, and to have parents who can pay for it.

At some point during the summer I went to the DMV office in Hyannis to take my driver's test. I don't know when I got my learner's permit, but I'd had it for a while and had a fair amount of driving experience, not all of it with the requisite adult in the car. The high school made it easy to get a driver's ed certificate by offering it at the school, but to do that you had to make room in your schedule, and I didn't have any wiggle room. So after a little bit of practice parallel parking – and would somebody explain to me why it's so important to know how to parallel park? I mean, if you're no good at it, you can just keep looking for a parking lot or a double open space somewhere – Mom and I took the '63 Lancer to the DMV and signed up for the exam. A wiry little older guy got in the front seat next to me and off we went. I was doing fine until he directed me to a long, straight, barely inhabited stretch of road a little ways behind the DMV office. I drove along it at what seemed a moderate rate, then saw a sign that said 25, so I slowed down, but it was too late.

When we went in to do the paperwork, the guy said, "You get off the line a little too fast for my money, sonny", and flunked me.

I found out later that the speed limit on that stretch of road is the most important thing to be learned in a year of driver's ed. Had I but known.....but I didn't, and I was pretty unhappy about going into my senior year without a license, and Mom was pretty unhappy about wasting most of a day for no good reason. It wasn't like her to vent for very long, if at all, but when the occasion called for it she could summon up a few choice words to let you know she was pissed. I heard a few choice words, and pretty soon life was back to normal.

I was back at work bussing tables at the Pancake Man by now; they must have granted me special dispensation for such a critical mission as Boys State. Gardner Lewis was now running the other PM down-Cape, and a young guy by the name of Baumgartner was managing the Falmouth joint. With the exception of a requirement that the busboys wear black bow ties, the job hadn't changed at all, and my status was somewhat elevated from before, partly because I was a returnee and partly because I'd gotten pretty good at the job. I don't recall any friction with Baumgartner or anybody else, but towards the end of June I parted ways with the Pancake Man. My new employer was ORE, who had something they wanted me to do.

ORE was Ocean Research Equipment, one of a growing number of spinoffs from the Woods Hole oceanography centers. This one was located in an unadorned warehouse style building on Falmouth Heights Road, about a mile around the foot of the harbor from home. There were a few people who did office work, at least a few with their own spaces who did designing and engineering, and a few who worked in the shop. I was one of those. My job was quite specific, repetitive and not hard to learn, but it did require a certain degree of common sense, hand-eye coordination and a good set of nerves. ORE had a contract to pressure-test a great number of glass balls that were going to be employed deep in the ocean. It was never made clear to me just what they would be used for or how deep they'd be going, but my job was to test them and not ask questions about them. This I did for the next six weeks at $1.50/hour.

The balls were a tad larger than a basketball and their walls of clear glass were about three quarters of an inch thick. The water-pressure generating device that I tested them in was a cylindrical tank set so that its top was a little above floor level. The walls of this tank were about six inches thick, solid steel. The inside of the top of the tank was threaded to receive the lid, which was threaded to screw down into the tank, kind of like a Thermos jug but infinitely tighter. The lid was about a foot thick and must have been awfully heavy, but I never found out because its weight was borne by a cable suspended from above and operated by me. I could test three balls at a time in this tank. First I put each ball in a burlap bag, I'm not sure why. Then I gently placed the balls into the tank and started the process of sealing it. To do that, I lowered the lid with a hand-held button, got the screwing-in process started, then spun the lid by hand while lowering the lid at just the right rate. Round and round and round. When it was all the way down, I did some final lockdown and retreated behind the control panel to start the test.

To look at the control panel, you'd surmise that the operator must have undergone a lot of training. There were all kinds of dials and gauges, but all that concerned me were the on/off switch and the pressure gauge. Turned on, the pressure in the tank came up rapidly for a while, but the inlet valve slowed down and labored mightily as it neared the required pounds per square inch. Gzhung…gzhung… gzhung…Was it 8000 PSI? 18,000? Whatever it was, getting near to it was a time of anxiety for everyone in the building, because if the balls imploded it made a sound like a Scud missile just hit us, and the whole building shook. If they held, I'd release the pressure and everyone could relax for a while. A failed test meant a big cleanup job for me, as the tank would be full of pulverized glass and shredded burlap. It was always a disappointment to me when an implosion occurred, and not just because I hated cleaning out the tank. By the time I'd taken a ball out of its box, folded it into its burlap sack and placed it with its teammates into the tank, I'd developed a slight sense of kinship with it, and I really wanted those balls to pass their test. There was a heavy price to be paid for those that didn't.

This was my first job where I had to show up at a reasonable hour in the morning and put in eight hours. I packed a lunch and took a half hour to eat it, usually on a picnic bench outside with the rest of the staff. I was a bit of an outsider, being the only kid and only there for a while, but everybody was pleasant to me. Bunny was a machinist who took pieces of raw metal and made precision parts out of them. We spent all day about 20 feet apart from each other but hardly ever spoke because we had to keep an eye on what we were doing. Ken Ketchum's dad, a former Oceanographic man, was an engineer I think, and there was a nice guy from Buzzards Bay named Bob who worked in the shop when I started but was turning into an engineer. The owner was Dave, who lived on Martha's Vineyard and crossed the sound on his boat every morning. He had the look and demeanor of the boss of a small business, able to mix with the employees and interact comfortably, but always a little preoccupied and prone to distraction. A day's work there felt to me a little like a long run: keep focused on what you're doing here, notice what's around you but don't get drawn in by it, keep doing this like you mean it, and when it's over you'll be glad you did it. Approaching mid-August, I was told that we were near the end of the glass-ball contract, thank you very much Tom. That was fine with me. There was something else I wanted to do.

I'd like to be able to put myself back into the frame of mind I was in when I decided to hitchhike around New England for the next two weeks. If I could do that, it would tell me something about how the emerging counterculture values of freedom and rootlessness were creeping into the mindsets of innocent young mainstream kids. I'd probably read "On The Road" by now, but "Me And Bobbie McGee" was still years away; I'd guess I just felt that things were very predictable and sensible, standard points on a preordained continuum, and I wanted to escape those constraints for a little while. To no surprise of mine at the time, my parents had a few words of caution but no objections. I did have a few destinations to give some body to the enterprise. I was bound for Sturbridge, Massachusetts, then Burlington, Vermont, then Old Orchard Beach, Maine. I well knew that a fair amount of the time would be taken up with getting from one to the other. I got a money belt for the journey, since cash was the only way to pay for anything and I didn't want to put it all in my wallet. I put a change of clothes and who knows what else in an adidas gym bag, got a ride to Palmer Avenue and headed out.

Neil Hicks was one of my fellow T-1 co-citizens at Boys State. He lived in Sturbridge and I had his home phone number, but I knew he had a day job at Old Sturbridge Village and my rides got me near there by mid-afternoon, so I went there looking for him. Old Sturbridge was and is one of those re-creations of a colonial-era community where the shtick is that the workers dress in period costume and assume the persona of an 18th-century resident. I found Neil describing some aspect of his work to a cluster of visitors, what work it was I don't remember. I stepped in among them and started asking him a number of impertinent questions that had no easy answer, just to watch him squirm. He kept his cool pretty well. At the end of the day, we went to his home where his mother made me feel very welcome and never asked me how long I'd be staying.

It turned out to be a couple of days. We went to visit another T-1 alumnus, John, whose family had a place on a nice lake nearby, where I water skied for the only time in my life. Neil's father owned an apparently successful ceramics research and manufacturing company – this wasn't art ceramics, it was industrial – whose home base was a big, modern building with lots of glass and an immense atrium with a swimming pool that we spent some time playing in.

It was raining the morning I left, but I had a raincoat and my adidas bag was of vinyl or some such waterproof material, so Neil dropped me off at the entrance to the MassPike and left me to my fortunes. There was another guy already trying to hitch a ride there, a little ways before the toll booths at the onramp. The etiquette of the road called for me to stand a little ways past him so that he'd get the first ride. This guy had been there a while in the rain and was getting pretty impatient. He was waving his arms at the cars driving past him towards the toll booth – most cars drive past most of the time no matter where you are – and soon he started shouting at them. A trooper walked down from the booths to tell him he'd have to be more courteous than that, but he couldn't stop himself. Before long, he was shaking his fist and shouting obscenities at all the drivers who passed him by. It was raining hard now and I know how he felt, but sometimes you just have to recognize your place. Trying to hitch a ride at the onramp to the MassPike with a state trooper looking on is one of those times. The trooper finally walked down to escort him away, and I ambled down to where he'd been. The very next car pulled over to let me in. As I got in, the escortee looked over his shoulder, saw this and erupted in a paroxysm of frustrated rage. Oh well, I thought, wherever he's going, at least he'll be dry.

My ride took me west on the Pike to Lee, where I got out and headed north on Route 7, a two-lane state highway that ran straight to Burlington. My first ride dropped me off in Williamstown, where I got a look at the very pretty, precious Williams College campus. The sky was clearing and I went on my way. My hitching luck ran out late in the afternoon when I was left on a picturesque but lightly-traveled stretch of road a little ways into Vermont. I was there for a couple of hours, the sun went behind the mountains and it cooled off in a hurry. I was in the process of formulating a plan for what to do when it got really dark and cold, when someone stopped and took me to Rutland. Rutland had a whole lot of guest houses along the main drag. These were people's homes where the owners had enough rooms upstairs to take in overnight guests, and a sign out front announcing that fact. I was surprised at how uncomplicated it was for me to secure a room for the first time in my life. I walked in the front door, a pleasant middle-aged lady met me and brought me over to a little desk where she took my money – it wasn't much – and pointed the way to my room. This was the first night in my life where nobody knew where I was. I had a dinner at a nearby diner and spent it at a guest house in Rutland.

Back on Route 7 in the morning, I headed north towards Burlington. I must have been cognizant of Middlebury College along the way, because it's right in Middlebury and the road goes right through town, but if I spent any time there it escapes me now. My contact in Burlington, though he didn't know it yet, was Joe Rivers, who'd been in Falmouth for the chorus festival in March. I was aware that you really shouldn't drop in on people without at least letting them know you're coming, especially if you don't know them very well and all the more if you expect them to put you up. And yet, here I was doing it, and it wasn't for the last time by any means. I did this sort of thing, probably all too often, for some years to come, always under circumstances that allowed me to persuade myself that the customary rules of etiquette don't apply in this instance. Nobody ever expressed to my face any dismay that I was suddenly there, which probably only goes to show that my friends had better manners than I.

Another reason not to show up unexpectedly is that the person you're counting on finding might not be around. That almost happened to me this time. I'm not sure whether I had Joe's phone number or address or what the sequence of events was, but I do know that I wound up at his family's home and met his father, who told me that Joe wasn't living there. Uh oh. But no, it was cool, he just had a place of his own and his dad called him and he came by and got me. If my being there was putting him out, he didn't let on, but greeted and treated me like we'd known each other a long time. He had an apartment in a big old house, I think, and the place was pretty nice. He had a roommate who was in college and friendly, and you could tell they weren't slobs. We made up some dinner and sat around talking and a couple of college girls came by to hang out. It's only occurring to me now that my being there might have kept Joe from going out partying, but if that was the case he didn't say so. I was a little intimidated by his guests, but not so much that I clammed up. I had a nice evening, of which the dominant inner theme was consideration of the fact that here was this guy who was a year older than me and had a damn good life of his own, as far as I could see. When I headed out in the morning, I was going down the front walk and Joe stood on the porch and said, "Your time's coming, Tom." I never saw Joe again, but I thought of him often.

With no interstate highways in existence or possibly even contemplated yet for northern New England, getting across first Vermont, then New Hampshire en route to the Maine coast involved going from one little town to the next on roads that were state highways with numbers, but essentially local roads. With the Green Mountains in central Vermont and the Whites in NH, many changes of direction were involved, and many short rides. The proportion of Vermont drivers willing to stop for a hitchhiker was relatively high, but most of them weren't going very far, usually just to the next town. The day was lovely, the scenery breathtaking at times, and every little town had its own appealing features, so it was okay with me that progress was slow. Nearing the eastern edge of the state, I was picked up by a girl maybe just a year or two older than me. She was driving a Jeep and was wearing jeans and boots and a checkered work shirt. She could have come from a camping trip or a horseback ride or from working on a farm. She was chatty, smart, self-possessed and knew how to drive the Jeep. She looked like she didn't worry much about whether she looked just right, which caused her to look authentic and natural and, hence, just right. I didn't know there were girls like this.

She told me her family ran a store in Fairlee called Chapman's. It was right on the Connecticut River, Vermont's eastern border. I live near there now and patronize Chapman's from time to time. They sell toys, jewelry, hand-knit hats and scarves, fishing gear, wine, used books, exotic chocolate, things like that. It's not really a general store because you can't buy groceries. The woman who seems to run the place is named Alida, and she does a good job of it. In the interest of connecting past and present, I'm tempted sometimes to enlist her help in figuring out whether she might have been the driver of the Jeep who gave me a new perspective on womanhood.

- Alida, do you remember late in the summer of 1966 picking up a young guy hitchhiking?
- Of course! How could I forget?

  Nah.

My next ride took me down Route 5 and across the river into Hanover. I must have been aware that Hanover was the home of Dartmouth College, but I had no idea I'd ever been there until I got out in the center of town and things looked familiar. It came to me that I'd been there with the family in the early stages of Eric's looking at colleges. My cousin Jon Hopkins was still a student there at the time, and I know we'd spent some time with him, but my lasting recollection was of the weather, which had been kind of cool and drizzly but thoroughly pleasant, kind of like my favorite nights for running. Now it was late summer, late afternoon, clear and sunny, more pleasant yet. I walked around the campus a bit and gained a sense that this school was powerfully rooted to the ground and beneficently open to the sky and the countryside around it. I thought of trying to move on towards the coast, but pictured myself getting dropped off in the middle of farm country with night coming on, so I thought better of it. I asked about a room at the Hanover Inn overlooking the campus, but it was going to be expensive. Heading down Main Street, a very short walk, I found the Green Lantern Inn. The Green Lantern was the only other place in town where a room could be had, and was kind of a poor man's Hanover Inn. Being a poor man, I took a room there.

As all inns should, the Green Lantern had a dining room and full dinner menu. It wasn't very big, but it nodded in all respects to the traditional ways of New England hostelry: linen tablecloths and napkins, true silverware, rough plastered walls and lots of dark posts and beams; if it weren't August, there'd have been a fire going in the fireplace. Turn the electric lights into whale oil lamps, and I could have been some important personage in the Federalist era, holding over for the stagecoach to Boston. And it didn't cost a whole lot. That was probably, or certainly, its undoing. Like most of the old buildings that remained in downtown Hanover, it was torn down some years later to make room for a four-story brick office building with an outfitter's store or a boutique or restaurant or some such thing on the first floor. There is once again an alternative to the Hanover Inn downtown, but it costs even more, markets itself as a luxury joint and is not an attractive building.

Next day, I took Route 4 all the way to Portsmouth, then along the Maine coast to Old Orchard Beach. The southern Maine shore isn't a bit like what most of the world thinks of when they think of the Maine coast. They think of Down East Maine, with its rocky shoreline and bays and inlets and offshore islands and quaint little fishing/lobstering towns. Southern Maine has broad, sandy beaches that go uninterrupted for miles, and the region is not at all subtle about its tourist attractions. Old Orchard Beach offered a true honky-tonk experience, with a permanent carnival located on its famous Pier. There were rides, arcades, fried dough, corn dogs, Shoot-Til-U-win games, photo booths, you name it, and the town had a healthy measure of fleabag hotels and fried-food joints to keep all the visitors going. I got there and looked around and wondered how Kalpy fit into all this.

Kalpy fit into it because, for one thing, he grew up there, and it's an easily overlooked fact that all vacationers' destinations, other than remote wilderness areas, are sustained by local year-round residents, not all of whom make their living off of the seasonal visitors. For another thing, Kalpy would find a way to fit in anywhere. When you know how to operate, and you like to be in people's company and they in yours, you're going to fit in. I'm pretty sure that Kalpy knew I'd be along, but he didn't know when, since neither did I. I knew that he owned and worked at a restaurant called the Pineland Grille, and I found him there late in the day. His was one of the few eateries in town where you could sit down at a table and be served. I got a hero's welcome from Kalpy, who introduced me around to the staff and set a righteous meal before me. I'm sure that everybody up there knew that he was a highly successful high school track coach and that this was an important part of his life, but I might have been the first of his athletes to appear in the flesh.

Kalpy's home, where I stayed during my time at Old Orchard Beach, was a large, handsome place on the water a little ways north of town. I can't remember whether that was his boyhood home and he was sharing it with his family and his parents, or whether it was just him and his wife and their kids. His wife was Angel, a beautiful, gracious, high-bred totally Grecian woman whom I've spoken of; Tommy was about 11 years at the time, and Betty, probably 7 or 8. I stayed for a couple of days at least. I hadn't run for over a week and was quite aware of that, so I got in a couple of runs in the hard sand along the shore. I think I brought the kids to the attractions on The Pier, and I went with Kalpy one evening to a racetrack nearby where I placed a few bets on the horses. I did some lazing on the beach, and swimming, but the Maine waters aren't to be stayed in for very long. I had a good time, felt the summer slipping through my fingers and headed home.

I got back with a few days to spare before school started up, and beautiful late-summer days they were, so I spent part of each of them at Surf Drive Beach. There was a residual group of local kids hanging out there, soaking up the last sunrays and free days, as I was. I became good friends with a girl named Ronna, who was a little younger and unknown to me previously, but smart and easy to be with. Our liaison carried over into school, where we looked for each other and got together when we could. We weren't going steady, which was what it was called when a pair was romantically involved, but she was a good, comfortable friend who I felt easy around, the first girl I'd let myself know like that. After the year got under way, she had an AFS sister from South Africa who later got in trouble back home for being a white girl actively opposed to apartheid, or so I heard. She also had a father who I met many times, liked a lot, and discovered later was the local interviewer for Falmouth applicants to Harvard. I realized as I got into the process of looking at and applying to colleges what a serendipitous happenstance this was. They were also one of not many Jewish families in Falmouth. The cross-cultural impact of this wasn't of great importance, but they all count.

* * *

My last year at LHS looked to me like it'd be an interesting one. Except for the anticipation of adventures in track, I hadn't ever felt that way before, but there were going to be some new takes this year. I was in the journalism class that put together the student newspaper. I was taking physics and calculus. The English department had a program set up for the seniors that would have us working with different teachers for different disciplines. We had a new French teacher. American history was the seniors' course in social studies, and I thought I'd like that. And I was signed up for drivers' ed for the first half, just to make sure there'd be no more screwups at the DMV office. On top of all that, I was a senior, with all the privileges of rank implied by that. LHS had a long-standing tradition that the central set of stairs that ran from the cafeteria up to the center of the topmost hall was reserved for the seniors; were known, in fact, as the Senior Stairs. I'd always felt that was a contrived bunch of crap, but I observed the ban for five years and just couldn't wait to walk up and down those stairs.

Drivers' Ed did me a lot of good, in that nothing ever happened in the class and I was able to use the time to get most of my homework done. Our teacher was Mike Gaddis, whose greatest glory in his association with LHS was not teaching kids to drive, but coaching the boys' basketball team for several years, including the heaven-sent 1963 season. He also coached football for a while and had some success there as well. I'd guess he was deep into his 50's which then meant you were getting pretty old, and he showed it. He had a white crewcut and a frighteningly flushed complexion, spoke hoarsely and breathed loudly. He didn't seem to take much pleasure in being a drivers' ed instructor. There were days when he really didn't want to be there, which we divined from the mood he was in, and others when he wasn't there at all. There were probably some course requirements, but I can't say what they might have been. Everybody in the class was just there so their insurance rate would be lower, or to heighten the odds of passing their driver's test. This was known to Mike, so he made little effort to engage us in learning about driving. On his good days, he could be fun to talk to, because however he may have felt about his duties as an instructor, he was very down to earth.

When we went to the DMV for my test, I drew the same officer who'd flunked me over the summer. He and Gaddis were old pals, but I still had to get all the maneuvers right. I was going up the fateful straightaway behind the DMV at 25 MPH when a schoolbus coming towards me pulled over to let kids out. The law about stopping for a schoolbus unloading kids was a recent one, so the busses didn't have any flashing lights or flipout signs or anything to warn you, you were just supposed to know. I knew, so I came to a stop. The tester looked at me funny, like I was doing something wrong, so I pointed to the bus. He reflected for a moment, nodded his head and spent the rest of our drive talking to Gaddis in the back seat. When we were all getting out, Mike said, "Turk, you gave me that book, didn't you?" Book? What's he talking about? "You know, the one with the questions you answered at the end of every chapter." Pause. "Oh yeah, I gave that to you last week." I got my license. The really good news is that eight or nine years later, I was living in a cottage on Perch Pond next door to Mike and Trudy Gaddis. I couldn't have asked for better neighbors. I saw a lot of Mike, who was always cheerful, still down to earth, and seemingly happy and in good health. He had me worried there for a while.

Later in the very afternoon of my driver's test, I was in the VW in front of the school chatting with Lynn Botsch. Lynn was the proud operator of a vintage Citroen, a luxury French sedan with features that American automakers never dreamed of and a comfort level on a par with your favorite easy chair. How she wound up with that vehicle I never knew, but it was a joy to ride in. I wanted to add a little zest to my departure and went up the drive in the VW at a high rate of speed, which I sustained for too long. I hit a patch of sand when I tried to turn onto Lakeview Avenue and went into a spin, which ended in the middle of the Galassos' front lawn. They were nice enough about it, but I had to do a little free landscaping work to make good on it. First day with my license, and I'm already causing property damage. I can almost, but not quite, say that that was my last accident in a motor vehicle. It was certainly my most avoidable one.

I was starting to get some notice for being a good taker of multiple-choice tests. I'm not sure when the National Merit test was administered, but at some point in the fall the results came in and everyone who'd taken the test was called into a classroom to get their results and have them explained. Hugo Tassinari was the LHS guidance counselor leading the meeting. He had a few three-digit numbers written on the blackboard. After going on a bit about how the colleges look at the scores, he directed our attention to the numbers: "THIS (142) is the score that achieved Letter of Commendation status last year. Two of our students scored THIS (144) and one scored THIS (146). THIS (148) was the score that achieved semifinalist status last year. One of our students scored THIS (150), and if Mr. Turkington would like to stand up and take a bow, he may." I didn't take the bow, but I admit

I felt a little rush. There was a second round of the SAT's coming up soon, and I felt like I was getting in good shape for it. Not that I was doing anything to prepare for it – nobody was, as far as I know – but I liked the direction my Saturday morning test binges were taking.

For the record, the three Letters of Commendation went to Linda Bennett, Mark Denman and Ken Ketchum. There were any number of bright kids in our class who could outsmart any of us on a given day. Why did we get these high scores, and the gold stars on our college applications that tend to accompany them, and not Steve Troynak or Anita Barrow or Patty Ortins or Donnie Bumpus or Sydney Sheehan? Succeeding in these exams is a discrete ability, and I seemed to have it. There were plenty of things I was just plain stupid about, but I could ace a standardized exam in my sleep. As for that semifinalist business: my older son achieved it and asked me what he had to do to become a finalist. I told him, stay out of jail.

Another oddball class I was taking was Journalism. The class met every day and was for credit. Our task was to put together all the elements that would take up a full page in The Enterprise every Tuesday and report on the doings at LHS. Our teacher was George Moses, who was semi-retired and did this for fun, but did it well. There was a lot of life in his class, as well as a modicum of goofing around. He was also the town moderator at Town Meeting every spring, a considerably more critical and demanding position that he executed as well as is humanly possible: with tact, humor, command and a thorough understanding of the rules of order. The class was fun. Every week, everyone would get their assignment, get it accomplished by the end of the week, and leave it to Mr. Moses to assemble it into publishable form. He anointed me editorial editor, which may have been the plum position, if only because it required no research or legwork. I could just think about some issue that affected LHS at the time and write up how I felt about it. What's not to like about that job? There was another substantial benefit of being in the class that didn't become known to me until later in the year.

The cross country season got under way with a bunch of experienced runners who'd won the state meet in 1965 and a few newcomers who looked very good. Vadala was gone, off to Providence College, but we were otherwise intact and full of high expectations. Everybody was in good shape; without saying it often or loudly, we felt that we ought to be able to win every meet we were entered in, wherever or whatever it was. Geoff was stronger than ever, to a point where I found that just training with him was a challenge. Racing with him was more than that.

The most prominent newcomers were the Binghams. Pete was a junior who'd already established himself as a force in the hurdles and long jump in the track seasons. These aptitudes don't often translate into distance running ability, but Pete took to it quite nicely. His brother Mark was a freshman, but had the build and the self-confidence of a thoroughbred and ran accordingly. Jim Peters wasn't new to the team, but he was coming along quickly and looked to be in the mix, if still a little behind. All three of these guys were from Mashpee, the town just to the east of Falmouth that sent its high schoolers to Falmouth. Mashpee had been established many years before as the home for the Wampanoags who lived here before the white settlers came in and took over. I believe the Binghams were Wampanoags in large part, Jim Peters entirely so. It will never be known to me how welcome minority kids may have felt when they entered into an activity dominated by a pre-established group of white kids. I would hope that, at least on this team, these guys felt they were wanted, because they most decidedly were, by everybody involved.

It's bemusing to me that I should have such distinct memories of my first five days on this team as a lowly freshman, and such a hazy recollection of the entire season when I was an exalted senior and co-captain of a feared and respected squad. We trained; we raced; we won. There was a certain sameness to the routines, and to the races. Just about every time we competed, Geoff and I ran together a little ways ahead of the others for most of the race, then at some point Geoff would pull away and I'd try but fail to stay with him. Sometimes I'd finish close behind him, sometimes not so close, but he was always our first man and I was nearly always our second. There'd be a bunch of LHS guys not far behind me, and we'd win. We won all our dual meets and the league meet and the Catholic Memorial Invitational. With enrollment growing at LHS, we were in Class C now, but we won the state meet with plenty of room to spare. It's easy to say this in deep retrospect, but this would have been a good time for Kalpy to have looked beyond the usual competition and get us off to a big-time race or two, maybe to one of the big invitationals in Van Cortland Park in the Bronx. Kalpy rarely missed a trick, but he may have overlooked one here. He got on board with the idea in the winter and spring, but we may have been most ripe for success in the fall.

The only discontent attached to this season without defeat was that we didn't get to run in the New England championships. For some reason, Massachusetts had no all-state meet on the schedule to bring together all the best teams and individuals from all the classes, just to see who's the boss in head-to-head competition.

What they did was, they added up the total team times from everybody's results in the class meets and sent the three teams with the best aggregate times to the New Englands. This year, the second and third-place teams were tied; we were a total of two seconds behind them. It kind of left every one of us thinking, If I'd known we'd be going to the New Englands if I ran two seconds faster, I'd have run two seconds faster. Well, yeah, maybe. It's one thing to think that way an hour after it's over, but what if someone had told you that half a mile from the finish line? Those two seconds can be very hard to find.

I was beginning to have some distractions from my narrow focus on the running teams, though the most engaging and ego-boosting of them came about as a result of it. Not too long after getting my college applications submitted late in the fall, I started hearing from the track coaches at some of those schools, inviting me to come visit for a weekend, see the school, meet the team and such. This came as somewhat of a surprise to me, because I hadn't yet and never did reach the elite level of competition where I'd expect college coaches' interests to lie. I suppose when you factor in the grades and test scores it takes to pass muster with the admissions offices, the pickings get fairly slim, and I looked like a good candidate. So I got to sample the wares of a number of upper-crust schools in greater depth than I could have gained from the standard campus tour and Q&A session.

I stayed a weekend at Harvard in a luxurious ancient apartment at the top of Lowell House shared by the school's top miler and hurdler. Geoff went with me down to Princeton where we stayed with Richie Stafford of Salem and his roommate, Eamon something. Good guys, good runners, and there was nothing I could see that was not to like about their school, or Harvard either. These places are dripping with tradition, excellence, privilege and self-esteem. If anything, I got an even stronger sense of that at Yale, where I didn't apply but did get a look at on my Brown weekend, when I went there with the Brown team to a meet. Only trouble is, I felt no sense of identity with these schools. I felt they were too rich for my blood, and couldn't picture finding a niche for myself in them. I can hear it now: Well, you just go there and make your own way, you know. Okay, but I had four years to do that in high school and didn't do such a satisfying job of it. I wanted to feel some sense of belonging with the place before I went there.

I never did hear from the Dartmouth coach, but my application was in and I already had a nice impression of the school, so I figured I ought to go up and get a longer look at it. My friend Neil Hicks had the same notion, so we made arrangements for me to pick him up in Sturbridge and head north one October weekend. I figured it was a small college where everybody knew everybody, and since I was friends with Dave Burwell and Charley Johnson, we'd locate one of them and have a place to stay. A few years later, when the Aquarian Age was upon us, this might have been a reasonable approach, but this was 1966 and it was presumptuous as hell, not to mention risky. We got to the campus about 9 at night to find a bonfire as tall as a skyscraper blazing in the middle of the Green and thousands of people, not all of them students, milling around it, not all of them sober. This was a football rally for the big homecoming game the next day, and this was the most festive weekend of the year at Dartmouth. And here were two high school kids, far from home and needing a place to stay.

There was no turning back now, so we left the Green, found a dorm and checked out the list of residents inside the front door. No Charley, no Dave. We tried another. No luck, but a guy asked who we were looking for, said he knew Charley and directed us to his dorm. I can still see the look on Charley's face when we barged in. "Tom!" He was sitting in a dorm chair with a study board across its arms, reading and taking notes. He was either happy to see us or putting on a good show of it: he talked for a while, introduced us around and spent some more time back with his books while we sat in the hall and drank beer moderately with a bunch of other guys without dates. It was nice; nobody was getting shitfaced, the talk was of interesting matters and Neil and I were included. Charley was in a two-room double, so there was room for us on the floor, though the roommate seemed a little put out, but who can blame him? Charley gave us a mini-tour the next day, we ate in the dining hall, walked around the library and the arts center, and in all, the visit was a positive.

My visit to Brown was quite the opposite, and has long served me as an example of how initial impressions can be deceiving. I was there on a cold, raw, blustery January weekend, so whenever I was outside I saw people walking hurriedly with their heads down, and nobody talking to each other. I was put in the charge of a Brown Key member whose task it was to serve as my host for the weekend, but he didn't seem to like doing it and probably shouldn't have been. He had someplace to go that evening, so I hung out in his dorm and met a few nice people, but was left pretty much on my own. I went with the team to Yale the next day for the meet and was impressed, though not tempted, by the intense Olde English model/blueblood/privilege/heritage atmosphere I found there.

The Yale dinner was great, too, served as it was in a wood-paneled dining room straight out of Hogwarts. On the bus coming back, I got to talking with Greg Oullette, a superstar long jumper from Wareham who filled me in on how much he enjoyed Brown and asked me what the plans were for that evening. I told him actually, Greg, I think I'll head back to Falmouth. Oh – well then - could you drop me off in Wareham? I've had many reasons since then to realize that Brown is a fine and vital institution, but my weekend there killed the deal as far as my interest went.

My nighttime running had for two years now been as regular a feature in my life as doing my homework or putting on clean socks; i.e., I didn't always do it, but I usually did. Sometimes I'd make arrangements with Mark or Kevin or Salt to meet up and do it together, but usually I got out on my own. The loop from 287 Scranton Avenue that went around via Queen Street and King Street was 1.42 miles, which was about what I guessed it to be before I got an accurate measure on it. I rarely ran that loop just once, but when I did, I blasted it. I had a 4.78 mile course that was a favorite of mine, especially when the wind wasn't blowing too hard. It took me along the beach, down to the Mill Road anchor and back via Elm Road. As with all workouts, there were plenty of times when I didn't feel very into it, just got it done and told myself: Well, at least I ran. But there were many transcendent moments when I fell into a zen-like state where the road and my breathing and my feet hitting the pavement and the silence and darkness around me were all one body, heading for eternity as fast as we could. I nearly always had a stopwatch going on the front steps. Knowing the time gave me an objective perspective on the run, outside of the quality of the experience.

My interactions with people I came across on a night run were rare, brief and widely variant. If I went the distance without seeing or being noticed by another soul, that was fine with me. Early on, I too often had encounters with passing cars containing critical or downright nasty people. Nothing spoils a run more than hearing someone shout, "TURKINGTON, YOU ASSHOLE!" as the shouter and his pals zoom past, or hearing a thrown bottle break at my feet or on a stone wall behind me. The commentary seemed to change with time; it was as if the town got used to having boys running around the streets at odd hours, maybe even came to appreciate that the results of this peculiar activity were state championships for Falmouth teams. By my senior year, I was hearing a lot more encouragement than scorn, when I heard anything at all. One cool, calm, clear autumn night, I was on my long loop, feeling great and running like a deer as I approached my friend Ronna's house. The banging of a trash can alerted me to her father putting out the garbage. I could tell that he stopped to watch as I went by. A month or two later, he was conducting my alumni interview for Harvard, and he brought the moment up. Thought it said good things about me. Who was I to dispute him?

English instruction for seniors introduced a team teaching element to the curriculum. My usual instructor was Mr. Reid, a young, lively fellow who ran the class well and enjoyed the kids, but left me with the impression that he was just kind of sliding through it. We spent a few weeks with Mr. McKee, a Dartmouth grad with a very sharp wit, a trace of aloofness, and an oblique and somewhat cynical view of the world that was not a mismatch with a lot of high school seniors. Mrs. Pierce got us for a few weeks of creative writing. In her class, I did one of my best pieces of work ever. It was a short story assignment for which, no surprise, I wrote a piece about a young American kid who's in the finals of the 10,000 meters in the Olympics. I told it well: it got into what was going through the kid's mind as the race drew near, then how after he settled into the race, he was too intent on his running to notice anything around him, then how he came around and bore down on the last lap. This was patterned after Billy Mills's race in Tokyo in 1964, so the kid was racing with the Tunisian and the Australian to the finish line. He feels the tape against his chest, crosses the shadow of the telephone pole and staggers across the front yard to grab the stopwatch on the steps. I was reading this aloud to the class, and after the last line - "The boy reset his watch, and went indoors" – I looked up at Mrs. Pierce and saw her jaw drop. That's a hackneyed expression, but she knew she'd just heard something good, and she showed it. With some alterations, I used the same story a couple of years later in a college class and got a similar reaction from Professor Levitin.

The culture of the track team extended beyond what transpired in the daily workouts and the frequent meets. As we accumulated major championships, there came to be a certain cachet in being known as a serious member of the team. At a time when we're thrashing about trying to establish some identity for ourselves, there's a real security in knowing we're respected for something that we do. And there were activities that kept us plugged in, almost like secret handshakes. Kalpy had a theory that high jumpers and pole vaulters, who must come down after they've gone up, will feel better about going up higher if they don't have to fall so far and can count on landing on something soft. At the beginning of every winter track season, he'd order in a pile of burlap feed bags and a big load of furniture foam remnants. Down in the lower lobby of the gym, we'd all take an afternoon or two and stuff those bags with the foam so that Kalpy could stitch them up with a big needle and thread, then tote them off to the jumping pits. This was before any high schools were buying big expensive landing pits made for the purpose, so our pits were as comfy as anybody's. Did it make any difference? Kalpy kept developing state champion high jumpers and pole vaulters, despite having absolutely no background in those events. You be the judge.

The winter track team appeared to be stacked with talent. We had a potential state meet scorer in every event, and two in some of them. I was a captain along with Geoff Cahoon and Greg Anderson. This elevated status did nothing to make me a better runner, and in fact I felt I'd been flatlining for some time, including the entire cross country season. I was putting in the daily workouts and keeping up with my night runs, but I didn't feel that I was striving, and couldn't figure out where that little touch of magic had gone. To add to that, I had to deal with my first lasting injury, which befell me early in January. We had a clear but cold day and I felt my knee tighten up on me while doing some high-speed intervals. I was feeling good and wanted to keep going, so I did, but the knee locked up tight and gave me frequent trouble for weeks. I'd had a couple of pretty respectable dual meet efforts earlier, so I felt I was going in the right direction and didn't want any interruptions, but the knee became a regular issue. I started having to sit out some practices, and a few meets.

I can't blame the injury for what happened at the YMCA meet in Boston, because that was over Christmas break. Jim Peters, Salt Handy and I were in the seeded heat of the mile, and we performed horribly. We all can live with a stinko race from time to time, but our shame was exponentially compounded this time by being broadcast to viewers of the late news all over Massachusetts. I was home watching it, and there must have been a dearth of sports activity that day because all the sportscaster had to talk about was the YMCA meet. The format was that while he read his commentary about the meet, they showed our race on the screen behind him. Viewers saw a pack of about ten runners taking off, then immediately there they were coming up the home stretch of the first lap, with three guys in Falmouth uniforms in the back of the pack. A moment later we saw the end of the second lap, the three Falmouth runners now ten yards behind the pack. A moment later and we were twenty yards behind. Next lap, thirty, and the guy kept talking. I was cringing in my chair, knowing that hundreds of thousands of people were seeing this, and anyone who was paying attention could clearly see that these Falmouth kids were in way over their heads. By the time the sports segment was done, we were entering into view stage left just as the pack was exiting stage right. Of all the damn times to show a race of mine on TV.

The BAA meet in Boston Garden came up in mid-January. Having lost some training time and missed some races, I didn't go into it with a whole lot of confidence. What little I had escaped me early in the race, where I felt flat, awkward and unprepared. A group of four, including Bobby Jayes, pulled away over the first half. I struggled along in the next bunch, hoping some kind of magic would happen late in the race to springboard me out of there, but of course it didn't. I wound up sixth in 4:38, a few yards behind Wayne Silveira of New Bedford and far behind the top four. What really irked me was that Geoff won the 1000, Greg won the 300, Carl Gonsalves won the high jump and the relay team placed fourth, so we scored 16 points. The winning team had 18, so a couple of points out of the mile would have come in very handy. Had we won, we would have been the first team not from Class A ever to win it, or so we were told. The BAA meet was the equivalent of an all-class state meet, and Falmouth wasn't used to scoring many points in it, but here we almost won it. It was a good day.

It stayed good, too. It was a fairly select group that went up to the BAA, and Kalpy took us all over to the waterfront. This being Boston, it wasn't a long walk. This is the Quincy Market district now, jam-packed with stores and bars and eateries and tourists, but then the Durgin-Park restaurant was the only place with the lights on. We had a fun dinner there, then headed back to the Garden by way of Haymarket Square. The Haymarket exists today in a severely truncated form, hemmed in on all sides by high rents and luxury condos; then it went on for blocks, rows and rows of shabby pushcarts and smelly basement shops selling meats and produce of a variety and quality and price that couldn't be found anywhere else. Kalpy, who did a lot of cooking at home as well as at his restaurant, looked around a bit until he found a leg of lamb that he liked. We all went back to the Garden to watch the K of C night meet, where we saw a lot of collegiate athletes we knew about and a lot of Olympic-caliber athletes we'd heard about competing on the very same track we'd been racing on a few hours earlier. This was all fun, every bit of it.

We were back in the Garden for the state meet two weeks later. I'd been sitting out races in the interim, but was able to get in some workouts, some of which were terminated when my knee stiffened up. I didn't feel I was totally out of condition. What made me nervous about the Class C mile was the depth of the field: John Vercollone, who'd won the BAA mile, was in it, along with Jayes, Mike Malone, Al Arsenault, other guys with pedigree; I could run a pretty good race and still get bumped back quite a ways. At least I wasn't feeling that my team's fortunes were riding too heavily on the outcome of the mile; we went up there feeling that we'd be scoring points from a lot of different places, and we weren't too far into the day before it became evident that we were right. Nevertheless, Salt and I went to the starting line as anxiety-stricken as ever. There were about a dozen in our heat; Vercollone went out hard and immediately opened up daylight on the rest of us, who stayed clustered in a pack.

Did I say clustered? I meant congealed. At any given moment for the first three quarters, I was within arm's length of at least two other guys and sometimes more, and the cast kept changing. I don't know why nobody got tripped up, because everybody spent the whole race either passing or getting passed, and at close quarters. Experience helped me out a whole lot here. I was able to respond instinctively to the constant changes in position, rather than have to think about what to do, so I stayed focused on my running. I swung out into the second or third lane when I had to, ran to the inside when there was room. The pace kept accelerating, but things never broke up. Just over a quarter mile to go, I sensed that two guys ahead of me were about to draw up side by side, and one on my shoulder was pulling up on me, and in two seconds I was going to be boxed in. When it's time to go, you better go. I slipped between the two ahead of me, passed the next kid on the left, the next one on the right, and I was in the clear. For the next 65 seconds, I felt like a cartoon character running a step ahead of a buffalo stampede. The sound of all that banging on the boards was terrifying, but I kept it behind me. 4:33.1, second place, four points for Falmouth. Salt came in 15 yards behind me and was out of the money. Considering the congestion and the extra yardage I ran out in the outer lanes, this might have been the best race I ever ran.

It was also the last one I ran that season. I ramped up my training as my knee came around, but Kalpy and I agreed that there wasn't much point in testing it in a race. I did my job at the state meet, and my teammates did theirs. Geoff won the 1000, Robb Hart got third. Donnie was third in the 600. Greg broke the state record in the 300, but George Carter of Danvers beat him to it. Mark Bingham took third in the two mile. His brother Pete won the hurdles. Carl Gonsalves won the high jump. The relay team took third. Randolph and Andover were in the habit of fighting it out for the Class C title, but we were well ahead of both of them and everybody else.

One of the officials at the meet was Jock Semple, a crusty little Scotsman who'd been American for quite some time but still sounded like he was just off the boat. Jock was one of a number of underappreciated older guys who kept the running sports alive and active for those who'd moved on from school. Geoff and I knew him pretty well from participating in his summer track meets in South Boston, and road races. He was the trainer for the Celtics back when that job was not a lofty perch, and had himself a little office deep in the bowels of Boston Garden. He collared us on the track that afternoon and asked if we wanted to watch the big-time meet that night from down on the floor. Well, yeah, Jock, we'd like that. So he told us where to go to get into the Garden using his name, where we'd find his office, and when to be there. I can't remember whether the whole team was staying for the night meet, but Geoff and I and a couple of teammates met up later with Jock, who led us through a rabbit warren of subterranean corridors and elevators and passageways and finally out onto the floor. The uppermost point of the banked turn was about chest-high, so we stood there with our elbows on the edge of the track and watched some of the world's most accomplished runners compete. Great.

Jock unwittingly but somewhat deservedly became a symbol of male chauvinism in sports a few months later, when Kathy Switzer entered the Boston Marathon by signing up as K. Switzer. The rules against women running middle distance races were just starting to soften. A woman in a marathon was unimaginable to most of the world, strictly against the rules, and Boston was no exception. Well, Jock was a stickler for the rules. When he saw K. Switzer out on the course, he felt he must tear her number off to render her unofficial, and ran after her to do so. He did this in full view of the press truck, so the next day the world was treated to a photo sequence of Jock running after Kathy, reaching for her number, and getting tossed to the side of the road by her large boyfriend, who was running alongside her. It was an important moment in consciousness-raising in the sporting world, but Jock was pilloried for his role. He was seen as the face of chauvinism, and understandably so. The exclusionary rules were changed over the next few years, and Jock did as much as any of the old guard to bring that about. He was all about participation, and once he understood that women and girls wanted to participate, he helped open the sport up to them.

* * *

Considering that I spent more of my waking hours in the classroom than anywhere else, not a whole lot of my time there made a deep impression on me. I had an American History class with Mr. Craig. He was a portly, kindly old gent who never seemed to get out of his chair and whose voice and method of delivery was nearly as sonorous as those of Mr. Roberts, whose two years of instruction in World Cultures left me with no memories more distinct than breaking a desk once and sleeping often. What is it about social studies? Here in my adulthood, I derive much of my reading enjoyment from the fields of history, politics, modern issues, cultural trends: social studies, y'know? Yet in high school, where I had a course of study all laid out for me and a professional in the field to guide me, my engagement was so tenuous that I can't even remember what was offered me in my junior year. I had to have taken something in the department, but I have no idea what it was. Maybe the problem is in the static nature of the subject matter. When you teach history, there must come a time when you realize you're teaching the same thing, year after year: no evolution, no new material. Get someone in there for 30 or 40 years, and they can sleepwalk through it, and I guess some do. It should come as no surprise that the students join the teacher in that activity.

French was another matter, not in terms of enthusiasm for the subject matter, but for wakefulness in the classroom. Madame Colton had moved on, and my new teacher was Mae Childs, a Falmouth product who'd gone on to college, gotten a teacher's credential and landed the job of French teacher at LHS. She was all of, what, 23? She was not a very demanding instructor, though she stayed on task most of the time. What I noticed above all was that she was very pretty, cheery and lively, and that I spent much of my time in her classroom in a state of erotic excitement. She moved around the room a lot as she taught, but every day there was almost sure to be a time when she'd come over and sit on my desk with her legs crossed while she taught the class. I could have wrapped my right arm around her hips without even leaning forward, and believe you me, when Miss Childs sat on my desk, that possibility was the sole occupant of my mind. She never gave me any reason to think that this was a come-on of some kind, but it was an overwhelming distraction to which I had no objection.

I was in LHS's inaugural calculus class along with the half dozen other whizzes who'd doubled up on the math courses the year before. Our teacher was Gail Cavanaugh, who was male. So right off the bat, he was joke material. His appearance and his ways did the rest. He was ultra-thin, wispy even, with a tiny little head and prominent google eyes magnified by a set of powerful spectacles. There was an avian look to him that radiated timidity and delicacy. He spoke softly and with great deliberation. He was a heavy user of the opaque projector, as high-tech a device as existed in the classroom then, allowing him to have his scribblings on a sheet of paper projected on the chalkboard, which he seldom used. He knew his stuff and used every minute of his class time to focus on the subject, but he wasn't very good at understanding why one of his pupils who didn't understand some point, didn't understand it. If you asked him to clarify some element of the lesson, he'd very carefully repeat what he'd said to introduce it in the first place, in hopes that you'd get it the second time around. He couldn't very well determine what it was about his explication that you'd missed, so he wouldn't come at it from another angle that might shed new light on it.

Pretty well into the course, this was not a problem for me, but it became one. There began to be gaps in my understanding of calculus that led to greater gaps down the road. This is where a student of ambition would have checked in with Mr. Kinney to see whether his perspective might tie things back up, but it never occurred to me to do so, even though I'd always found that learning math from him was easy. And it wasn't that I didn't want to do well in calculus; I just never thought of getting outside help as an option. I sat in the classroom, absorbed what I could, did my homework most of the time, and figured that was about all I could do. As the year went on, I found it wasn't good enough. One example of the type of snag I ran into was an early encounter with f(x), a real bedrock piece of beginning calculus, which means, more or less, that everything that we do with x here is what we'll be doing with x from now on. A simple enough concept, but one that wasn't clear to me at the outset. So I asked Mr. Cavanaugh for clarification, and our conversation went something like:

- Mr. Cavanaugh, what exactly does f(x) mean?
- (pleasant smile) It means "function of x".
- Well, what I mean is, what are we really saying when we say, f(x)?
- (repeat smile) We're saying, "function of x".
- But what does "function of x" mean?
- It means "this is x's function".
- (Nod head, shut mouth, think "Oh for Chrissake")

Fewer problems came my way in physics class, also taught by Mr. Cavanaugh, where the material could be as obtuse as calculus, but where there was reference to the observable world, complete with labs and illustrations from real life. There, I could find applications of the theoretical matter that made things clear to me, so I didn't have to ask any dumb questions or get any useless answers. A meek and ultra-restrained teacher named Gail, of course, is going to be referred to, though not addressed, by that name by his students. In down times in his class, some of us dreamed up a Life Of Gail that he lived after hours. In this life, Gail races around the back roads of Falmouth at night in his Ferrari, swerving to mow down ducks in the road, tearing up the football field, laying long patches of rubber on quiet residential streets. Gail breaks into feeble old folks' homes to steal jewelry, clubbing barking dogs with a baseball bat. An unoccupied summer home burns to the ground? Gail again.

Sometime early in the spring, Columbia University hosted the Columbia Scholastic Press Association conference, an annual event that brought together staff members of student newspapers from all over the country. Our Student Intelligencer was a member of the association and every year, attendance at the conference was a huge perk for its principal contributors and George Moses, our advisor. Mr. and Mrs. Moses were New Yorkers from way back and enjoyed the trip as an opportunity to revisit their old haunts. They and nine members of the class, six girls and three boys, took the train into Grand Central and set up in our digs at the Waldorf-Astoria. Yes, THAT Waldorf-Astoria. Upon arrival, we all dropped off our bags, said so long to the Moseses and headed uptown to check in at the convention. We went into a crowded auditorium to hear a speaker or two, milled about in a reception hall with many other students, took note that we'd won an award for being the best paper in our class, went to the Brass Rail for burgers and beer (NY's legal drinking age was 18, and I was close enough), headed back downtown, and that was the last we saw of Columbia and the conference.

Having gained some familiarity with NYC on my family trips there, I played some part in suggesting places to go and the means of getting there. The nine of us did not all stick together, but I had companionship where I wandered. I know some of us took to the streets of Greenwich Village, from which the folk revival of a few years earlier had moved out, but whose echoes remained in an emergent countercultural scene that was a source of fascination to young rubes like us. At some point, I went on a search for a recorder. There was a movie out at about this time, "You're A Big Boy Now", which was about a young fellow's coming of age in NYC, for which the music had been recorded by the Lovin' Spoonful. There was an uncomplicated instrumental piece in it, Amy's Theme, that I liked and wanted to be able to play, so I found a recorder store and bought a low-grade recorder, which became a prop through the trip, on the train ride back and beyond. Somehow, somewhere, everybody saw some of the city, ate and got back to the Dorf before it got late, but I recall none of those details. The one ritual that was implicitly expected of us was that we all drop in on Mr. and Mrs. Moses, whose room or suite was not on our floor, to sit around a while, talk about what we'd been doing, mainly to let them know we were all sober and accounted for. They were such gracious and trusting people, I think we all felt we just mustn't do anything to trouble or embarrass them.

And we didn't. The latter part of our evenings we spent in one of the girls' suites, sitting around drinking beer and shooting the breeze. We recognized that this posh hotel was full of people who didn't want to be disturbed by a bunch of teenaged yahoos, and we respected that. But we did drink a lot of beer and talked, talked, talked until pretty late. At some point, my roommates – Larry and Buzzy – and I went back to our room and got ready for bed. Next thing we knew, there was a knock on the door and a visit from three of the girls who just didn't want the party to end. They sat on our beds and the talking went on. Then they lay down on our beds, and before long they got under the sheets, and the talking ended. These were sweet girls of good repute, as were the boys, and I don't think anybody's activity advanced to intercourse – not in my bed, at least – but we all enjoyed a hearty makeout session that to me was introductory, exciting and seemed to come quite naturally from somewhere. And yet, I didn't have any sense of turning a corner of some kind, or of wading into a part of life that I'd denied myself before. Maybe it's the age, maybe it's the circumstances, but I wasn't that reflective. As best as I can recall, my conscious reaction amounted to: Well, that sure was nice. I'm glad that happened.

We all knocked around the city in our own way, but what I came away with from this trip was that in at least a few important ways, I was a normal, regular, sociable guy. I'd had doubts about this. The fellowship of our parties at the hotel, on the train trips to and fro, in our encounters in the city, was new to me and felt right. I was dropped into a situation where the close company of girls – and they in the majority – was part of the territory, and I found that I fit comfortably into that place and enjoyed it, and was enjoyed in turn. I had access to all the alcoholic drinks I wanted and never got trashed. I felt no need to defend myself or to take measure of what I let out. These revelations may sound like no big deal for a bright boy of 17 years, but when they come around with authority for the first time, they're a big deal, even if the boy doesn't recognize them as such at the time.

April 15 of 1967 was probably the only day in four years that I skipped practice after school. All the seniors had Kalpy's imprimatur to do this, because that's the day that the letters are delivered from the college admissions offices. I went home to a mailbox full of fat envelopes, whose bulk indicated a bunch of papers to fill out and news from the financial aid offices. The SAT's, the mile times and the recommendations from various older folk who were sure that I'd be a standout in college and had a bright future, all of these things plus good fortune falling my way left me with my choice of schools for my higher education. I probably knew where I had in mind to go, but sometime in the next two weeks I made one more pilgrimage to Dartmouth to check on the vibes there, and they were good. The financial aid was satisfactory. The cost of a year's tuition plus room and board was to be, as I recall, $3200, of which my parents were expected to kick in $1200 and I $500. Can do. Did.

The Senior Class Play was gearing up at about this time. I capitalize its initials because of its long-standing status as an institution in every senior class's year at LHS. The director had for some years been Bill Fraher, my junior year English teacher and, as I've mentioned, a dramatist from his early days. Mr. Fraher's choice of the play of the year was presumably based on his assessment of the talent he would have to work with. In 1966, they'd produced "Rhinoceros", with Ray Rodrigues starring. The themes there were alienation and conformity, big issues in 1966. In Neils's year, there'd been two plays, one of which was "Everyman", whose theme was – well, you know. So Bill Fraher wasn't averse to presenting a meaningful piece of work. That was not what we got. We did "Teahouse of the August Moon", a piece of fluff along the lines of a lame situation comedy that took place in American-occupied

Japan after WW II. Most of the cast played Okinawan villagers who spoke no English, which severely limited their roles. All but one of the speaking parts were Army men, which left the girls out. Carl Soderland and Bob Olenick had major roles, Salt Handy and I had lesser ones, but none of us was born for the stage.

The non-American speaking part, Sakini, was a huge one, and Donnie Bumpus played it, to the salvation of the show. Donnie was wry, personable, credible and above all, audible. As long as there is some constant element in a play that makes it worth sitting through, it can claim a measure of success, and Donnie provided that. But the whole cast put a lot of time into it and had fun with it. We got a Jeep on the stage, and a goat, and staged a pretty convincing wrestling match. Margo Carreiro, our only trained talent, performed an eye-catching dance. The sets were well done. Aside from the script being so lame, and the cast providing just the one captivating performer, the production did what it was meant to do: provide focus and group activity for a bunch of seniors who were running short of reasons to come to school.

I tried to keep senioritis from affecting my performance with the track team, but it crept in there. My knee issue from the winter cleared up gradually, and I felt that my work was up to par by the middle of March. Trouble is, I went into the season with no feeling that this was my last chance to make a big push and leave my signature on the proud legacy of LHS track and field. Far from it: I viewed the next two months on the track as a customary obligation that I would fulfill in an honorable manner. That is hardly the burning ambition required of a champion. I suspect I sensed that my signature was already on the document, and that at this point I was just sweeping up on my way out.

There was a changing of the guard going on, as a lot of younger guys were stepping up and becoming statewide performers. I felt that I was in a loftier position of honor and respect now than I was when I was actually earning it. If the high school years are viewed as a career, then the spring season of the senior year is time for the gold watch. It doesn't happen to everyone, but it happens a lot, and except for a few bright moments, it happened to me.

It would have been nice if one of those bright moments had been in Philadelphia, but it wasn't. The Penn Relays were and are an ancient, honored weekend event that drew great numbers of top-ranked collegiate and high school teams from all over the East. Kalpy sent four runners and our best pole vaulter, Don McLane (aka Deputy Dawg), down there to go up against some top-flight competition. There was a degree of humor in our failure to meet expectations, starting in Logan Airport. Not many flights to Philly had a hold that could accommodate Dep's pole, so we sat around for about as long as it takes to drive to Philadelphia, waiting for a plane that could take us all and the pole too. Eventually we got there and somehow transported the pole to the Penn campus, where Eric had set up rooms for us to stay in. Or did we stay in a hotel? Not sure. The next day, we got dressed and went over to Franklin Field, where Dep was entered in the pole vault and Geoff, Donnie, Salt and I were to run in the distance medley relay. Dep had been gaining some consistency at close to 12 feet and had been a little ways over it a couple of times. When he got to the pit, he saw that they were warming up at 12-6. Warming up! "I ain't jumping." said Dep, and nobody argued with him. That did it for our pole vault entry.

The rest of us went down on the field when they called for our race, but when we got there, they told us that we couldn't run in it because the qualifying time that had been submitted was from the year before, and was supposed to be from this year. Or something like that. There was some disappointment in this, and some relief. Salt and I were the most afflicted with senioritis of our group, and the distance the two of us were to cover made up 7/10ths of the race. Marty Liquori was in this race, and Jim Jackson, and other guys knocking on the door of a 4-minute mile, and we just didn't belong on the same track with them. We would have gotten buried deep, but the experience of running on the track might have helped us the next day, when we were to be in the two-mile relay. This was an artificial surface and a good one, but it had a bit of softness and bounce in it that took some getting used to. In our race the next day, I couldn't stop being conscious of how odd my stride felt, how my feet weren't landing the way I expected them to. Not a good thing to have on your mind when you're trying to run a fast half mile, and I didn't. Salt was even worse; Geoff and Donnie ran closer to their capabilities and we came in at 8:20. but we all felt we should have been 8 or 10 seconds faster and were glad it was over with.

Kalpy's assistant coach, Frank Rhodes, accompanied us to Penn and handled our failures with aplomb. Mr. Rhodes had a shining background in the sprints and hurdles, which were largely his bailiwick with the LHS team. He had the habit of telling you after a really good race that you can do better, which is not what you want to hear after you've done something worthy of praise, but this time, when we could have and should have done better, he took it in stride. While in college, Frank Rhodes was a well-regarded hurdler, and a committed participant in the civil rights movement. We were lucky to have him in our track program.

One Saturday in May, a dilemma presented itself in the scheduling of two major meets on the same day: the official state relays in Belmont and the D-Y Invitational at Dennis-Yarmouth. Falmouth had never won the state relays, and never lost the D-Y meet, and Kalpy wanted to win them both. His solution was to split the team up: send enough guys to Belmont to win that one, and the rest of the team to D-Y to win that one. A risky move, one that might appear to have the quality of arrogance that so often leads to a fall, but Kalpy didn't do arrogance and neither did his runners. We all liked a challenge, and Kalpy put a good one on our plate that day. Most of the varsity runners went to Belmont; the JV's and the varsity field event guys went to Dennis-Yarmouth.

I was in Belmont for the two-mile relay (4x880 in modern parlance), the first event. Kalpy had me running third leg, which puzzled me, because as well as our anchor man Jim Peters had been running, he was a sophomore and I felt I was still a little ahead of him. As it turned out, I was right where I'd have wanted to be. Mark and Salt kept us among a pack of leaders through the first two legs. When I got the baton, I shot out of there to clear out from the crowd and settled into second behind Mike Malone. Belmont wasn't a very fast track, but the conditions were good and I felt good, and I knew I'd get Malone. I also knew that the very audible Bobby Jayes was just off my shoulder, and that he'd bide his time until he felt he could blow by me. I was determined not to let that happen. We went through the first lap and well into the second in that order; I opened it up on the backstretch of the second lap, went past Malone and could hear Jayes hanging with me, but there he stayed. I ran a 2:03 and handed the lead to Jim, who ran 2:03.5 and won going away.

We kept scoring in every race, until it came down to the 440 relay, which is always a dicey proposition, what with the blind handoffs and lane violations and such. Greg Anderson ran the anchor, got the baton five yards behind and finished five yards ahead. That's a lot to accomplish over 110 yards. Kalpy was very happy with the title and justifiably proud of his own work. He knew just about what everyone on his team was capable of doing and set his relay teams up so as to maximize the scoring from what he had to work with. Except for Geoff and Greg, he didn't have any superstars in there, yet he took 12 guys and managed to win an important meet that everybody else wanted. A crafty guy. We got back to Falmouth about in time to meet the bus returning from D-Y, where the rest of the team had won that meet with room to spare.

Senioritis is not just for athletes. One of its common symptoms is a devil-may-care attitude towards the requirements of classroom work. I was slacking off in a number of ways, including, for vir tually the first times, cutting classes when I felt I had something better to do. Dave Swain and Mark Denman and I were sitting around in Gail Cavanaugh's physics class one sunny May day, pondering fried clams and the beautiful day and the view from Nobska Point and how well all these things would go together. Gail hadn't gotten to the classroom yet, so we got up and left. We drove down to Woods Hole, ordered fried clams at Cahoon's fish market (this was run by Geoff's dad), and enjoyed them at Nobska Point. We were in somewhat the state of mind that hard-working people on vacation feel when they're laying on the beach on Tortola or having a souvlaki and retsina at a Greek taverna: this is so enjoyable, why don't we do it for the rest of our lives? Well, you can't. To do so would not be responsible, and being responsible is the bedrock value that attends all those who aim for success, however unclear the target may be. The last stages of the senior year in high school are, for many or most of us, a quasi-vacation that offers many opportunities for self-indulgence.

Some of the teachers recognize this as an inevitable fact of senior-year life, and accommodate themselves to it. Some feel that their purpose in that school is to teach their subject at full bore every day, and they bend not at all. I can understand the feelings of the latter, but I find the former to be more my kind of people, then and now. Playing it loose with the sanctioned routines when on an approach to the end of a long haul is simply not inappropriate behavior, even when engaged in by those of generally dependable commitment. There is, of course, such a thing as too much. Several years previously, the LHS senior class had been treated every spring to a trip to D.C. At some point, it was felt that as the classes got bigger and the kids more restive, taking them all to a faraway place for several days was just playing with fire, so the trips got shorter and closer to home. The final senior class expedition was a day trip to Martha's Vineyard a few years before my time, when it was reported that some boys got ahold of some alcohol and wound up throwing a bunch of rented bicycles into Oak Bluffs harbor. That was it for the senior class trips.

We had a Class Day that was held in the auditorium and attended by everyone in school. I think it served as a stage for presenting a bunch of year-end awards to upperclass kids who'd done something especially praiseworthy, but the meat and potatoes of the assembly was the senior class skit, where the creative seniors present some entertaining way of running through their years at LHS. Ours was pretty good, or maybe very good. "The Time Machine" was a popular TV show right then, so our skit was based on that. Donnie and I played a couple of research scientists who'd just perfected a device that could bring us back in time. We were there to emcee the trips back to the main events of the class's four years. When we activated the device, the curtains opened up and there was a big round of applause for the set, which had been executed by the art students and was very impressive. One by one, we called back mini-acts that played out peak moments or successes of our time there. Mr. Marshall, our aging and dignified principal, collared us afterwards and spoke with some emotion about how much he'd enjoyed the show. It was a nice part of wrapping things up.

One of the appearances in the show was made by the duo of Jane Howard and George Williams, the most accomplished artists in the class. Jane was a reserved, formidable figure who gave those of us who didn't know her well the impression that she had other things on her mind than the egocentric concerns that customarily plague teenagers. Besides her reputation as an outstanding artist, she acquired some note as the girlfriend of Moultie, the leader of a rock band from Provincetown called the Barbarians. The Barbarians had a song, Are You A Boy Or A Girl, that made the charts and got a lot of radio play in our parts. They had hair down to their asses, wore skin-tight jeans and played music that was quite removed from teen pop rock. When Moultie came by the school on his motorcycle to pick up Jane, it was a sign that some sort of rejectivist world out there was knocking on our doors.

George Williams, had we been astute enough to recognize it at the time, was an avatar of that world, was sitting right next to us in class, and had been since seventh grade. He was no troublemaker, but he made no effort to confine his behavior to the clear parameters defined by authority or the fuzzier ones engendered by his peers. He observed the rules for the most part, but not the norms. One day in junior high, I was sitting next to him on a schoolbus that was stopped in traffic just as an old woman named Marie, one of the town's unconventional characters who was often to be seen walking around town, was walking past. George pulled down his window and shouted out: "Hey Marie! Been gettin' some on the side or what?" She shouted back, "Nope George, gettin' it in the middle!" This exchange gave me pause: How is it that Marie and George know each other? And what are they doing shouting a crude exchange back and forth here on Main Street? George was a boy of many mysteries, but he was distinctly his own person. His artwork was legendary in our little world, including a series of Mystic Eyes that anticipated Peter Max. I still have a couple of his works, and I treasure them.

There was one other notable spring track event that season that sticks with me for a few reasons. The Falmouth Commodores of the Cape Cod League of collegiate baseball players played their home games at Fuller Field, which was also the football field and our home track. The Commodores had lights set up for their night games, and Kalpy had the notion that an evening track meet might draw some more spectators out than the scattering of parents and friends we generally saw in the afternoon. He scheduled a dual meet against one of our league opponents for late in the day, and publicized it through announcements at the school and a mention or two in The Enterprise. About 500 people showed up.

Really. No admission fee, no food stand, no Pep Squad, no band, just a plain old track meet the likes of which had been held here countless times before. But because it was going on at a time that folks could get away to watch it, and because Kalpy pumped it up it as the last chance to see the state champion LHS team in action, a crowd turned out. I suppose the football and basketball players get accustomed to competing before an audience, but it was kind of a kick for the track guys.

The folks saw some good competition, mostly between members of the home team. This was not a meet between equals; it would have been hard to find a team that could offer that. I was in the mile of course, with Salt and Mark and a few opponents and younger kids. I paced it much of the way and started pulling away in the last lap. This is nice, I thought, that I'm running well and winning when there are so many people watching. In the middle of the backstretch, I heard Kalpy shouting over the loudspeaker: "Here's a race in itself! Tom Turkington and Mark Buguey!" What? Mark? I didn't expect to see Mark there, but he pulled up with me coming out of the last turn. I asked him, somewhat breathlessly, if he wanted to tie for first. "No", he said with great resolution, as he powered it up on the straightaway. I really tried to draw him back in, but he was an inspired young man tonight, and he wasn't going to let me. His time was just over 4:42 and I was right behind him, not a bad result for a dual meet on a crummy track. I was pleased with the time, satisfied with second place and happy for Mark.

That about did it for my tenure as a track star at Lawrence High. I tried to get ramped up for the state meet, but there was little sense of urgency generated by the needs of the team, and the fire within was burning low. We all knew that we had far and away the best team in the state, mile race or no mile race, and my distractions were becoming of greater interest to me than my performance on the track. I finished up my LHS career with a 4:48 in the Class C meet, nowhere near in contention. Geoff, on the other hand, was putting it all together. He won the Class C meet, ran 2nd in the all-class state meet and 3rd in the New Englands. It helped his cause that this wasn't a bumper year for 880 runners, but 3rd in the New Englands says a lot in any year, any event.

It's taken me a long time to have much to say about Geoff. This may be because he was such a constant in my life through my high school years that I don't associate him with any particular event, or period, or activity. Our friendship grew out of the running sports, but we crossed paths in many other ways and places. When I draw up an image of Geoff, I'm as likely to picture him with me throwing snowballs at cars below Harbor Hill, or eating lunch in the cafeteria, or visiting Richie Stafford at Princeton, as doing a training run in Beebe's Woods. We just connected a lot, often by design but not always. We were both unalterably hooked on distance running and the LHS teams from the day Kalpy greeted us as newcomers in the cross-country locker room. Geoff's arc of progress in the sport took longer than mine to get going, but it went further.

I've known few people as spontaneously expressive as Geoff. If something struck him funny, his laugh was abrupt, heartfelt and audible from great distance. He had a rare talent for making funny sounds in unorthodox ways. He could clap his hands an inch in front of his mouth, adjust the tone by opening and closing his mouth and play any tune, right on key. I've spoken of the hoarse, extremely loud coughlike eruption that he could bring up from deep in his voice box. He could yip like a dog and truly sound like one in distress. He could cup his hands, put his lips to his thumbs, and play a tune by modulating his breath and raising and lowering his fingers like the valves on a trumpet. He did these things not to attract attention or to show off, but as a logical extension of his unfiltered, unfettered personality. His smile upon greeting a friend was broad and immediate. He held neither his thoughts nor his feelings back.

It's not surprising that people, especially those in the world of high school track in Massachusetts, started associating us with one another. I was a trace taller than Geoff and had a little more bulk, but we were both blonde, both quite competitive distance runners twelve months of the year, and clearly were good friends as well as teammates. During the summer, we got up to Boston frequently for Monday evening track meets put on by Jock Semple and Fred Brown at the South Boston Naval Annex. We showed up at a lot of AAU all-comers' meets, never with any hope of winning, but just because they were there and were part of a scene that we knew well, and where we were known. We often had teammates with us for some of these events, but we were the constants. One day we appeared at a meet being run by Ralph Colson, another of the old fellas who lent himself to keeping the running sports thriving. He saw us, grinned and said, "Here they are, the gold dust twins!". I got a nice sense of belonging out of that. It's a good thing there weren't any video games or smartphone screens to absorb us, or we probably wouldn't have done any of this stuff.

One thing that I found peculiar about Geoff's company was the frequency with which he would attract the attention of older kids, or men, whose interest seemed to reach beyond the normal congeniality we extend to outgoing, interesting people. My understanding of sexuality, though still quite murky, was broadening, and I couldn't sometimes help but suspect that there was an erotic flavor to their engagement. I didn't understand this. Geoff seemed every bit as much the awkward, frustrated heterosexual as I or anybody else. I guess I just figured that his slightly quirky, highly accessible personality evoked a more personal response in some guys than most of us did. I stayed in touch with Geoff for a few years more, and came to find out that he went through his youth with inclinations and longings that were unexpressed by him and unknown to me.

* * *

The senior class enjoyed, or endured, the standard celebratory and obligatory rituals and routines that most high school seniors share. We had a class banquet at some big restaurant - the Seacrest, I believe - that I attended and enjoyed. I can't remember much about it except that the Bol Jaggers played after the dinner, and I thought they were pretty good. The senior prom was a much bigger deal. I think I rented a tuxedo for it. My date was Linda, a smart, unconventional girl whose relationship with me began at the Waldorf-Astoria and had encountered fits and starts in the interim, largely due to my uncertainty as to what was expected of me. By prom night, we were on good terms and ready to bow to most of the traditions of the event: fancy duds unlike anything we'd wear for any other occasion, dinner with friends at the Coonamessett Inn, and a few peculiar rituals at the prom, including a promenade by all the couples around the floor of the gym, to help the orchestra (I think it was) select the queen and her court.

We went to a party at Margaret Vieira's house afterwards, and it wasn't very long before Linda and I went our separate ways. I'm not sure just how this happened, but there weren't any histrionics or hurt feelings attendant to it. It's not like we'd had a close, long-term relationship that ran aground on Prom Night. Kids were coming and going to this party and that all night, and at some point Linda went elsewhere. I wound up hanging out with Sharon, an old friend who I'd always thought it'd be fun to pair up with, but had always been too uptight to take the initiatives that would effect that. This night, it was unplanned and easy. We watched the sun rise from Surf Drive Beach and called the evening a success.

Academically, the last weeks of senior year in high school hardly exist. The grades are all determined, college acceptances aren't impacted by anything short of felony, they've run out of fun activities that can hold the kids' attention, summer's coming on and there is no use in trying to keep your seniors committed to anything. The one carrot that can still be held out there is graduation, and the threat to bar the kids from participation in it if they do something really bad, like not come to any of the rehearsals. Our last week of school called for us to show up in the auditorium for an hour a few times to practice marching. I believe a lot of schools don't impose the marching order on their graduates any more, and probably haven't for years. Now they're more likely to arrive on the scene in complete disorder, whooping it up and trailing a bagpiper or something. I'd have a hard time judging such indiscipline to be an inferior mode of appearance. Acting goofy in joy, or feeling goofy in solemnity? You decide.

Being the largest graduating class ever, it was decided that we'd hold our ceremony outdoors if weather permitted. It did, so there were 221 seats set up on the parking lot in front of the school for us. We marched up to our places to Pomp And Circumstance (does anybody know what that title means?) and fried in the hot June sunshine while people made speeches. I don't remember anything about any of them, or any other part of our ceremony, but I do recall feeling good about it all, maybe even a little sentimental. Half of the days of the last six years of my life I'd spent in this school, and here I was saying goodbye to it with everyone else who'd had the same experience. It's not exactly tearjerker material for skeptics like me, but I was not unmoved.

Curiously enough, what I do recollect in scorching detail is the Lawrence High School anthem, which we did not sing at graduation (maybe another first for the Class of '67) or at any other time that I know of. It was a song that was written at a time when a pompous, flowery ode to one's alma mater was something to be learned by all, and sung, and cherished. As such, it had long outlived its relevance by 1967. I don't know if there's anyone else alive who can recall the lyrics and melody of this song. The details of how, where and why I learned it are lost to me, but learn it I did. One of the verses goes like this:

> Oh! Lawrence High, thine ancient mission serving,
> Create in us a spirit ringing true;
> Teach us to walk life's pathways still unswerving.
> Ready to meet life's problems old and new.
> Oh! Lawrence High School, whate'er betide,
> We still shall deem thee our mentor and our guide.

Would somebody please tell me why I remember these things?

* * *

Before I Go

I stand by my recounting of all these people, places and events from my youth under the presumption that if I remember them, they must have happened as I say they did. There is a logic to this, but it's not unassailable. Eric had a sneak preview of the manuscript and called me out on one detail. My parents, says he, did not have that wall taken down between the bedroom and the sewing room to create a space for him and Neils to share. They did that after Neils left to create an enlarged bedroom for themselves. Neils lived in the sewing room, which was just long enough to accommodate a twin bed, just wide enough to swing the door open, and had no closet. I was 14 and not wasting my attention on things that didn't immediately affect me, so I'll go with Eric's recall and give myself a Mulligan on that one.

> "So, did your host family have a nice room for you, Neils?"
> [translated from the German]
> "Uhhhh…."

Also pertaining to 287 Scranton Avenue: Since I described the place, it has acquired new owners, who have thoroughly and tastefully updated, upgraded and upscaled my boyhood home. My only regret is that the place has missed its chance to get in the National Register of Historic Places. Sic transit gloria mundi.

* * *

Thanks beyond measure are due Rebecca, Simon and Brian, three inquisitive young minds who I felt would someday want to know what their old man was like before he grew up.

I am grateful to Lyme author Ed Gray and to Brian, who applied their high-tech experience to those many navigational skills which have always eluded me.

And thanks to Eric, who first suggested this manuscript ought to exist in a more corporeal form than as an icon on my desktop. Eric has observed that many years from now, long after the Cloud has been hacked to death and our tweets and blogs and postings and e-titles have vanished in obsolescence, we'll still have the books.

Made in the USA
Middletown, DE
02 January 2024

47056345R00208